Perimeter Security

Michael J. Arata, Jr.

McGraw-Hill

New York Chicago San Francisco Lisbon London Madrid
Mexico City Milan New Delhi San Juan Seoul
Singapore Sydney Toronto

ISBN 0-07-146028-4

The sponsoring editor for this book was Larry S. Hager and the production supervisor was Pamela A. Pelton. It was set in Bembo by Lone Wolf Enterprises, Ltd. The art director for the cover was Anthony Landi.

Printed and bound by RR Donnelley.

 This book is printed on recycled, acid-free paper containing a minimum of 50% recycled, de-inked fiber.

McGraw-Hill books are available at special quantity discounts to use as premiums and sales promotions, or for use in corporate training programs. For more information, please write to the Director of Special Sales, McGraw-Hill Professional, Two Penn Plaza, New York, NY 10121-2298. Or contact your local bookstore.

DEDICATION

This book is dedicated to my wife, Karla, for putting up with me during the writing of this book; and to my daughter, Kristen; and son, Jimmy, without whose patience and understanding of late nights and weekends spent writing and rewriting, this book would not have been possible.

ACKNOWLEDGMENT

Thank you Victoria Roberts of Lone Wolf Enterprises for the excellent, expert job you did in editing and guidance; without it this project would not have been possible.

ABOUT THE AUTHOR

Michael Arata has over 15 years of security experience that includes positions from manager to vice president and consultant. He has developed and managed successful security programs from the ground up for several large organizations including the Director of Corporate Security for a major West Coast construction company.

He holds a master's degree in Public Administration, a B.A. in Business/Public Administration, and a B.S. in Safety and Fire Protection Technology. He has attended numerous seminars and training programs relating to security and holds CISSP, CPP, CFE and ACLM, professional certifications.

He has spoken at various professional organization seminars on the subject of security and written articles about security for trade publications. He has guest lectured at the Oklahoma State University and the University of California, Berkeley on safety and security related subjects. He is an adjunct instructor of Criminal Justice at a local college.

Contents

Introduction

The news today is filled with heightened awareness and sensitivity about physical or perimeter security due to the threat of terrorism. What does perimeter security mean? We will explore perimeter security in depth in the book. Perimeter security is defined as the protection of the outer boundary of your facility. With the advent of network security, perimeter security is defined as the protection of outer boundaries of the network. We are only going to focus on physical perimeter security in the book.

What does perimeter security entail? Perimeter security starts at the property line. This is either a natural or manmade barrier. In most cases it is the fence line. Then there are gates, lighting, the building or structure itself, walls, windows, doors, alarms, etc. Sometimes intrusion detection is used to monitor the perimeter fence line or the detectors are located in the ground. In the chapters that follow we are going to explore in detail each of the elements that make up perimeter security.

In Chapter 2 we will examine the security survey and threat assessment. You can't design effective perimeter security that also brings value to the company or the owner without first understanding what you are protecting and who you are protecting it from. Therefore the security survey and threat assessment is the first step. One important aspect is to obtain and understand the crime statistics for the area your project or building is located. The statistics can be obtained from the local police departments. There is also a company that will provide the information and you don't need to purchase any software. All you need to do is to give them an address and they will provide scores for that address based on certain data. The scores are a predictor of the occurrence of crime by type. There are checklists for performing a risk analysis and checklists for completing a security survey.

Chapter 3 will outline the specifications for chain-link fences. The specifications are the Federal DOD requirements which are a standard in the security industry. The types of fences will also be discussed along with their uses. Sample design specifications are also presented.

Chapter 4 is all about protective barriers and how they are effective in physical security and protecting the perimeter. The types of barriers will be presented. The designs and their uses will be discussed. Portable and permanent barriers types and uses are explained.

Chapter 5 addresses protective lighting the types of systems, uses and the design of the protective lighting system to enhance perimeter security. The proper illumination of lighting for security purposes is discussed and the definition of a foot-candle and its importance to security lighting is presented.

Chapter 6 is about access control systems and what is available and the benefits of using dual technology systems. Sample detailed design specifications are provided for the access control system. The integration of alarms and CCTV into one system is discussed.

Chapter 7 presents intrusion detection systems (IDS). The use of dual technology systems when deploying an IDS is discussed. All the types of IDS systems are presented and how they work. Sample design specifications a re included in the chapter for use as a guide for developing a set of specification for a project.

Chapter 8 concentrates on parking garages and parking lots and how to include security into the design and construction of them. The type of lighting that enhances security in parking garages and lots is outlined. The use CCTV and other security devices to help make the users of the parking garage and lots feel safe. As with the other chapters sample design specifications are included in the chapter.

Chapter 9 looks at the world of CCTV. The types of systems used are presented but emphasis is on the digital systems since this is the current trend of the CCTV today. Deign issues are also discussed and as some of the problems that may be encountered in the design and installation.

Chapter 10 is all about locks and keys. The uses of the various locking devices are discussed. Key control programs are also presented. Sample design specifications for deigning locking devices into a project are presented.

Chapter 11 windows and doors are on the perimeter and a likely point of entry for intruders. The ways to protect the windows and doors by using two types of IDS and better locking devices is explored. The chapter has a sample design specification document for designing secure windows and doors.

Chapter 12 the concept of defense-in-depth is explained and how it can improve security in a new facility by designing layers of security. The layered approach will help enhance security because when one layer is defeated there is another layer to tackle for the intruder. The defense-in-depth approach helps to harden the target by making it harder to gain entry and the possibility of being detected.

Chapter 13 secure areas in buildings like storage areas for high value cargo are important to certain types of facility designs. Warehouses that have or will have high value cargo must have a way to protect the cargo to keep the losses to a minimum.

Chapter 14 is the design of perimeter security for new facility for a fictitious company. The company makes vaccines to be used for biological agents and could be the target of various groups so protecting the facility is important to its operation. By designing the security the company can make sure the security meets its security needs and also be part of the architectural design. Also included is a figure showing the security devices on a sample floor plan for the new facility.

Chapter 15 protection of utilities is a sometimes forgotten part of perimeter security since the utilities traverse the perimeter to enter the facility or building. The utilities are the life blood of the facility brining electricity, telephony, and water in. Without the utilities the facility could not operate.

Chapter 16 protecting against explosions either intentional or accidental is important. There are new designs of building structures that can help the building with stand the effects of an explosion. This means that the protection can be designed into a new facility like the walls, structural members, windows and other openings to with stand the effects of explosions and limit the loss of life. Part of the design process is picking a location that can be defended and not be destroyed or severely damaged by being located to a value target.

Chapter 17 outlines fire protection system types including detection. Fire sprinklers and gaseous systems and how they work are presented. Sample design criteria documents for sprinkler systems are included in the chapter. The different types of detection system and how they work are explained. There are also sample design specifications for detection systems provided in the chapter.

Chapter 18 protecting companies from eavesdropping is becoming more of an issue especially if the company works on Homeland Security work like vaccines for biological agents, or new technology for IDS, etc. The types of eavesdropping devices are explained as is the how to design a soundproof room. Other countermeasures that can be added to the design are also discussed.

Chapter 19 shipping and receiving areas are a large vulnerability and need to be designed to help mitigate the possibility of an explosive device being introduced into the facility or building by way of the shipping and receiving dock. In Chapter 20 all the forms and checklists will be in this chapter separated by category.

Threat Assessment and Risk Analysis Basics

Properly designed and implemented perimeter security planning is the key to success. Threat assessment and risk analysis are both important to the process. Perimeter security countermeasures cost money to implement and, to help justify the expenditures, threat assessments and risk analyses are good tools. Threat assessment is the process of determining what the vulnerabilities are and the likelihood that they will result in a loss. To put it simply – what can go wrong resulting in a loss? Risk analysis is taking the vulnerabilities (threats) and determining the likelihood of whether a threat will cause a loss. The purpose of the risk analysis and threat assessment is to make sure the most cost-effective solutions are proposed. So the steps to the process are as follows:

1. Identification of the assets

2. Identification of the threats

3. Analyze the threats (risk assessment)

4. Determine what countermeasure (security feature) will mitigate or minimize the impact of the threat

5. Do a cost analysis so the benefit of the countermeasure selected can be quantified.

Using the survey and the risk analysis, the design specifications for perimeter security of the facility can be developed to meet the threats of the facility. This way the most severe threats and risks are addressed. To identify the threats you need to first identify the assets. Table 2-1 outlines the risk assessment steps and provides a brief description of each one. This is a good summary of the process.

TABLE 2-1   Risk Assessment Steps

STEP	DESCRIPTION
Identification of the assets	People, equipment, buildings, etc.
Identification of the threats	CAP Stats, etc.
Analyze the threats (risk assessment)	Probability of occurrence
Choose countermeasure	Alarms, access control, etc.
Cost analysis of countermeasure	
Cost benefit, ROI	

This chapter is an overview on how to do a threat assessment, including some useful tools to aid in the process such as a cost benefit analysis. To fully understand the concepts in the chapter there are some terms that need to be defined:

1. Threat assessment—What can or will cause harm or loss to the people, facility, and products - vulnerabilities

2. Risk assessment—The evaluation of the threats and determining which ones pose the greatest potential to cause harm. The analysis is used to categorize the threats in rank order by the highest probability of occurrence.

3. Risk management—The process used to minimize the exposure to loss

There are entire books devoted to risk management that include risk assessment, analysis, and mitigation. Formulas are used to determine the probability of a potential loss occurring and what the dollar of the loss would be. For the purposes of our discussion, we will keep it basic. The basics outlined in this chapter are effective tools and are easy to use.

HOW TO DO A THREAT ASSESSMENT

A threat assessment is the first step in determining what perimeter security will be needed. The assessment is the first step in risk analysis and is used to determine the threats and vulnerabilities. Conversely, the first step in risk analysis is identifying the threats. Why do we need do a risk assessment you may be asking? The following will give the reasons why:

1. Security costs and money is limited.

2. Justify the expenditures

3. Be a part of the risk management program

The risk management program has two methods for achieving the goal:

1. Pay for loss prevention countermeasures

2. Purchase insurance

The risk management program has the following steps:

1. Identify the risks

2. Analyze the risks for probability of occurrence

3. Choose the method of mitigating the risk
   a. Risk avoidance
   b. Risk reduction
   c. Risk segregation
   d. Risk acceptance
   e. Risk transfer (purchase insurance)
   f. Combinations of any of the above

4. Continually re-evaluate the steps above

Identify the Risks

Now let's look at how we can identify the risks. The security survey is a tool that can be used to identify the risks. The survey starts by looking at the location of the building or structure. The purpose of the survey is to provide the information necessary to make decisions on what level is security is needed. To effectively perform the survey, you need to collect some background information about the crime statistics in the area of the proposed or existing building or structure. The survey form and the crime statistics are used to determine the threat to the facility, which is the first step in risk analysis. What you are looking for is the type of security features that will best meet the need. So looking at crime statistics is an important first step. The following steps are an abbreviated version of what the security survey is all about:

1. Where is the facility located or where will it be located?

2. Crime statistics for type and frequency?

3. What type of facility or structure will be or is at the location?

4. What is it you are trying to protect?

5. Who are trying to protect it from?

6. What is the best way to protect the facility, people, and process?
   a. External intrusion detection
   b. Access control
   c. Video surveillance (CCTV) monitoring
   d. Locks and keys
   e. Clear zones
   f. Security officers
   g. Controlling vehicular and pedestrian traffic

7. What natural barriers can be used in the protection and design plan?
   a. Rivers
   b. Cliffs
   c. Beaches
   d. Other rugged terrain

The most effective way to collect the information necessary to identify the risks is to have some kind of form or checklist. These forms are extremely helpful and make the job easier by ensuring that all the information is collected and recorded. The forms can be simple to comprehensive. The more comprehensive the form, the more accurate the survey and risk analysis will be.

Analyze the Risk for Probability of Occurrence

So we want to know if an event will happen that will cause a loss. This is also known as the probability of risk occurrence. There are various methods used to determine the probability of risk occurrence. Some are simple, such as the Simple Probability Formula. Others are more complex and will left for the risk management books and books on statistics. For our discussion we will look at the simple formulas.

A simple explanation of probability is given by the action of tossing a coin. The action will generate one of two outcomes, either heads or tails. If the coin used is perfectly symmetrical, the probability would be 1/2 (.5 percent) for heads, 1/2 for tails (.5 percent). The probability measure of an event can be defined as the ratio of the number of outcomes. Therefore, when you toss the coin, the odds are that heads will come up in half of the tosses and tails will come up in the other half of the tosses. Thus if you toss the coin 100 times and you get tails 50 times, then a probability measure of 50/100 to the event that the coin will come up tails on the toss.

$$\text{Simple Probability} = p(\text{Event 1}) + p(\text{Event 2})$$

The Probability of Event 1 plus the probability of Event 2

Then there is the probability of related events.

$$\text{Probability of Related Events} =$$
$$p(\text{Event 1}) \times p(\text{Event 2}) = p(\text{Both Events})$$

The Probability of Event 1 times Probability of Event 2 gives the probability of both events occurring.

Let's look at an example of how you can use the simple probability formulas. Event 1 and Event 2 are two independent events and the probability that both events will occur is determined by the product of their separate probabilities. The probability that either of the events will occur is the determined by the sum of their separate probabilities minus the probability that they both will occur. Event 1—there is an unprotected window on the first floor. Event 2—the burglar forces entry through the unprotected window and steals computers with company secrets. So we add the probability of each event together to see the likelihood that the events will cause a loss.

To use the formula we need to assign numbers to the events. The probability Event 1 will happen is 0.5, the probability that Event 2 will happen 0.8. The probability both events will happen is $0.5 \times 0.8 = 0.4$ and the probability that either Event 1 or Event 2 will happen is $0.5 + 0.7 - 0.4 = 0.8$. So there is an 80 percent probability that one Event will occur and a 40 percent that both events will occur.

There are matrices that rate an event for low to high as seen in the tables that follow. Matrix tables that rate probabilities from high to low are used to predict frequency. They are based on past performance and other data such as the CAP crime statistics of an address. A company called the CAP Index provides excellent crime statistics and tables to aid in the decision making by providing information to determine the type and probability of crime occurring at the chosen location. More will be presented about the CAP crime statistics later in the chapter. They are an accepted method of rating risk.

The numbers in Table 2-2 can be used to explain the severity of an event from "Low" to "High". The numbers can take on any number of representations. For example, take our earlier example of the unprotected window and the burglar.

TABLE 2-2   Risk Matrix

SEVERITY	PROBABILITY OF OCCURRENCE		
	HIGH	MEDIUM	LOW
High	1	2	3
Medium	4	5	6
Low	7	8	9

If the crime statistics show from the CAP report that burglaries have a high incidence of occurrence, you would select the probability of occurrence as 1. Now if a burglary does occur, you have determined that the loss would be severe so you give the severity a 1 as well. The result is a "High". "High" in the matrix means the severity is high as is the probability of occurrence. Action should be taken on reducing the exposure by implementing some countermeasures.

Calculating the Cost of a Loss

Now that we have calculated the probability of a risk occurring, we need to go one step further and calculate the cost of the loss so we then calculate whether the cost of avoidance is worth the expense. This is an important step in the process because expenditures for security, like any business expense, need to be justified. This is also known as a Return on Investment (ROI). If the cost of the security countermeasure is greater than the loss, the measure will not be implemented. For example, let's say the cost of the countermeasure will be $20,000 but the potential loss is only $2,000. Then the countermeasure will not be implemented. The process will also aid you in decisionmaking by prioritizing where the dollars will do the most good. To do this we can follow the steps below. (Based on information from http://www.epmbook.com/risk.htm "Risk Management: Who, What, Why", Simon Wallace copyright 2002).

1. Calculate the expected loss. There is a basic equation used to determine the cost of a loss.

   Probability of the Risk × Cost if it happens = expected cost if it happens

2. To justify the avoidance actions the following can be used to calculate the net benefit of the cost avoidance and/or reduction.

   Quantifying Risks and Justifying Avoidance Expenditures

   Probability × Financial Impact = Expectation of Losses

   .8 × $50,000 = $40,000 Expected Loss

Where .8 is the probability of an event occurring times the $50,000 the financial impact equals the expected loss.

Below is the amount of the expenditure to prevent or reduce the loss.

$15,000

Probability after effect of avoidance and/or reduction actions × Financial Impact after effect of avoidance and/or reduction actions = Revised expectation of losses

.1 × $50,000 = $5,000

Quantifying Risks and Justifying Avoidance Expenditures

Probability × Financial Impact = Expectation of Losses

0.$	50,00	40000	.8 is the probaility of occurrence

Cost of avoidance measure
$25,000

Probability after effect of avoidance and/or reduction actions × Financial Impact after Effect of avoidance and/or reduction actions = Revised expectation of losses

0.	$50,00	5,000	.2 is the corrected probability after the preventive measure has been implemented.
$15,00	$5,00	10,000	Actual benefit from the cost avoidance/reduction measure
$100,00	$10,00	$110,000	Total cost avoidance including the $100,0000 insurance deductible and the countermeasure

FIGURE 2-1   Sample spreadsheet

.1 is the corrected probability after the preventive measure has been implemented.

So the actual benefit from the cost avoidance/or reduction measure

$15,000 (cost of avoidance or reduction) - $5,000 = $10,000 Net Benefit

Now take the deductible for the insurance + the net benefit to determine the total cost avoidance of the countermeasure.

A deductible of $50,000 + $10,000 countermeasure = $60,000 cost total cost avoidance

Figure 2-1 is sample spreadsheet that illustrates the information discussed in quantifying risks and justifying cost avoidance expenditures.

The Survey Form

Figure 2-2 is a sample survey form. It is one that I have used. The form is broken into eight parts. It is one that was compiled from other forms. The following is a list of each part:

- Part 1 Building and Site Physical Features

- Part 2 Social and Political Environment
  Crime statistics
  Crimes against persons
  Crimes against property

- Part 3 Perimeter
  Grounds
  Exterior doors
  Exterior Windows
  Other openings
  Exterior lighting

- Part 4 Interior
  Interior lighting
  Interior doors
  Offices
  Keys
  Locks
  Access control
  Alarm systems

- Part 5 Warehouse Activities

- Part 6 Employee Training

- Part 7 Security Loss Reports

- Part 8 Security Policy and Standards and Procedures

The security survey form in Figure 2-2 is one of many that are being used. In the Appendix of this book, you will find several other survey forms to choose from. Each section of form needs to be completed. Each question in Parts 3-8 has a check box to the the right of the question. In Figure 2-2, the section is Grounds and there are a total of 66 points possible for the section. Each question requires a Yes or No answer. The total number of possible points is listed for each question. To complete the form all you need to do is to put an **✗** in either the Yes or No box after the question in Parts 3 through 8.

(Text continues on page 20)

SECURITY SURVEY
PART 1
BUILDING and/or SITE PHYSICAL FEATURES

1. Location of facility: _____

2. Job: _____

3. Street Address and Zip: _____

4. Telephone: _____

5. Number of structures on the Site:

   (a) 1 story _____   (b) 2 story _____   (c) 3 story _____   (d) 4 story _____   (e) 5 story or higher _____

6. Number of structures interconnected: (a) At grade level or higher _____   (b) Below grade _____

7. Total working population on:

   a) First (day) shift 3 story _____   (b) Second shift 3 story _____   (c) Third shift _____

8. Estimated number of daily visitors: _____

9. Number of automobiles parked daily: _____

PART 2
SOCIAL and POLITICAL ENVIRONMENT

10. Is the facility in a: (a) City _____   (b) Town _____   (c) Incorporated village _____

    (d) Agricultural _____   (e) Unincorporated hamlet _____   (f) Rural area _____

11. Estimated percentage of neighboring area: (a) Residential _____   (b) Commercial _____

    (c) Industrial _____   (d) Agricultural _____   (e) Undeveloped _____

12. Estimated percentage of residential area: (a) One family homes _____   (b) Two family homes _____

    (c) Multiple dwellings _____   (d) High rise multiple dwellings _____

13. Police department having jurisdiction: _____

14. Total sworn officers in the department: _____

15. Average response times for emergency calls: _____

16. Is the jurisdiction separately reported in the Standard Metropolitan Statistical Area section of the _____

    Uniform Crime Reports?

    _____

17. If 16, is yes, what are the most recent indexes for: (a) Total crime _____   (b) Violent crime _____

    (c) Property crime _____   (d) Murder and Manslaughter _____   (e) Rape _____

    (f) Robbery _____   (g) Aggravated assault _____   (h) Burglary _____   (i) Larceny over $50 _____

    (j) Car theft _____

FIGURE 2-2   Sample Security Survey Form

(continued on next page)

EXPLANATION OF ELEMENT SCORING

(X0) - Score No = Zero; Yes = Points Indicated

(%) - Score up to the points indicated based on the percent compliance

(Part Whole) - Award points indicated for each part up to the whole number indicated.

(PJ) - Score up to the points indicated based on your professional judgment.

PART 3
Physical Security Survey
Perimeter

1. GROUNDS (66)		Yes	No
1.2	Does the fence meet the minimum specifications for security fencing? (.5/3)		
	(1) Chain-link?		
	(2) No. 11 gauge or heavier wire?		
	(3) Mesh opening not larger than 2 inches square?		
	(4) Selvage twisted and barbed at top and bottom:?		
	(5) Fence bottom is within 2 inches of solid ground?		
	(6) Is the fence top guard strung with barbed wire & angled outward & upward at a 45-degree angle?		
1.3	Are boxes or other items placed a safe distance from the fence? (X0-5)		
1.4	Is there a cleared area on both sides of the fence? (X)-5)		
1.5	There are not any unsecured overpasses or subterranean passageways near the fence?		
1.6	Are fence gates solid and in good condition? (X0-5)		
1.7	Are fence gates' hinges secure and non-removable? (X0-5)		
1.8	Have unnecessary gates been eliminated? (X0-5)		
1.9	Are locks and chains used to secure gates? (X0-5)		
1.10	Do you regularly check those gates that you have locked? (X0-5)		
1.11	There are not weeds or trash adjoining the building that should be removed? (X0-5)		
1.12	Is shrubbery near windows, doors, gates, and near entrances kept to a minimum? (X0-5)		
1.13	Stock, crates, pallets, etc. are not allowed to be piled near the building? (X0-5)		

FIGURE 2-2   Sample Security Survey Form *(continued)*

(continued on next page)

2. EXTERIOR DOORS (55)
Yes No

2.1	Are doors constructed of sturdy material? (X0-5)		
2.2	Are all hinge pins located on the inside? If No, are they pinned or welded? (X0-5)		
2.3	Are all door hinges installed so that it would be impossible to remove the closed doors without seriously damaging the door or Jam? (X0-5)		
2.4	Are all door frames well constructed and in good condition? (X0-5)		
2.5	Are the exterior locks double cylinder, dead bolts, or jimmy-proof type locks? (X0-5)		
2.6	The breaking of glass or a door panel then will not allow the person to open the door? (X0-5)		
2.7	Are all locks working properly ? (X0-5)		
2.8	Are all doors properly secured or reinforced? (X0-5)		
2.9	Are all unused doors secured? (X0-5)		
2.10	Are all padlocks, chains, and hasps case hardened? (X0-5)		

3. EXTERIOR WINDOWS (20)

3.1	Are all windows securely fastened from the inside? (X0-5)		
3.2	Are windows within 14 feet from the ground equipped with protective coverings? (X0-5)		
3.3	Do those windows with locks have locks that are designed and located so they cannot be reached and/or opened by breaking the glass? (X0-5)		
3.4	Windows cannot be removed without breaking them? (X0-5)		

4. OTHER OPENINGS (25)

4.1	Are all ventilators or other possible means of entrance to the buildings) covered with steel bars or wire mesh? (X0-5)		
4.2	Are exposed roof hatches properly secured? (X0-5)		
4.3	Are the accessible skylights protected with bars or an intrusion alarm? (X0-5)		
4.4	Do fire exit doors have a portable alarm mounted, to alert if door is opened? (X0-5)		
4.5	Entrance cannot be gained from an adjoining building? (X0-5)		

FIGURE 2-2 Sample Security Survey Form *(continued)*

(continued on next page)

5. EXTERIOR LIGHTING (45)   Yes   No

5.1	Is the lighting adequate to illuminate critical areas? (X0-5)		
5.2	Is there sufficient lighting over entrances? (X0-5)		
5.3	The protective lighting and the working lighting system are not on the same circuit? (X0-5)		
5.4	Is there an auxiliary power source for protective lighting? (X0-5)		
5.5	Has the system been tested? (X0-5)		
5.6	Is the auxiliary system designed to go into operation automatically when needed?: (X0-5)		
5.7	How are the protective lights controlled? (5/10) 1. Automatic timer 2. Photo cells		
5.8	Are the switch boxes and/or automatic timer secured? (X0-5)		

PART 4
INTERIOR

I. INTERIOR LIGHTING (20)

1.1	Is there a back-up system for emergency lights?: (X0-5)		
1.2	Is the lighting provided adequate for security purposes? (X0-5)		
1.3	Is the lighting at night adequate for security purposes? (X0-5)		
1.4	Is the night lighting sufficient for surveillance by the police department? (X0-5)		

2. INTERIOR DOORS (30)

2.1	Are doors constructed of a sturdy and solid material? (X0-5)		
2.2	Are doors limited to the essential minimum? (X0-5)		
2.3	Are outside door hinge pins spot welded or bradded to prevent removal? (X0-5)		
2.4	Are hinges installed on the inward side of the door? (X0-5)		
2.5	Is there at least one lock on each outer door? (X0-5)		
2.6	Is each door equipped with a locking device? (X0-5)		

3. OFFICES (20)

3.1	Are offices locked when unattended for a long period of time? (X0-5)		
3.2	Are maintenance people, contractors, vendors, other visitors, required to show identification? (X0-5)		
3.3	Are desks and files locked when left unattended? (X0-5)		
3.4	Items of value are not left on desks in an unsecured manner? (X0-5)		

FIGURE 2-2   Sample Security Survey Form *(continued)*

(continued on next page)

4. KEYS (33)

Yes No

4.1	Are methods taken to control the issuance and management of keys? (X0-20)		
4.2	Do these controls include: (1/13) 1. Total keys issued? 2. Total master keys? 3. Is there an adequate log maintained of all keys that are issued? 4. Key holders are not permitted to duplicate keys? 5. Are keys marked "DO NOT DUPLICATE"? 6. If master keys are used, are they devoid of markings identifying them as such? 7. Are losses or thefts of keys promptly reported to security? 8. Is there a person responsible for issuing and replacing keys? 9. Are visual audits made of the keys? 10. Are locks changed immediately upon loss or theft of keys? 11. Are the duplicate keys stored in a safe and secure place? 12. Are keys returned when an employee resigns, is discharged, or suspended? 13. Are records maintained indicating buildings and entrances for which keys are issued?		

5. LOCKS (35)

5.1	Are entrances equipped with secure locking devices? (X0-5)		
5.2	Is the lock designed or the frame built so that the door cannot be forced by spreading the frame? (X0-5)		
5.3	Are all locks in working order? (X0-5)		
5.4	Are the screws holding the lock firmly in place? (X0-5)		
5.5	Is the bolt protected or constructed so it cannot be cut? (X0-5)		
5.6	Are locks' combinations changed or rotated immediately upon resignation, discharge, suspension of an employee having possession of master keys?		
5.7	Are locks changed after a major security violation resulting in large loss?		

6. ACCESS CONTROL (20)

6.1	Are methods taken to control entry and movement of people and vehicles?		
6.2	Do these controls include: (1/10): 1. Employees? 2. Service people? 3. Truck, rail, and other delivery/pickuup vehicle operators? 4. Outside contractors? 5. Visitors? 6. Sales personnel? 7. Employees' vehicles? 8. Other vehicles? 9. Intruders? 10. Other: &		

FIGURE 2-2 Sample Security Survey Form *(continued)*

(continued on next page)

	7. ALARM SYSTEMS (25)	Yes	No
7.1	Does the alarm system have an intrusion alarm system? (X0-5)		

7.2	Does the alarm system have the following features: (2/20)
	  1. Is it connected to a central station?
	  2. Is it a proprietary system?
	  3. Is the system tested before activating it for non-operational periods?
	  4. Is the alarm system inspected and tested annually?
	  5. Is the system tamper resistant?
	  6. Is the system weather resistant?
	  7. Is there an automatic emergency power supply?
	  8. Is the alarm system properly maintained by trained technical specialists?
	  9. Are frequent tests conducted to determine the adequacy and promptness of response to alarm signals?
	  10. Other:		

PART 5

1. WAREHOUSE ACTIVITIES (30)

1.1	Are methods taken to control entry and the movement of people and finished products and raw materials? (X0-16)		

1.2	Do these controls include: (2/14
	  1. Is there separate lounge facilities for truck drivers?
	  2. Trash collectors are not permitted in the warehouse?
	  3. Employees/vehicles?
	  4. Contractor's vehicles?
	  5. Are shipping and receiving platforms free of trash?
	  6. Are pin locks used for loaded trailers parked on company property?
	  7. Other? N/A		

PART 6

1. EMPLOYEE TRAINING (50)

1.1	What percentage of employees receive an orientation to security program standards? (%-10)		
1.2	Are written materials included in the orientation? (X0-5)		
1.3	Are signs and notices posted in appropriate places to reinforce knowledge of security standards? (X0-5)		
1.4	Are training manuals used to aid and reinforce security training?		
1.5	Are records kept to verify security training and identify employees who need training?		

FIGURE 2-2   Sample Security Survey Form *(continued)*

(continued on next page)

PART 7

	SECURITY LOSS REPORTS (24)	Yes	No
1.1	Are security losses investigated with the findings and actions reported on a standard incident report form? (X0-10)		
1.2	Does the security program require a complete investigation of incidents involving the following: (2/14) 1. Cash funds? 2. Irregularities in financial accounts? 3. Equipment and materials shortages? 4. Production losses from disturbances? 5. Expendable supplies and inventories shrinkage? 6. Computer theft? 7. Other security losses:		

PART 8

SECURITY POLICY (50)

1.1	Is there a written policy signed by the site manager emphasizing the importance of protecting people, property, and intellectual property against loss by taking or intentional destruction? (X0-15)		
1.2	Does the security policy include: (1/10) 1. Theft of property? 2. Burglary? 3. Theft of process or trade secrets? 4. Assault on employees and visitors? 5. Bomb threats? 6. Arson? 7. Civil disturbances? 8. Other security losses?		
1.3	Is the security policy: (2/10) 1. Communicated in writing to all employees? 2. Referred to during new employee orientation? 3. Referred to in group meetings? 4. Contained in some manual? 5. Referred to in management program?		
1.4	Does senior management support the security policy: 1. By periodic written communications? (X0-5) 2. By regular security tours? (X0-5) 3. By participating in security program audits? (X0-5)		

FIGURE 2-2   Sample Security Survey Form *(continued)*

(continued on next page)

·

		Yes	No
2. SECURITY STANDARDS AND PROCEDURES			
2.1	Are there written standards for management performance in the security program? (X0-5)		
2.2	Are security program standards communicated to all levels of management? (X0-10)		
2.3	Are security instructions and procedures defined in a program manual? (X0-5)		

Total Points Scored for Security _____

Total Possible Points: _____

Percentage Score for Security: _____
  (Total points scored divided by total points possible multiplied by 100.

Figure to nearest 1/10 of 1%) _____

FIGURE 2-2   Sample Security Survey Form *(continued)*

The survey form is the key to helping you choose the protection necessary based on the threat, making the solutions cost effective. The advantages to using a form are as follows:

1. You will have a plan to follow.

2. The important areas to be analyzed will be evident.

3. Any deficiencies will be noted.

4. You will have documentation and history.

5. Your decisions will be based on facts rather than subjectivity.

6. The design of the perimeter protection will zero in on the mitigating the risks.

Table 2-3 is a physical security features for basic level security. The spreadsheet is not exhaustive but it can be used to give a quick look at the physical security status of a facility or property. Each checklist list specifies what the elements that are required for that level covering the three levels of security from basic to high. Each level calls for progressively more security based on company standards. The spreadsheet is used to check a location against a set of predetermined standards. The standards can be used for an existing facility or for the design of a new facility.

The purpose of the spreadsheet is to visually spell out the requirements of the security policy as it relates to physical security based on location and the critical nature of the operation. Crime statistics play a part in designing and planning the security. The higher the rates of crimes against persons such as homicide, rape,

TABLE 2-3 Basic Level Physical Security Standards Features

LOCATION	CCTV	INTRUSION	GUARDS	KEY CNTRL	DURESS	LIGHTING	PERIMETER FENCE	SEALS/PAD
EXTERIOR								
Grounds				R		R		R
Parking Lots				R		R		R
Docks	X	R		R		R		
Doors		R		R		R		X
Roofs		R		R		R		
Windows		R			N/A	R		N/A
Gates		R		R		R		X
Rail Sidings		R		R		R		
INTERIOR								
Lobbies		R		R		R	N/A	N/A
Reception				R		R	N/A	N/A
Elevators		R		R		R	N/A	
Stairwell		R		R		R		
Office Suites		R		R		R		
Common Areas		R		R		R		
Service Areas		R		R		R		

FOOT NOTES
X   Denotes Option for meeting standard
R   Denotes required feature
N/A Denotes no action

robbery, aggravated assault and crimes against property such as burglaries, larceny, and motor vehicle theft will dictate if more perimeter security may be needed. Across the top of the sheet you will notice that the main elements of physical security are listed starting with CCTV and ending with perimeter fence. The list is not in order of importance. The headings for the rows are listed with a main heading of exterior, interior, and a description location for each area. There is a legend at the bottom of each sheet under the heading "Foot Notes". An "X" in the box denotes that the feature is optional. The "R" denotes the feature is required to meet the level of security listed on the top of the form. Finally, "N/A" means that the feature is not applicable to the location.

Table 2-4 outlines the requirements for the intermediate level of security. Any thing marked with an "R" is required to meet the standard. As you can see the

TABLE 2-4   Intermediate Level Physical Security Standards Features

LOCATION	CCTV	INTRUSION	GUARDS	KEY CNTRL	DURESS	LIGHTING	PERIMETER FENCE	SEALS/PAD
EXTERIOR								
Grounds	X		X	R		R		R
Parking Lots	R		X	R		R		R
Docks	X	R	X	R		R		
Doors	R	R	X	R		R		X
Roofs		R		R		R		
Windows		R		N/A	N/A	R		N/A
Gates		R		R	X	R		X
Rail Sidings		R		R		R		
INTERIOR								
Lobbies		R	X	R		R	N/A	N/A
Reception			X	R		R	N/A	N/A
Elevators		R		R		R	N/A	
Stairwell		R		R		R		
Office Suites		R		R		R		
Common Areas		R		R		R		
Service Areas		R		R		R		

FOOT NOTES

X   Denotes Option for meeting standard
R   Denotes required feature
N/A Denotes no action

intermediate level requires progressively more elements than the basic level does. Table 2-5 outlines the requirements for a high level of physical security.

The Crime Statistics

There is a company that provides the crime statistics on any specific address in the US and Canada. The company is called CAP Index. (This is the name of the company; it is not an acronym.) In Figure 2-3, the name of the company is displayed as well as a legend on the right side of the map.

The data used in the CAP Index is based on US and Canadian census figures and other government data. A scientific approach is used. The methodology is based on a cause-and-effect relationship of the amount of crime in a neighborhood and what CAP calls the "social disorganization of the neighborhood". CAP combines the social information, crime indicators, and survey information, providing the most accurate scores indicating the area's risk of crime. The area can be as specific as an address. This makes the statistics more meaningful and accurate about the type of crimes and the rates. The CAP site at www.capindex.com explains how the system works in detail and you can request further information. The numbers are compared to county, state, and national averages. The "social disorder" number is based on the known indicators of crime and has 21 demographic values such as population, mobility, economic data, education data, and others. 90 crime vulnerability assessment scores are provided for each address reported to CAP. The data used is standardized across the US and Canada. The data for the police and FBI Uniform Crime Reports (UCR) are not uniformly available and therefore not as accurate as the CAP scores. The reason for the inconsistency in the Uniform Crime Report is that reporting is voluntary and some jurisdictions do not report everything. The UCR data can be up to 18 months old.

TABLE 2-5   High Level Physical Security Standards Checklist

LOCATION	CCTV	INTRUSION	GUARDS	KEY CNTRL	DURESS	LIGHTING	PERIMETER FENCE	SEALS/PAD
EXTERIOR								
Parking Lots	R		X	R		R		R
Docks	X	R	X	R		R		
Doors	R	R	X	R		R		X
Roofs		R		R		R		
Windows		R			N/A	R		N/A
Gates		R		R		R		X
Rail Sidings		R		R		R		
INTERIOR								
Lobbies		R	X	R		R	N/A	N/A
Reception			X	R		R	N/A	N/A
Elevators		R		R		R	N/A	
Stairwell		R		R		R		
Office Suites		R		R		R		
Common Areas		R		R		R		

FOOT NOTES
X   Denotes Option for meeting standard
R   Denotes required feature
N/A Denotes no action

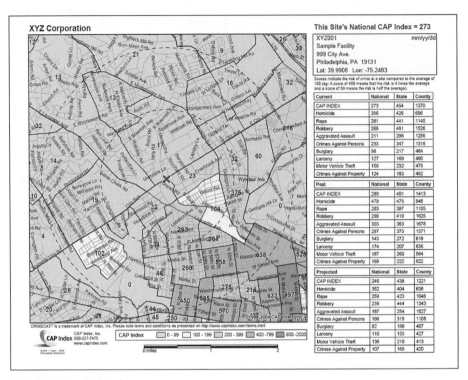

XYZ Corporation

This Site's National CAP Index = 273

XYZ001   mm/yy/dd
Sample Facility
999 City Ave.
Philadelphia, PA 19131
Lat: 39.9908 Lon: -75.2483

Scores indicate the risk of crime at a site compared to the average of 100 (eg: A score of 400 means that the risk is 4 times the average and a score of 50 means the risk is half the average).

Current	National	State	County
CAP INDEX	273	454	1370
Homicide	386	426	696
Rape	281	441	1140
Robbery	288	461	1526
Aggravated Assault	211	296	1286
Crimes Against Persons	233	347	1316
Burglary	98	217	464
Larceny	127	169	490
Motor Vehicle Theft	158	232	475
Crimes Against Property	124	183	482

Past	National	State	County
CAP INDEX	288	401	1413
Homicide	479	475	846
Rape	283	397	1105
Robbery	290	410	1625
Aggravated Assault	303	363	1678
Crimes Against Persons	297	375	1571
Burglary	143	272	619
Larceny	174	207	636
Motor Vehicle Theft	187	260	564
Crimes Against Property	169	222	622

Projected	National	State	County
CAP INDEX	246	439	1221
Homicide	352	404	636
Rape	259	423	1046
Robbery	239	444	1343
Aggravated Assault	167	254	1027
Crimes Against Persons	196	315	1108
Burglary	82	199	407
Larceny	110	153	427
Motor Vehicle Theft	136	210	413
Crimes Against Property	107	165	420

CRIMECAST is a trademark of CAP Index, Inc. Please note terms and conditions as presented on http://www.capindex.com/terms.html

CAP Index, Inc.
800-227-7475
www.capindex.com

CAP Index   0 - 99   100 - 199   200 - 399   400 -799   800 -2000

0 miles   1   2

FIGURE 2-3   CAP Index map

CAP, on the other hand, updates their data every year. The data is a good tool to predict the vulnerabilities associated with crime for a given address. By reviewing the data you can more accurately assess what types of crime will occur where the building is or will be located. Armed with this information, you can make more intelligent decisions about countermeasures that will mitigate the threats. There is no software to buy to get the CAP Map for your address of interest.

Risk Analysis Steps

Now that you have identified the risks using the tools we described, you must now interpret what you have collected. There are six steps for analyzing the risks. The following outlines these steps:

1. Identify the assets of the facility (Security Survey) — people, facilities, equipment, etc.

    The form in Figure 2-3 can be used to collect the information to identify the assets. A separate asset table can be used to collect information about assets by location or department.

2. Now a value must be assigned to the assets. Assigning value is not a simple task. For equipment or products, the value can be the purchase or the replacement costs. To determine value, you would answer the following questions:
   a. How much revenue does the equipment and facility generate?
   b. How much does it cost to maintain?
   c. How much would it cost if the equipment were lost?
   d. How much would it cost to replace?

3. Now that the assets are identified, the risks need to be identified. The various risk categories are examined and the various factors are applied until a list of possible threats is created. Since there is not a scientific way to determine which risk categories apply to an asset; it is a subjective determination. Common sense should prevail.

4. The next step is to go through the various assets and the threats to estimate how much would be lost if the threat causes a loss. Building and equipment replacement costs can be calculated. What about business loss because patrons are afraid to go to the business because it is in a high crime area or the crime rate is increasing?

5. Now calculate the probability of occurrence by using the formula below or use a matrix chart as depicted if Table 2-1.

$$\text{Simple Probability} = p(\text{Event 1}) + p(\text{Event 2})$$

The Probability of Event 1 plus the probability of Event 2

Then there is the probability of related events.

$$\text{Probability of Related Events} = p(\text{Event 1}) \times p(\text{Event 2}) = p(\text{Both Events})$$

The Probability of Event 1 times Probability of Event 2 gives the probability of both events occurring.

6. The frequency of occurrence is then used to determine cost of the expected loss the on a particular asset because of a threat. The following formula is used:

$$\text{Probability} \times \text{Financial Impact} = \text{Expectation of Losses}$$

The corrected probability $\times$ the expected loss after the countermeasure has been implemented = The corrected loss

The cost of the counter measure $-$ the corrected loss = The net benefit of the countermeasure

Cost of deductible savings $+$ the net benefit of the countermeasure = Total cost avoidance

TABLE 2-6   Risk Analysis Checklist

STEPS	DESCRIPTION
Identify Assets	People, equipment, etc
Set Value of Asset	Cost of replacement or loss of use
Identify Risks	What could cause a loss
Estimate Loss of Asset (formulas below)	

Calculate Probability:
   Simple Prob = p(Event 1) + p(Event 2)
   Prob of related Events
      p(Event 1) × p(Event 2) = p(Both Events)
	How to calculate Simple Probability

Calculate Cost of Loss:
   P × (Financial Impact = EL (Expected Loss)
   CP (corrected probability) × EL =
      corrected loss (CL)
   CM (cost of countermeasure) − CL =
      Net benefit of CM
   Cost of deductible + net benefit CM =
      Total cost avoidance
	Calculating the cost of a loss and the cost avoidance

Table 2-6 provides a snapshot of the seven steps to performing a risk analysis. The checklist can be used as a guide to make sure the steps are all completed.

Choosing the Method to Mitigate the Risk

After the risks are identified you need to select a method to mitigate the risk. The mitigation method we are talking about here is now whether to add an intrusion detection system. The risk management program methods are as follows:

- Risk avoidance
- Risk reduction
- Risk segregation
- Risk acceptance
- Risk transfer (purchase insurance)
- Combinations of any of the above

Table 2-8 is a synopsis of the risk mitigation methods. Each method is outlined and a brief definition is included. This is quick reference guide to risk mitigation.

Risk avoidance is when you cease doing or simply don't do something. An example is not driving in a snowstorm because of the high risk of getting into an

TABLE 2-7 Asset Identification Table

ASSET	DESCRIPTION OF ASSET, NUMBER, ETC.
People	
Buildings	
Computers	
Intellectual Property	
Equipment	

accident. You simply avoided the risk by not driving in the snowstorm. Businesses can choose to not do something that has a high risk or potential loss. An example would be to not allow customers in a work area that is dangerous, like your local mechanic shop's garage while work is being performed.

Risk reduction is used to lower the severity of a potential or actual loss. Fire sprinklers are a good example of risk reduction. When a fire occurs in the facility, the fire sprinklers will activate, controlling or extinguishing the fire. The fire sprinklers will limit the spread of a fire and therefore reduce the loss.

Risk segregation has two components. First is the separation or spreading out of the activity to minimize the exposure. An example is having a policy that all the top executives don't travel together on the same flight. In the unlikely event the plane crashes, all the top executives are not lost in the single event. Another example is to not locate a business or operation of the business in an area that is at high risk for causing a disruption, like placing the only data center of a company in an area prone to earthquakes. To offset such a decision, a company would need to have an update disaster and business continuity plan that calls for a back up data center to be used in the event of the loss of the primary data center and to back up the critical company data regularly.

TABLE 2-8 Mitigation of Risk

METHOD	DEFINED
Risk Avoidance	Avoid the risk
Risk Reduction	Reduce the potential loss
Risk Segregation	Separation/duplication
Risk Acceptance	Accept the risk
Risk Transfer	Purchase insurance or self insure
Combination	Any combinations of above

Second is duplication or back up. This is where you back up your company's critical data on a regular basis in case there is a server or disk failure. Critical data can be identified as anything that is important to keeping the business running like accounts payable and receivable. Other data such as orders, payroll, etc. may also be needed to be backed up. The backed-up data can be used to keep the business running (continuity). There are entire books written on the subject of disaster planning and business continuity and are beyond the scope of this book. Another example is to have back up power for perimeter lighting so the facility will still have lights in the event of a power outage.

Risk acceptance is when the company management decides, after doing an analysis, that the potential loss from the risk is not significant and nothing needs to be done about it.

Risk transfer is when a company purchases insurance, thereby transferring the liability of the risk to the insurance company. Companies pay an insurance premium to transfer the risk. Premiums can be high so to offset the cost, there is a deductible. The higher the deductible, the lower the premium. We all do this and a common example is automobile insurance which transfers the cost of the liability to the insurance company. If you are involved in an accident, the insurance company pays for the damages of your claim if the other motorist was uninsured and you are responsible for the deductible which is usually $500.00. For companies the deductible can be as high as $250,000 or more, so using risk mitigation techniques is a good business financial consideration.

Businesses can also transfer the cost of the risk to an insurance company by purchasing a property and casualty policy. The insurance company will not accept all of the risk and, in some cases, will not accept the risk at all. There are deductibles that we have outlined in our automobile insurance policies and businesses also have deductibles for their property insurance. These deductibles keep rates down. As previously stated, it is not unheard of for a business to have a deductible of $250,000 or more for a loss experienced from a property casualty claim. This is why the whole concept of risk analysis and mitigation is important to the business's bottom line.

Other risks that need to be considered are natural disasters such as tornados, hurricanes, blizzards, and earthquakes and the effect on the perimeter security. Is there back-up power available? How long will it keep critical systems operational?

There are combinations of the risk mitigation methods by using one or more of the five risk mitigation methods. For example, you can transfer part of the risk and reduce the other part. To transfer the risk you purchase insurance for part of the risk and then you implement a countermeasure for the other part of the risk. For example the insurance company will only consider insuring the risk for part of its value for a burglary of computer equipment by only insuring the hardware and not the critical data. To offset the remaining exposure from the loss of the data, you decide to implement a countermeasure of locking the computers down and encrypting the data to prevent easy theft of the intellectual property along with an intrusion alarm system to protect the remaining exposure. You have now used a combination of mitigation methods, risk transfer and risk reduction, to address the exposure of the company's computers.

PLANNING AND DESIGNING

Now that we have identified the threats and analyzed the risks, we need to choose the countermeasures necessary to mitigate the exposures. There are some things to keep in mind when completing this phase:

- What does the countermeasure cost to implement?

- What amount of the project budget has been allocated to security?

- Does it make sense?

- What is the cost benefit of the countermeasure? (see sidebar example)

- Can the cost of the countermeasure be justified?

- Is there a benefit?

- Does the cost exceed the potential loss?

XYZ CORPORATION

XYZ Corporation which makes computer software for the financial industry is building a new two-story office building. The architectural conceptual design drawings include windows on the first floor. The CAP statistics for the address of the proposed building show a high incidence of crimes to property, especially burglaries. The windows are designed to go around the entire first floor including the back end of the building which is not visible from the street. After analysis it is determined that the cost of a potential loss from a burglary would be $250,000 in computer equipment since every workstation has a desktop computer. The average cost of each computer is $10,000 including the software development tools and special software for each machine. The company has a $300,000 deductible for its property and casualty insurance policy to keep the premiums low. The probability of occurrence is 80 percent.

FIGURE 2-4   XYZ Corporation Floor Plan

The countermeasures to mitigate the risk include installing Lexan glass in all the first floor windows in the rear of the building and installing dual technology glass breaks on the inside of the building. Also in the design, the rear door is designated as the employee entrance door which will be alarmed and be card-access controlled. The cost for the countermeasures is $180,000.

The drawing in Figure 2-4 depicts the addition of window contacts, door contacts and glass breaks.

Now we would use the formula to determine the whether the countermeasure will net a cost avoidance when it is implemented:

$$\text{Probability} \times \text{Financial Impact} = \text{Expectation of Losses}$$
$$.9 \times \$250,000 = \$200,000 \text{ Expected loss}$$

Cost of countermeasure $180,00

$.4 \times \$250,000 = \$100,000$ .4 is the corrected probability after the preventive measure has been implemented.

$\$180,000 - \$100,000 = \$80,000$ net benefit of countermeasure

Cost of deductible savings + the net benefit of the countermeasure = Total cost avoidance

$300,000 + $80,000 = $380,000 the cost avoidance of the countermeasure.

So the countermeasure is worth the cost since the total cost avoidance would be the cost of the installation. The design will include the countermeasures since they are cost-effective and a cost avoidance.

CHAPTER 3

Perimeter Fence

The perimeter fence usually marks the boundary of the property. It helps delineate private and public property. To mark the boundary, the fence does not have to be high, since it is not meant to help secure the property. However, there must be a clear zone around the perimeter fence. The view should not be obstructed from outside the perimeter. This will aid in detecting an intruder that has gained access to the property. The clear zone also will assist in detecting the intruder attempting to gain access by climbing or cutting the fence.

Some perimeter fences enhance security if they are higher and topped with barbed wire. The purpose of a perimeter security fence is to slow down the intruder by adding a layer to prevent or deter entry, but the perimeter fence is not designed to stop the intruder completely. The perimeter security fence is a delaying tactic to slow down the intruder and to control vehicular and pedestrian access to the property.

The perimeter fence can take many forms. It could be a block or concrete wall, or a chain-link, wrought-iron, or wooden fence to mark the property line or be the perimeter security fence. Chain link is the most common type used for commercial properties. There are federal guidelines for chain-link fences, and we will explore those guidelines later in the chapter.

Chain-link fence helps provide the clear zone on each side of the fence, because the chain mesh allows the property to be viewed from outside the fence. The block wall also is used for commercial properties. Even though the block or concrete wall does not provide visibility from both sides of the property line, it is still a good perimeter fence for some applications, since it can be harder to climb over or get through. The wooden fence is more common for separating single and small multi-family properties.

The perimeter fence has openings called gates. You can use several types of gates for vehicular and pedestrian traffic access. Each of the gate types will be explored later in the chapter. The various gates are as follows:

- Roll/slide

- Cantilever

- Lift

- Motorized

- Swing

In this chapter we will explore the types of fences, their components, the types of barbed wire, gates designs, and uses of the perimeter fence. A table at the end of the chapter outlines the advantages and disadvantages for each type of fence. Sensors also can be used to detect intruders that climb, cut, or otherwise disturb the fence. Fence sensors will be discussed in Chapter 7, "Intrusion Detection Systems and Alarms"

TYPES OF PERIMETER FENCES

Perimeter fences are constructed of four types of materials:

1. Chain link

2. Wrought iron

3. Wood

4. Concrete or block wall

The most widely used material is chain-link mesh. Wrought iron is gaining popularity, as is the concrete wall. These fences are used primarily around the perimeters of industrial sites, such as water treatment plants and power substations. The use of these materials has been around for a long time, but since September 11, 2001, they have become more popular and are being used at new installations, even replacing some of the chain-link fences at existing sites. Concrete or block walls usually are topped with barbed wire. Openings in concrete or block walls are limited for allowing vehicular traffic access. To allow vehicular traffic access to the property, you must have some type of motorized gate. Because the walls are installed around a high-security site, the gate motor is operated by an access control card or a keypad. The gates are either wrought iron or chain link to allow ease of movement. When a pedestrian opening is installed, it is sometimes made of a metal door to prevent easy access to unauthorized personnel.

Chain Link

Chain-link fence is the mostly widely used type of perimeter fence. The federal government uses chain-link fences as a boundary around many federal buildings, facilities, and especially parking lots. The federal specifications for chain-link fence have become the industry standard for designing and constructing a perimeter chain-link fence. These specifications are found in Federal Standard RR–F–191/1A. The requirements include the barbed wire, as well as the components of the fence and how it is to be constructed. Below is a summary of the federal specifications for chain link fences, taken from Defense Logistics Agency (DLAI 5710.1):

1. Fabric made of chain link

2. No. 9 gauge or heavier wire

3. Seven feet high

4. Fence fabric mounted on metal posts set in concrete

5. Mesh opening not larger than 2 square inches

6. Fence bottom within 2 inches of solid ground

7. Fence top guard strung with barbed wire, and angled outward and upward at a 45-degree angle

The chain-link fabric is to be constructed of galvanized, aluminized, or plastic-coated woven steel. The fabric is to be secured to the posts with at least 9-gauge wire. If the fence is constructed of 10-gauge wire, then the anchors used to secure the fabric to the posts also shall be made of 10-gauge wire. The anchor wire gauge must be equal to the fabric gauge. Only nonreflective paint should be used on a chain-link fence to reduce glare and maintain the clear zone on both sides of the fence. The mesh openings in the fabric should not be larger than 2 inches square. A larger opening in the mesh will make it easier for an intruder to climb the fence.

The fence is to be mounted on metal posts, using the proper gauge wire, as outlined above. The posts are to be secured in concrete at the proper height of 7 feet. All openings and corners are to be secured with additional bracing (see Figure 3-1 for details). All the posts, bracing, and other structural members are to be located inside the fence fabric and of equal structural strength.

The minimum height of the fence is 7 feet. Some locations may not permit fences to be constructed higher than 6 feet without a permit from the planning and zoning or building department. Check with the local codes before constructing the

FIGURE 3-1   Security fence corner with truss braces & tension rods

fence. Remember, if you are going to add barbed wire set at a 45-degree outward angle, it will add another 12 inches to the overall height of the fence. On top of the fence, the federal standard calls for three strands of barbed wire placed on an 18-inch outrigger, facing upward and outward at a 45-degree angle. This makes the perimeter fence harder to climb from the outside. (See Figure 3-2 for more details). Make sure the angled barbed wire faces outward at a 45-degree angle.

To prevent intruders from being able to lift the fence from the bottom to gain easy entry, the bottom of the chain-link fabric should be extended 2 inches into the ground and be anchored, not allowing an opening of more than 5 inches in

FIGURE 3-2   The 18" outrigger for the barbed wire

height. To anchor the 2-inch extension into the ground, you may use horizontal bottom rails, concrete curbs, or sills. This is sometimes overlooked, but it is important. Finally, the fence needs to be stabilized in areas where there is loose sand, shifting soil, or surface waters that may cause erosion and expose an opening in the perimeter fence. When surface stabilization is not possible, concrete curbs or sills (or other similar permanent anchoring system below ground level) can substitute.

Some chain-link fences have a mesh fabric size of 3/8-inch coated vinyl. Since the mesh is smaller, it is more resistant to damage. For example, a projectile would hit a greater number of strands of the 3/8-inch mesh than on a wider mesh. This makes for a stronger fence. Narrow mesh fabric fences are used in high-security areas. There also are chain-link fences that have slats in the chain link to obscure the view into the area within the perimeter fence. The problem with the so-called privacy slats woven into the chain link is that they block the view inside, voiding the clear-zone concept. However, there are uses for this type of fence. The slats make it very difficult, if not impossible, to climb the chain-link fence. The woven-slat fence is found around:

- Construction excavating sites, to block the public view of the site

- Swimming pools and tennis courts, providing privacy

At high-security locations, such as prisons, you will see two fence lines. There is an interior fence line with a clear zone of approximately 10 yards, then another outer fence. Both fences have three coils of razor wire. This type of double fence installation can be seen around other high-security locations, including military facilities and nuclear power plants. We will cover razor wire later in the chapter.

Wrought Iron

Wrought-iron fences come in all shapes and sizes. Some wrought fences are decorative and are found mainly around residential properties, especially single-family residences in affluent areas. To be effective as a perimeter security fence, it must be at least 6 feet high. An example of a wrought-iron fence can be seen in Figure 3-4.

The specifications of the wrought-iron fence in Figure 3-3:

1. The fence is 7 feet tall.

2. The top has rounded ends facing downward toward the outside and has pointed ends on a 45-degree angle facing outward, similar to the barbed-wire outrigger on a chain-link fence.

3. The ends are sharp, and climbing the fence would not be easy. The diameter of the pickets ranges from 1- to 18-gauge tubular steel.

4. The fence in Figure 3-3 is a two–rail fence, one rail at the bottom and one at the top, and the pickets and slats are 2 inches in diameter.

5. The pickets on the fence are called spade pickets, because they look like a spade found on a playing card.

6. The posts are 4 inches in diameter and are set in concrete.

7. The bottom of the fence's wrought–iron slats is 3 inches above the ground. The fence is built around a water treatment plant facing the road.

The wrought-iron perimeter fence in Figure 3-4 looks formidable and cannot be climbed easily. This type of fence is good for an industrial site, such as a water treatment plant. Before designing and constructing a wrought-iron fence that is 6 feet or higher, check with the codes. Some jurisdictions require a permit to construct such a fence, and others may not allow the fence at all.

The wrought-iron fence is a good deterrent to the uncommitted intruder looking for an easy target. The design in Figure 3-4 would be time consuming to defeat, and even the somewhat motivated intruder may think twice about attempting entry. Time is important to the intruder to evade detection, and the average time spent at a location in the commission of a burglary is 10 minutes.

FIGURE 3-3   Example of a wrought-iron fence

FIGURE 3-4   Wrought-iron perimeter fence

So if it takes time to penetrate the perimeter fence, the intruder may think twice for fear of being detected.

Wood Fences

Wood also is used for perimeter fences. There are various types of wood fences. For wood to provide some sense of security, the fence must be at least 6 feet high. Remember, the fence is intended to slow down the intruder, and wood fences are not as secure as chain-link or wrought-iron fences. Some wood fences are constructed using steel posts. The steel posts tend to last longer than wooden ones, and they are not subject to rot. The types of wood fences are:

- Privacy

- Decorative

- Shadowbox

- Solid board

Privacy wood fences are usually 5 feet or higher and are made using solid board slats with top and bottom rails to secure the slats, which are known as the

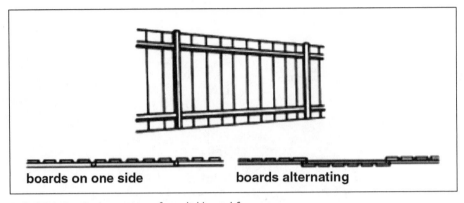

boards on one side   **boards alternating**

FIGURE 3-5 Construction of a solid board fence

board-on-board fence. There is limited visibility from either side of the fence because the boards are placed close together with a small space for the expansion of the wood. There also is a kick plate at the bottom. These fences are made from either redwood or cedar and are used to mark property boundaries in single-family residential lots. This fence type also is used to enclose swimming pools.

FIGURE 3-6 Shadow box fence

Wood fences higher than 5 feet are not easy to climb. Wood fences usually are not topped with barbed wire, since the predominant use of the wood fence is for residences. Openings in wood fences are primarily swing gates. Swing gates that provide access for pedestrians to backyards with swimming pools or spas usually have spring-loaded self-closures installed to prevent the gate from being left open and allowing open access to the pool. The wood fence has its uses, but for a high-security facility, it is better to use a wrought-iron or a chain-link fence. Figure 3-5 is an example of the construction of a solid board fence.

Concrete Walls

Concrete walls often are constructed around industrial operations, such as power substations. Concrete or block walls that are less than 6 feet tall sometimes are used around residential properties such as apartment complexes and single-family homes that back up to commercial property. The walls are used to delineate and not for security, although they provide some security by being an obstacle to intrusion:

- The concrete wall is between 8 and 15 feet high, and is topped with barbed and razor wire.

- The walls often are constructed of filled reinforced concrete cinderblock or precast reinforced concrete, making the wall 4 inches thick. The precast concrete is made off site in sections and put together on site.

- The razor and barbed wire is attached to the wall using the same outriggers found on the chain-link fence set at a 45-degree angle (see Figure 3-2). There are three strands of barbed wire, and on top of the barbed wire is the razor wire.

- The columns for the concrete walls are anchored to concrete footings (piers) that are set below grade. The columns are attached to the footings. The column sits down on the rebar protruding from the footings.

Concrete walls may not be permitted by zoning laws in certain areas if they are over a certain height and are topped with barbed and razor wire. You do see these walls in residential areas to separate a subdivision from a main road, in which case, the walls are rarely topped with barbed and/or razor wire. Concrete walls also are used as sound walls along freeways and other highways to deaden traffic noise.

FENCE OPENINGS

Openings are vulnerable points to the integrity of the perimeter fence. To ensure a secure opening, the designer should follow these recommendations:

- Make sure to use the same material to construct the opening as well as the fence.

- Limit the number of openings to the essentials.

- Use self-closures on any pedestrian gates to prevent them from being left open.

- Monitor the openings in high-security perimeter fences using sensors (to be discussed in Chapter 7) or security officers.

- Provide a latch and lock to secure pedestrian gates when they are not being used.

- The posts that support the gates may ease climbing access. To prevent this, string barbed wire across them.

These are the five types of gates found in perimeter fences:

- Roll/slide

- Cantilever

- Lift

- Motorized

- Swing

The roll/slide, cantilever, and motorized types allow vehicular traffic into the property. The swing gate also is used as a pedestrian gate, which sometimes can be locked electronically with PINs or access cards to gain access.

Roll/slide gates slide open from one side or from both sides. The gates have small wheels on the bottom and are easy to open and close by sliding the panel(s) laterally. On some roll/slide gates, the wheels run along a track, which helps guide the gate. Roll gates usually are used to allow vehicular traffic through the perimeter fence. If the gates are not motorized, they need to be opened manually. At many locations, the manual roll/slider is opened at the beginning of the work day and is left open all day. This creates a large opening in the perimeter fence and is a breach in perimeter security.

The roll/slide gate is constructed of the same material as the rest of the fence. Roll/slide gates are found primarily in chain-link and wrought-iron fences and are used to allow vehicular traffic access.

The cantilever gate operates as a roll/slide gate (see Figure 3-7). The gate is used in places that are too narrow to permit the use of a two-panel roll/slide gate. This type of gate can be operated manually or motorized. The motor-driven gate closes automatically when the vehicle trips a loop inside the perimeter by driving over it. The gate is constructed of the same material as the rest of the fence, which in most cases is chain link or wrought iron.

The lift cantilever gate opens like a roll/slide gate, except it lifts at a 45-degree angle. The gate is used in places that are too small to permit the use of a two-panel roll/slide gate. This type of gate is not usually operated manually, so the

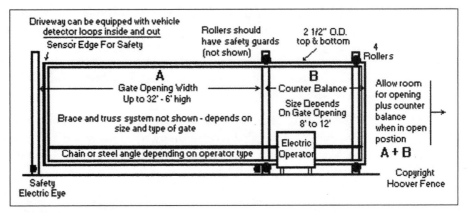

Driveway can be equipped with vehicle
detector loops inside and out
Sensor Edge For Safety

Rollers should
have safety guards
(not shown)

2 1/2" O.D.
top & bottom

4
Rollers

A

Gate Opening Width
Up to 32' - 6' high

Brace and truss system not shown - depends on
size and type of gate

Chain or steel angle depending on operator type

B

Counter Balance

Size Depends
On Gate Opening
8' to 12'

Electric
Operator

Allow room
for opening
plus counter
balance
when in open
postion

A + B

Copyright
Hoover Fence

Safety
Electric Eye

FIGURE 3-7 Cantilever sliding gate

gate is not left open after entry. The gate is constructed of the same material as the rest of the fence, which, in most cases, is chain link or wrought iron.

Some lift gates lift straight up. These usually are chain link and are used in areas without enough room for roll/slide, cantilever, or swing gates. Lift gates are motorized and lift up like a garage door, except the gate lifts in one piece, rather than folding panels.

Motorized gates usually are used at industrial sites for roll/slide, cantilever, lift, or swing gates. They are operated either by a keypad or access card reader. The keypad or access card reader will activate a ground loop or the gate's motor. Motorized gates close either at a preset time (usually a few seconds after being activated) or after the gate is fully opened and the ground loop is activated inside the perimeter. To prevent damage to vehicles that are entering the site, use sensors in the ground loop to prevent the gate from closing prematurely. Exiting through a motorized gate is activated by the ground loop sensor. Sometimes the ground loop for exiting is activated by an access card or a keypad. A motorized gate operator must be sized properly. If the motor is too small, it will either burn out or not open the gate completely.

Swing gates are used for both vehicular and pedestrian openings. The gates for vehicular traffic sometimes are motor operated. Swing gates are hinged on the same side that swings open. If the gate swings to the left, the hinges will be on the left. Swing gates for pedestrian traffic usually are not motor operated but oftentimes have a spring self-closure.

BARBED WIRE

Barbed wire is used to top the perimeter security fence. Without the barbed wire, climbing the fence would not be much of a deterrent. Barbed wire is attached to the top of the fence either by outriggers (discussed earlier in the chapter), or it is strung between other connectors (posts) spaced at intervals along the fence:

- Barbed wire has sharp edges at set intervals along the wire. The barbs are designed to cause discomfort or injury to anyone attempting to climb over or pass through the wire.

- The wire is made of two strands of twisted wire, and the barb is made of a piece of wire tightly coiled around the two strands of wire. The barb has four sharp edges protruding, which are the ends of the wire coiled around the twisted strands.

- The barbs are placed strategically along the twisted strands of wire, making it difficult for an intruder to climb over or pass through the barbed wire.

- Twisted-strand barbed wire can be cut with wire cutters, as can the mesh on a chain-link fence. Since the barbed wire sits on top of the fence, it usually is not easy to reach from the ground. The determined intruder will be equipped to get through the barbed wire and the fence. However, barbed wire is an effective deterrent for less motivated intruders.

These are the methods for stringing barbed wire:

- Outriggers - Barbed wire strung through the outriggers can position the barbed wire strings at a 45-degree angle facing outward.

- Straight barbed wire - These are strings of twisted-strand barbed wire strung between the straight posts, not at an angle but horizontal to the ground. Climbing the straight strands of barbed wire is not as difficult as the angle wire. The straight strands of barbed wire usually are strung across gates.

RAZOR WIRE

Razor wire is similar to barbed wire but is sharper. Razor wire first was used by the military to install a perimeter quickly, because it comes in rolls. One roll covers 50 feet, and several rolls together span a large distance quickly. Sometimes the razor is laid out two rolls side by side for more protection. Razor wire looks intimidating, which is enough to deter some intruders.

For commercial use, the razor is atop the barbed wire on the outriggers. Some commercial locations also have razor wire at the bottom of the fence. The razor at the bottom of the fence is used to deter those who may be thinking of climbing over or crawling under the fence. As stated previously, no fence or razor wire will stop the determined intruder, but the razor and barbed wire can at least slow them down.

- The wire comes in coils and gets its name because the sharp edges look like the old double-edge razor blades, except the ends are very sharp and have a point on each of the four ends.

- Razor wire is used on high-security fences like prisons, government installations, and industrial sites.

- Razor wire, when used at high-security installations, often has three coils, one at the top of the fence, one halfway down, and one at the bottom. The wire on top of the fence is strung over the top string of barbed wire on the outriggers and under the bottom string. On prison fences, razor-wire coils cover the entire length of the fence, making it impossible to climb. It usually takes more than four coils of razor wire to cover the entire fence. The other two coils of razor wire are attached to the fence with anchors.

- The wire is made either from galvanized or stainless steel. This keeps the wire from rusting and needing replacement.

- Many jurisdictions do not permit razor wire, so check local codes before you specify razor wire.

- Razor wire cannot be cut with conventional wire-cutting tools, which makes it more desirable than barbed wire.

Industrial locations with razor wire generally have no more than two coils, but most have only one at the top of the fence. Razor wire also is used on top of vehicle gates, and it is strung through the straight strands of barbed wire.

There are many options for perimeter fence materials. Your choice will depend on the risk analysis you performed to determine what level of security is needed for your site. Barbed and razor wire are important considerations, and local ordinances will dictate what can be used.

FENCE DESIGN SPECIFICATIONS

Most fence companies have specifications. The chain-link fence design specifications are outlined earlier in the chapter. Below is a sample of general specification document headings. The outline can be used for all specifications, and when designing an entire system, all the information can be outlined in one document. Another part of the specifications is the "Instructions to Bidders or Final Specifications Instructions."

PART 1 GENERAL

1.1 Related Documents

1.2 General Requirements

1.3 Submittals

1.4 Quality Assurance

1.5 Delivery, Storage and Handling

1.6 Warranty

PART 2 PRODUCTS

This part outlines the type of fence and the construction materials the dimensions, diameter, etc. This section also outlines finishes and related topics, as well as automatic gate controllers and the motors and electrical, if applicable to the project.

PART 3 EXECUTION

3.1 Examination

3.2 Installation

3.3 Field Quality Control

Related Documents, Section 1.1, outlines what other sections or documents are related to this document or are included in other sections of the document in the sections that follow and any related sections. General Requirements, Section 1.2, outlines what is required for the project.

Submittals, Section 1.3, outlines what is expected to be presented:
- Drawings and how many copies
- Hardware and fence fabric schedule
- Copies of approved hardware and fence fabric schedule for the subcontractors (fence installer)
- Installation instructions
- Other

Quality Assurance, Section 1.4, addresses such things as:
- The length of time the installer has been in business
- Contractor's license number
- Attend a pre-installation meeting
- Ensure fence fabric and material meets the standards set forth in the submittals

Delivery, Storage and Handling, Section 1.5, addresses such things as:

- When and where deliveries are to made
- Where the materials are to be stored
- How the materials are to be handled especially those that are fragile.

Warranty, Section 1.6, addresses such things as:
- What is covered under the warranty
- The length of the warranty
- How to contact the installer for warranty work

Examination, Section 3.1, addresses such things as:
- Any acceptance testing to be performed
- Inspection of the parts

Installation, Section 3.2, addresses such things as:
- Any instructions on the installation
- Location for the installation of parts

Field Quality Control, Section 3.3 addresses such things as:
- How to install the cables and wiring
- All cables are to be tied using plastic ties.
- The location for all the devices for uniformity

Protective Barriers

In this chapter we will explore natural and man-made protective barriers, their uses, and the advantages and disadvantages of each type. Protective barriers are used to enhance perimeter security and usually are retrofitted by design especially those that are man made. Much of the work on the Alfred P. Murrah federal building in Okalahoma City since April 1995 has been retrofitting man-made barriers to prevent vehicles from getting too close to a building. One widely used method immediately following the bombing was to place K-rail (Jersey barriers), which is used to divide highways, around the access to the building to keep vehicles away.

Commercial buildings also added K-rail to provide a buffer zone between the street, driveways, and buildings. However, it was not a long-term solution, because the K-rail is not aesthetically pleasing. Since that time, more permanent and aesthetic solutions have been deployed, such as concrete planters and bollards to enhance the perimeter security. Aesthetically pleasing barriers such as decorative concrete planters are not only good at providing protection, but they help reduce the anxiety level of people using the space, because they do not feel like they are in an armed camp. The best protective barrier is incorporated into the original design and construction of the building or facility.

Protective barriers enhance the security of the perimeter fence or boundary. This is accomplished by incorporating the natural barriers into the scheme of the perimeter fence and enhancing the boundary by monitoring with CCTV or sensors. It is advisable to use more than one protective barrier. This concept is known as "defense in-depth." We will discuss the details of defense-in-depth in a later chapter. To put it simply, defense-in-depth is the process that accounts for the failure of one system allowing a breach to occur, so redundant systems prevent a breach. Protective barriers are usually one of two forms:

- Natural

- Man-made

NATURAL PROTECTIVE BARRIERS

Natural protective barriers are any natural feature that enhances perimeter security to the site. Natural barriers should be backed up with man-made barriers, since the natural barrier can be compromised by a determined intruder. Natural protective barriers consist of:

- Rivers

- Thick brush

- Mountains

- Ravines

- Canyons

Natural boundaries are in place before the design of the facility. In most cases, they cannot be removed (e.g., rivers and mountains), while other natural barriers require heavy equipment for removal (such as hedgerows). This makes the natural boundary difficult to defeat, especially by the less determined intruder. Even the determined and motivated intruder will have a hard time defeating natural barriers. Some natural protective barriers are permanent (such as mountains) and can be difficult to defeat without proper equipment or training. For example, with a facility on the top of mountain with one road in and out, the road can be protected and the rear of the facility can back up to a sheer cliff. The possibility of someone attempting to scale the cliff is very small, and if the intruder attempts to come up the road, he or she will be detected.

Another example of a natural barrier is a facility with a swift-moving river in the rear, used as the first perimeter fence. It would be prudent in some cases to add a second perimeter fence (for example, if the facility is an attractive target to terrorists or thieves). These types of facilities include places with large numbers of people, government buildings, and those housing infrastructure like power generators, chemical plants or refineries. The river would pose a challenge to most intruders, so you could concentrate your efforts on protecting the other three sides of the perimeter with man-made barriers.

Thick brush can be a combination man-made and natural barrier. The brush can be growing naturally, or it can be planted. An example would be planting some type of hedgerow and then letting it grow. A good example of the use of a hedgerow as a natural barrier can be found in France inland from the Normandy Beaches during World War II. The hedgerow provided excellent cover, and even tanks could not penetrate it easily, if at all. The hedgerow was there to provide wind breaks and separate one farm from another. Soldiers on one side of the hedgerow could not see the soldiers on the other side, let alone get through to attack. The only way through the hedgerow was to use tanks with special cutting blades.

Another example of bushes used as a natural barrier is the oleanders in California medians to divide the freeway. The bushes get thick and grow together, and they can slow down or stop an out-of-control vehicle. Also, the oleanders usually are high enough to prevent the opposite lanes of traffic from seeing an accident on the opposite side of the freeway.

Bushes with thorns provide an almost impenetrable perimeter boundary when planted close together. They are used on construction sites to prevent unauthorized people from entering the site. The bushes can be left on the site and used as a perimeter fence after construction is completed.

Natural protective barriers are useful and should be considered in the planning phase of the project. Natural barriers can be used on any site, from manufacturing facilities to college campuses. Any natural protective barriers on the site and could be used in the perimeter security should not be removed or altered in any way that would make them useless as a protective barrier. These natural protective barriers can add aesthetic beauty to the property and enhance perimeter security as well.

The advantages of natural barriers are:

1. They are already in place, so there is no added cost.

2. They cannot, in most cases, be removed or penetrated easily, as in the case of a sheer cliff.

The disadvantages of natural barriers are:

1. If the natural barrier is shrubbery, it needs to be maintained during construction.

2. The natural barrier may not be in the ideal location to provide the optimal protection. For example, a sheer cliff covering only half of the back section of the facility, with the other half a flat wooded area.

3. The main drawback to the natural protective barrier is that there is not a clear zone around the perimeter that is visible from both sides of the barrier.

MAN-MADE PROTECTIVE BARRIERS

The purpose of man-made barriers is to keep unwanted vehicles from accessing the site. The barriers should stop most vehicles from ramming their way through the perimeter. Man-made barriers can be used in conjunction with natural barriers or other man-made systems to provide a backup in case one system is compromised.

Types of man-made barriers include:

1. Decorative planters

2. Bollards

3. K-rail

4. Welded steel guard rails

5. Vehicle arrest barriers

6. Berms/ditches

Decorative Planters

Planters also are used as protective barriers. You can see them in pedestrian areas near the curbs of buildings in the downtown sections of most cities. They also are used to line streets that have been closed off permanently and transformed into pedestrian malls. Decorative planters keep traffic from entering the closed-off street. Decorative concrete barriers (planters) come in all shapes and sizes. Some are formed and shaped to look like planters; others are formed to look like large concrete benches (see Figure 4-1). Planters can be arranged to limit vehicle access to an area. Larger planters provide protection to roadways and buildings when strategically placed. The strategic placement of the planters creates a spatial

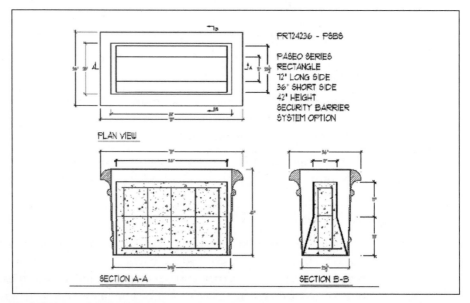

FIGURE 4-1   Concrete decorative planter

barrier between the building and the site improvements to prevent vehicles from accessing the buildings. Adding plants provides more strength to the planter, because the soil adds weight and fills in the open space, making the planter solid.

Planters can be any shape. They have rebar inserted into the concrete for added strength. To be effective as a protective barrier, the planters should conform to the following:

- The planters should have rebar reinforcement as a part of the design.

- Placement of the planters should be spaced so a vehicle-even a motorcycle-cannot fit between the planters.

- The planters should be placed along the curb if the building is located on the street.

- For buildings not located on the street, the planters can be located to prevent vehicular traffic from accessing the front of the building.

- The planters should be filled with soil and plants to increase their strength and aesthetics.

The advantages of using decorative planters to enhance perimeter security are:

- They are decorative and aesthetically pleasing.

- They are easy to deploy, because they are somewhat portable and can be moved using a forklift, or backhoe and sling.

- They are solid, especially if they are constructed using rebar and filled with soil and a plant.

The disadvantages of using planters to enhance perimeter security are:

- Because the planters cannot be moved easily, careful consideration must be given to deploying them.

- As with all man-made perimeter security, there is a cost involved in the purchase and installation of the planters.

- Traffic cannot be directed through the areas where the planters are located, so they may affect deliveries.

Bollards

Bollards are used to prevent vehicles from hitting and damaging equipment on manufacturing sites. They also are used to prevent vehicles in public areas from hitting and damaging fire hydrants, gas station pumps, electrical transformers in parking lots, etc. You usually see them at the ends of each pump island. They are good for anti-ram and traffic control but also can be aesthetically pleasing as well. Finally, bollards are aesthetically pleasing and usually fade into the background, so they are not noticeable to the users of the space.

Bollards are made from stainless steel, with the pipe being filled with concrete. The style used will depend on the location. Stainless-steel bollards are attractive and aesthetically pleasing, so they are usually used along the curb and next to buildings on the street. Bollards range in thickness from 12 to 24 inches in diameter. To place a bollard into position, a hole is bored into the ground a sleeve is placed into the hole where the bollard will be, and the bollard is lowered into the sleeve. Some bollards are then bolted to a plate secured within the concrete, covering the top of the sleeve. Most bollards extend 12 inches or more into the sleeve. This gives the bollard strength to withstand a vehicle.

There are four categories of bollards:

1. Fixed

2. Removable

3. Automatic retractable

4. Manual retractable

Fixed bollards are permanently anchored into the ground by bolting them to an anchor plate. They are used to protect large areas. Sometimes you see bollards lined up along the curb in front of a building. There is enough space to walk between them but not enough for a vehicle to pass through. The purpose of fixed bollards (as well as other types) is to prevent vehicles loaded with explosives from jumping the curb and getting close to the building.

Removable bollards can be lifted out of their sleeve to allow vehicle access. The bollards generally are not light, and therefore, are not easy to handle manually. However, smaller-diameter bollards can be lifted from the sleeve without special equipment, but since the bollard is heavy, it is not removed frequently. Usually two, three or more will be removable, depending on the diameter and spacing of the bollards, which creates an opening large enough for vehicles to enter. The larger-diameter bollards usually are lifted with a backhoe or forklift. These bollards do not allow easy access for authorized vehicles, which is why the retractable bollard is used where the flow of traffic in and out of the area is routine.

Another type of bollard is the automatic retractable. Like the removable bollard, the retractable bollard is designed to allow vehicle access. The retractable bollard slides into the sleeve until it is flush with the ground, thus allowing a vehicle to drive over it. The retraction is done electronically. The bollards in this type of system can be deployed quickly to prevent a speeding vehicle heading toward the location from entering. It takes less than 6 seconds to deploy the bollards from the lowered position to the full upright position. But the caveat of this system is that someone must be available to receive a warning that a vehicle is approaching at a speed and be able to operate the switch.

Bollards also can be lowered into the sleeve manually. A key bar is used to manually lower the bollard. It fits into a slot on top of the bollard and has two handles that extend on each side that turn to lower the bollard. The key bar looks like a key to shut off a water main valve. It is a bar with a key in the center and a handle on both sides above to turn the key and lower the bollard manually. These bollards are not removed often, since it may take time to find and use the key to lower the bollard. Manual bollards usually are not used for emergency vehicle access for this reason.

The advantages of using bollards to enhance perimeter security are:

1. They are more attractive than K-rail.

2. They can be removable or retractable, which will allow vehicle traffic to enter for deliveries, emergencies, etc.

3. They have been used for a long time, and the public is used to them.

The disadvantages of using bollards for enhancing security are:

1. They need to be installed, and the bollard sleeves need to be drilled into the concrete.

2. There is a cost associated with the installation, as well as a premium for more decorative bollards.

3. Because they are not as large as concrete planters or K-rail, the spacing is important and will dictate the number needed.

K-Rail

Another name for K-rail is Jersey barrier. The barrier got its name because it was first used on the New Jersey Turnpike and other New Jersey highways. K-rail is designed to deflect cars or trucks hitting the barrier. However, there are times that vehicles go over the barrier, especially if they are traveling at a high speed and become airborne. Therefore, when properly deployed, the barrier makes a good defense against vehicles attempting to get close to a building or onto the site. The proper deployment is to place the K-rail sections at angles and create a maze-like configuration. This will prevent a truck or car from defeating the barrier easily. The design of the barrier is important to achieving the goal of protecting the location:

• The barrier is sloped, with the slope being 13 inches from the ground. The purpose of the slope is to minimize damage to the vehicle, so the tires will ride up the lower sloped area, and to prevent the vehicle from going through the barrier.

- Hitting the barrier head-on will slow a vehicle down but may not stop it altogether. This is why you see barriers deployed at angles, so they can not be hit head-on.

- The barrier comes in sections that can be joined with reinforcing steel tie rods and concrete fill.

- The barrier is designed with reinforcing rods running the length of each section.

K-rail also is used as a temporary divider for road construction projects, so it's a well-known barrier. K-rail is used as a security perimeter barrier to protect buildings from truck and car bombs by creating buffer zones. The barriers are used to channel traffic to keep the buffer zone clear and not permit parking next to the building.

The advantages of K-rail are:

- K-rail can be deployed as a temporary perimeter security enhancement for special events or until a more permanent solution can be deployed.

- K-rail is used for crowd control at large special events because it can be deployed quickly with backhoes or bucket loaders.

The disadvantages of K-rail are:

- K-rail is not aesthetically pleasing.

- K-rail is a pedestrian nightmare to navigate when used in downtown settings, because it blocks sidewalks.

- Deliveries to areas using K-rail also are hampered because K-rail is not portable or easy to move.

- If a large bomb were set off near K-rail, the barriers may fragment and become a hazard.

Welded Steel Guard Rails

Welded steel guard rails have many uses. They are used as barriers in manufacturing facilities to prevent forklifts from contacting and damaging sensitive and/or critical equipment. The most visible use of guard rails is along highways as a divider or a barrier on a sheer cliff. Some guard rails have wooden posts and steel rails. We will discuss only the steel guard rail and post system. Guard rails for highway use are designed to:

1. Prevent a vehicle from leaving the roadway and crossing the center divider or from going down a steep embankment

2. Absorb some of the crash impact and keep the vehicle from rolling over

Guard rails can be placed strategically around the facility to be protected. The guard rail establishes a buffer zone around the building to keep vehicles from getting too close. Guard rails are not considered fences and usually range from 24 inches to 36 inches high. To be effective, the steel guard rail should be used in conjunction with another perimeter security feature, such as planters or bollards. Steel guard rail may not stop a truck coming head-on. Steel guard rails come in these sizes and dimensions:

- The rails are 11-inch-diameter corrugated steel.

- The posts are 4-square-inch steel.

- Heights vary from 18 inches to 42 inches.

The advantages of steel guard rail as a protective barrier are:

1. It is designed to withstand vehicle impact.

2. The designs are tested to ensure reliability.

The disadvantages of steel guard rails are:

1. Steel guard rail is not aesthetically pleasing.

2. It can be expensive to purchase and install large sections of guard rail.

3. How it is installed and the height of the guard rail will determine whether it can be penetrated easily by a large truck.

Vehicle Arrest Systems

Another tool in the arsenal of protective barriers is the vehicle arrest system. Some systems are designed for high-security environments, and then there are the everyday systems in parking garages, parking lots, and railroad crossings. A vehicle arrest system is defined as a system that will physically stop an unauthorized vehicle from entering an area. The most common system is the wooden or metal cross gate across the entry in public parking garages at airports and other places. The gate looks like a railroad crossing gate and is designed to allow vehicular access when a ticket is issued. Removing the ticket activates the switch to open the cross gate. When you leave the garage, the attendant operates the arm. These systems in the garages are not really security systems, since it is easy to drive through, breaking the arm. Security vehicle arrest systems are much more substantial.

Crash beams will stop a truck and are operated by hydraulics. These also are active devices to control traffic through a portal. The crash beam looks like the gates used in parking garages, except it is built of more a substantial material, like steel. Crash beams are designed to stop a vehicle traveling at low to medium speeds.

Retractable bollards are sometimes used as crash beams, as is retractable K-rail. These barriers rise out of the pavement when activated by a card reader and a ground loop, and they are the most substantial of the group. Some of the largest of these barricades are designed to stop a 30,000-pound vehicle traveling at 50 miles per hour. The medium-size barricades are designed to stop a 15,000-pound vehicle traveling at 50 miles per hour. The weight of the vehicle is important, because a load of explosives adds weight. The devices in this category are substantial and effective in stopping potential truck or car bombs from entering the protected zone. The retractable systems are passive. The designer of these systems needs to consider opposite-direction traffic, or the traffic leaving the site. An automatic device on the outgoing traffic side can be useful.

There are two types of vehicle arrest systems:

1. Active

2. Passive

An active system requires deactivation for entry. The garage system is active because when you drive up, the arm is in the down position, blocking entry until you take your ticket to deactivate the arm.

In a passive system, the arrest device is in the lowered position, allowing traffic to come and go freely. Passive systems are generally not as substantial as active devices.

Another vehicle arrest system is the plate barrier. There are two types:

1. Shallow mount

2. Surface mount

The shallow mount plate barrier is made of a 3/4-inch-thick plate that locks the plate in place when activated. This device is passive, as well. The plate is a shallow mount around 18 inches deep, so it can be deployed quickly. This device also is capable of stopping a 15,000-pound vehicle traveling at 50 miles per hour.

The surface-mount barrier is bolted down to the roadway. This device is passive as well. The device is capable of stopping a 3,000-pound vehicle traveling at 30 miles per hour.

The advantages of vehicle arrest systems are:

• They are effective in stopping vehicles that may be loaded with explosives.

• There are several variations from which to choose.

The disadvantages of vehicle arrest systems are:

• The installation can be expensive.

• They are not aesthetically pleasing.

Berms and Ditches

A berm is a raised portion of earth used to catch water or to block an unappealing view. They are sort of a manmade hill. A good example of a berm is a levee system around a river to prevent it from overflowing. Berms can be used as a barrier to stop a vehicle. The berm would have to be wide but also must be steep so a vehicle cannot roll over the top.

Ditches, on the other hand, are used as part of the property's drainage system and can be deep enough to prevent a vehicle from traversing easily to gain access to the site. A drainage ditch with a fence can be used as a part of the perimeter security protection plan.

The advantages of berms and ditches for perimeter security are that they are natural and may already be in place.

DESIGN CONSIDERATIONS FOR PROTECTIVE BARRIERS

Depending on the protective barrier chosen for the project, the designer will need to outline specifications. The following outline can be used as a guide:

PART 1 GENERAL

1.1 Related Documents

1.2 General Requirements

1.3 Submittals

1.4 Quality Assurance

1.5 Delivery, Storage, and Handling

1.6 Warranty-What the warranty covers, how long and how to get warranty service work completed.

PART 2 PRODUCTS

This part outlines the type of protective barrier, the construction materials, the dimensions, diameter, etc. This section also outlines finishes, automatic gate controllers, motors and electrical, if applicable to the project.

PART 3 EXECUTION

3.1 Examination

3.2 Installation

3.3 Field Quality Control

Related Documents, Section 1.1, outlines what other sections or documents are related to this document or are included in other sections of the document in the sections that follow and any related sections. General Requirements, Section 1.2, outlines what is required for the project.

Submittals, Section 1.3, outlines what is expected to be presented:

- Drawings and how many copies

- Hardware and fence fabric schedule

- Copies of approved hardware and fence fabric schedule for the subcontractors (fence installer)

- Installation instructions

- Other

Quality Assurance, Section 1.4, addresses such things as:

- The length of time the installer has been in business

- Contractor's license number

- Attend a pre-installation meeting

- Ensure fence fabric and material meets the standards set forth in the submittals

CONCLUSION

As you can see there are various natural and manmade barriers to enhance perimeter security. The natural barriers already on the site, such as rivers, mountains, and canyons should be used in the design of the perimeter protective barriers and physical security. Integrating natural barriers into the site perimeter security plan will enhance security as well as aesthetics.

CHAPTER 5

Security Lighting

ecurity lighting is an important part of the perimeter security plan. On most projects, however, little consideration is given to the security design and layout. Usually, lights are installed, and that is far as it goes. Then the owners, property managers, security directors, managers, etc., wonder why the images from the CCTV system along the perimeter of the property are not very good and usually are of poor quality.

For example, a vandal damages someone's vehicle in the parking lot at night and the CCTV images are not good enough to identify the perpetrator. The person's whose vehicle was damaged will not be happy however if the CCTV system and the security lighting is designed properly, you might be able to see the person, identify the person as male or female, and even possibly make a positive ID. Lighting is a usually on overlooked consideration when installing a CCTV camera system. This shortcoming of inadequate security lighting is discovered after the system has been installed and is needed for an investigation.

In this chapter we will explore the types of security lighting and their uses, as well as the integration of security lighting and CCTV. We will cover the concept of foot-candles, as well as the need for backup power sources and emergency exit lights. The design of a CCTV system will be covered in a later chapter.

Security lighting is used to light up the perimeter and property at night to closely simulate daylight. Security lighting makes an intruder visible, unable to use the cover of darkness to breach the perimeter security. Security lighting also will enhance the effectiveness of any security force on site by providing a clear view of the property through the CCTV.

To determine the security lighting requirements for the location, we need to know what we are trying to protect and from whom must be protected. For a quick reference to lighting requirements by foot-candle power, see Table 5-1 later in the chapter. This outlines the lighting requirements in the U.S. Army

Field Manual 3–18.30. FM 3–18.30 is the security industry standard for lighting requirements. The manual is an update of a previous version, and the lighting requirements have not changed.

When choosing security lighting for a project, also consider the energy efficiency of the lamps and systems. There are energy-efficient lamps and security lighting systems that also produce illuminations to meet the requirements outlined in Table 5-1. Remember, the goal of the security lighting is to provide illumination without shadows so potential intruders will not be able to enter the location without being detected by the security officers viewing the video surveillance system and/or roving patrols of security officers. The lighting also will aid the CCTV system by providing the necessary light for capturing useful images for security and investigations of unauthorized entries to the site as well as identifying any vandals. Finally, security lighting is inexpensive to maintain and will aid security forces by reducing the advantages of concealment and surprise for the motivated intruder.

Security lighting alone will not discourage an unauthorized person from attempting to enter the site, but the lighting will assist security personnel in detecting the unauthorized person. The lighting will enable the security force to observe activities around the site while minimizing the presence of the security force. To accomplish this task, security lighting must create contrast between the intruder and the background. For painted surfaces, grass, clean concrete, and brick walls, the lighting does not need to be as intense. The lighting must be more intense to contrast an intruder from a dark or dirty background. Eliminating shadowing is another important consideration in the design of the security

TABLE 5-1   Standards for the amount of lighting required for emergency and security lighting

LOCATION	FOOT-CANDLES ON HORIZONTAL PLANE AT GROUND LEVEL
Perimeter of outer area	0.15
Perimeter of restricted area	0.4
Vehicular entrances	1.0
Pedestrian entrances	2.0
Sensitive inner areas	0.15
Sensitive inner structure	1.0
Entrances	0.1
Open yards	0.2
Decks on open piers	1.0

lighting system. Along with more intense lighting, some things can be done to the background to assist the lighting. For example, painting stripes provides breaks in the background, which helps contrast outlines or silhouettes. These breaks will not provide any cover for an intruder to hide.

The goals of security lighting are:

• To create a psychological deterrent to an intruder

• To aid in detecting intruders

• To prevent glare that may blind security officers and produce outward glare to blind intruders

• To provide enough lighting for CCTV to depict and record colors accurately

One way to check for proper illumination is by using a light meter. The light meter will give you a pretty good idea if there is sufficient lighting in an area.

FOOT-CANDLE POWER

Foot-candle power is how lights are rated. It is a unit of measure to determine light intensity and is equal to 1 lumen per square foot, or the amount of light produced by one candle in a 1-square-foot area.

Foot-candles are measured using a light meter. Using a light meter is simple, especially with digital readout. Hold the meter where you want to check the illumination, and the meter will produce a readout of the foot-candles of light being produced by the lighting device. The higher the number of foot-candles, the more light is being given off. There are standards for the amount of lighting required for emergency and security lighting found in Table 5-1. Foot-candles are being replaced by lux. One lux is equal to 10 foot-candles and is a metric measurement. Light meters will give the reading in both foot-candles and lux.

Categories of Security Lighting

Security lighting is divided into four basic categories:

1. Continuous lighting

2. Standby lighting

3. Movable lighting

4. Emergency lighting

Continuous lighting is the most common security lighting system. It consists of a series of fixed lights arranged to flood an area with light continuously during darkness. The lamps are arranged to provide overlapping cones of light.

An example is the lights used in a chemical or oil refinery. The two types of continuous lighting are glare projection and controlled lighting. Glare projection lighting is also known as security lights. These lights will cause glare outwardly from inside the perimeter, causing any intruder attempting to enter the site to be blinded temporarily, thereby making it difficult to see inside the perimeter. The best example of controlled lighting is streetlights along highways, where the width of the lighted strip is adjusted to fit a certain area.

Standby lighting is similar to continuous lighting in arrangement, but it is not illuminated continually. The lights are tripped by a sensor or illuminated manually by security officers when an intruder or suspicious activity is detected.

Movable lighting can be moved and is not continuous. It is similar to a searchlight to track the movement of an intruder. A good example is the prison searchlight that watches several areas as it illuminates while it moves around.

Emergency lighting is used during a power outage or other failure that will cause the permanent lighting system to become inoperative. This includes an attack on the system. The emergency lighting is dependent on an alternative power source, either a generator or batteries.

Types of Lamps (Luminaries)

The bulb or lamp is the part of the light that produces the illumination. There are six types of lamps in security lighting:

1. Incandescent lamps are the most common bulbs in our homes. The incandescent bulb will provide instant illumination when it is switched on and also is the most common bulb used in security lighting.

2. Fluorescent lamps are most commonly found in offices and schools, as well as kitchens and bathrooms. The fluorescent bulb will produce 62 lumens per watt and is very efficient. The bulb is mercury vapor, which is temperature sensitive and should not be used outdoors in cold climates. Fluorescent lamps will cause interference with radio reception.

3. Mercury-vapor lamps often are used in security and produce a bluish cast when illuminated. The bulbs of mercury-vapor lamps last   longer   than incandescent lamps and can tolerate a 50 percent power dip. It takes considerable time for mercury-vapor lamps to illuminate when they are switched on.

4. Metal-halide lamps also are very tolerant of power dips. The illumination time also is considerable. However, a power dip of 20 seconds or more will cause the lamp to turn off.

5. Sodium-vapor lights are both high- and low-pressure lamps that produce a soft yellow light and are more efficient than mercury vapor lights. These lights are used in areas prone to fog and usually are found on highways and bridges,

because the yellow light will penetrate mist more effectively than white light.

6. Quartz lamps produce a very bright white light. The lamp illuminates almost as quickly as an incandescent lamp. Quartz lamps are high wattage, ranging from 1,500 to 2,000 watts in security lighting systems. Quartz lights are used along the perimeter fences and other barriers.

7. Halogen lamps are charged with xenon gas. The lamp produces a bright white light. The halogen lamp is popular, especially for vehicle headlights. Halogen lights are long-lasting.

Types of Security Lighting

There are four general types of security lighting systems:

- Floodlights are luminaries that use a narrow beam to focus on a specific area. The lights are very bright and concentrated, and therefore, produce glare. They are effective for directing glare outward from the site. Floodlights can be tripped automatically, using a passive inferred (PIR) device, motion sensors, or manually by security personnel. We will cover sensors in more detail in a later chapter.

- Fresnel lenses produce illumination in a long, horizontal beam. A good example is a lighthouse. Fresnel lenses were designed for use in lighthouses to warn ships of danger. In security, the illumination can be concentrated to produce glare for the intruder but not for those inside the perimeter. Fresnel lenses can be tripped by a PIR device, motion sensors, or manually.

- Searchlights are incandescent lamps that are focused narrowly. They can be moved around and focused on any location inside or outside the perimeter. Searchlights are used for grand openings of stores, restaurants, etc. Hollywood also uses searchlights to signify gala events.

- Street lamps also are considered a security light. Streetlights are used in parking lots and sometimes at vehicle entrances to the site. Street lights also are used along the perimeter. There are two types of street lights, symmetrical and asymmetrical. Symmetrical lights are used to disperse the illumination evenly, and asymmetrical lights are used to disperse the light by reflection.

LIGHTING REQUIREMENTS FOR PERIMETER PROTECTION

Each of the four types of security lighting has its uses, but no one type is good for all applications. When designing the system, you need to consider the following areas and lighting requirements (see Table 5-1). The table outlines the minimum amount of illumination needed and provides foot-candles based on the Department of the Army Field Manual 19.30 Physical Security. FM 3-19.30 dated January 8, 2001, supersedes FM 3-19, which was dated March 1979. FM 3-19.30, like the older version, is the standard used in the security industry for lighting requirements. The foot-candles have not changed from the older to the new edition of the FM. The minimum lighting recommendations in the table are based on FM 3-19.30.

Table 5-2 summarizes the security requirements of the Illuminating Engineering Society of North America. These standards are used in numerous local ordinances that call for security lighting as a part of Crime Prevention Through Environmental Design (CPTED). CPTED has gained wide acceptance in a number of communities across the United States and Canada. CPTED is the concept of prevention through the build out of the site to reduce the incidence of crime and the fear of crime occurring. The ordinances in most communities state that security lighting should not be directed above the horizontal plane of the project. The lights should have shields on the fixtures to keep the light from being visible on adjacent properties and roadways. The general use of floodlights as a part of the security lighting design is discouraged and may not be permitted.

Here is an outline of the requirements of some jurisdictions for security lighting. The requirements are usually part of an ordinance that outlines all lighting requirements that are acceptable throughout the jurisdiction. The ordinances usually are enforced as a part of the building permit process:

1. The illumination from security lighting will not illuminate vertical surfaces on buildings to a level of 8 feet above grade or 8 feet above the bottom of doorways or entries, whichever is greater.

2. Poles for mounting security lighting can be no more than 10 feet from the perimeter of the designated secure area.

TABLE 5-2   Illumination tables (foot-candles) permitted for security lighting applications Illuminating Engineering Society

LOCATION	FOOT-CANDLES REQUIRED AT LEVEL ON GROUND
Perimeter Fence	0.5
Buildings	0.5–2.0
Large open areas	0.5–2.0
Entrances	10
Gatehouses	30
Pedestrian walkways and access points	4–6

3. Perimeter security lights will have motion sensors to activate the lights, since the lights are to be in the off position until the motion sensor is tripped by an intruder within 5 feet of the perimeter.

4. The height of the pole on which a security lighting fixture is mounted is usually restricted to no more than 15 to 20 feet, depending on the jurisdiction.

5. The illumination tables (foot-candles) permitted for each security lighting application are based on the Illuminating Engineering Society of North America. Those jurisdictions that have adopted CPTED use the Illuminating Engineering Society of North America's security lighting standards outlined in Table 5-2.

6. The jurisdiction will review and approve the plans for security lighting as a part of the site lighting master plan.

Lighting requirements for the perimeter fence based on FM 3-19.30:

1. Where the perimeter fence is more than 100 feet or more from the building and there is a 100-foot clearance for 100 feet outside of the perimeter fence, the type of lighting recommended is glare projection.

2. For what is known as semi-isolated fenced perimeters, where there is not a clear zone within 60 to 100 feet outside the fence, controlled lighting is recommended.

3. For perimeter fence lines that are immediately adjacent to buildings, etc., controlled lighting is recommended inside the fence area.

Lighting needed for illuminating the entrances to the site based on FM 3-19.30:

1. Controlled lighting should be used for pedestrian entrances used to and from the site. The lighting should provide enough illumination to recognize people and examine ID badges. This requires a minimum of 2.0 foot-candles of illumination.

2. Vehicle entrances, on the other hand, should have enough illumination to complete a safe inspection of passenger cars, trucks, and freight cars (rail), including the contents.

3. Security officer gatehouses usually have a lower intensity of illumination inside the gatehouse, so officers can see approaching vehicles and pedestrians. If the illumination intensity inside the gatehouse is too high, the officer will not be able to see out as easily but would be easy to see from the outside.

Lighting illuminating other areas of the site and property based on FM 3-19.30:

1. Vacant land, storage, garages, and parking areas require illumination by controlled lighting of not less than 0.2 foot-candles.

2. Open areas adjacent to security officers and the perimeter fence require controlled lighting.

3. The decks on open piers are to be illuminated at a minimum of 1 foot-candle, and water approaches to piers within 100 feet should be illuminated to 0.5 foot-candles.

4. Areas beneath the pier should be illuminated with low-wattage floodlights. The floodlights are to be anchored to the pilings of the pier. Movable lighting also is used for docks and piers. Lighting on docks and piers must not be glaring to pilots or violate any marine rules and regulations. The U.S. Coast Guard has the authority to approve lighting adjacent to navigable waterways.

5. Lighting fixtures placed in outdoor storage places provide adequate distribution of illumination in aisles, passageways, and recesses to eliminate shadowed areas where an intruder could hide.

LIGHTING REQUIREMENTS FOR CCTV

Lighting is important for CCTV to capture images that are identifiable during hours of darkness. The intensity of the lighting of an area usually is overlooked when designing and installing a CCTV system. Qualified CCTV installation companies will address lighting issues, but the vast majority of CCTV installers don't consider lighting. Without adequate illumination, the CCTV system will not be an effective tool for monitoring perimeter security. To help make CCTV more effective, the following illumination and lighting arrangements should be considered in the overall design from the lighting guidelines of the U.S. Army Corps of Engineers Technical Manual 5-811-1:

1. Balanced lighting is obtained by illuminating the scene uniformly. This will provide the best image contrast. The lighting must illuminate the entire area within a single camera's field of view to ensure the that the maximum light-to-dark ratio does not exceed 6 to 1 and still provide the minimum faceplate illumination level necessary for the camera's entire field of view.

2. The camera and light source alignment is attained when the camera is located below the plane of the lighting fixture used to illuminate the area. No camera should be positioned to look directly into the lighting plane, especially if side light is used. To alleviate this problem, the camera and the lighting should be aimed in the same direction.

3. Spectral compatibility is another important point to consider when supplying lights for CCTV illumination. Spectral compatibility is when the amount of light put out by the light source is the same that is needed for the camera lens to operate properly. Since there are a variety of CCTV cameras available for

outdoor use, it is important that the light source spectra and the camera lens spectra match, so the light provides optimal illumination for the lens.

4. It is important to consider the coordination of the lighting restart capability with the CCTV system to make sure the cameras have the proper illumination. If the CCTV system is for surveillance of a critical area or function make sure any interruption in lighting will not create a problem for the camera lens chosen for the project. There are cameras that will adapt to low-light situations, but that will affect the quality of the image captured by the camera lens. The best recommendation is to discuss the proposed CCTV design with a competent, impartial CCTV system design installation company and not just a vendor that sells and installs certain systems. We will discuss CCTV systems in more detail in a later chapter.

ELECTRICAL POWER SOURCES FOR SECURITY LIGHTING

No discussion about security lighting would be complete without mentioning electrical power sources for the lighting. There are numerous things to consider, and the U.S. Army Corps of Engineers Technical Manual 5-811-1(TM 5-811-1) outlines a number of requirements. The requirements outline the need for alternative and backup power sources. The type of backup system will depend on whether the facility needs uninterrupted power for the security lighting system for critical and sensitive areas of the site. Following is a discussion of the types of alternative and backup power systems for security lighting, based on TM 5-811-1:

1. Alternative electric power is required in the event of an outage of the normal power source. The system used for the alternative power source must be reliable so continuous illumination will be ensured through the use of a battery backup system. Uninterruptible power supplies (UPS) are not used for security lighting because they do not perform satisfactorily for lighting applications. There two main types of alternative power sources:

   a. Battery backup – The battery backup is used when the demand for power is small. The lights are wired to the batteries, and when there is a loss of the main power, the UPS will take over and keep the lights on the system illuminated, or the lights themselves will have a built-in battery pack that will take over during a normal power outage. A battery backup system is more economical for small-demand systems; for larger-demand systems, a standby generator will be needed.

   b. Standby generator – The standby generator will have either an automatic or manual start. The generator is used to generate the power necessary to keep the lights illuminated during a disruption in the normal power source.

2. The restrike or startup time for some lamps used in security lighting has to be considered when designing a backup power source. For example, with high-intensity discharge (HID) lamps, the time for the startup is extended when using a generator, because of the time required for restriking the arc in a HID lamp. High-pressure sodium (HPS) lamps have the shortest restrike time for security lamps, which is less than one minute from a hot lamp. A lamp is hot for three minutes after loss of power. The total elapsed time from the loss of normal power to full HPS illumination includes the times for the standby generator to start up and the HPS lamp to restrike (four to five minutes).

The tolerable outage time of the security lighting system needs to be considered in the design phase. Tolerable outage time will depend on the project. Some projects have critical or sensitive locations that require backup and alternative power sources. The risk assessment will help determine the requirements for security lighting and alternative power sources. So the design and use of restrike systems need to be engineered carefully to achieve the desired level of minimum illumination for security lighting.

Wiring and Lighting Controls

The important points to remember in the design of security lighting system wiring and controls are:

1. The wiring must be installed in accordance with applicable codes and ordinances. The wire will need to be placed underground to minimize accidental damage, vandalism, sabotage, or weather-related issues.

2. To minimize illumination degradation during power surges, the feeders should be three-phase with a four-wire to its own breaker at the breaker box.

3. All lighting circuits need to be grounded.

4. The wiring circuit must be arranged so that if one lamp fails, it will not leave a large portion of the perimeter in darkness, especially any critical areas. The design of the lighting system must take into account the failure of lamps and make sure there is sufficient overlap to prevent a lamp failure from causing dark areas of the perimeter.

There are two types of on-off security lighting controls, manual and automatic. Manual controls are similar to a traditional light switch. These controls need to be accessible to and operated only by authorized personnel.

Automatic controls to switch on security lighting can be a sensor that is activated by darkness, by a passive infrared (PIR) device, or a motion sensor. The type of activation used to automatically control the security lighting will depend on the needs of the location. Usually a combination of automatic control systems is used to activate security lighting.

A good use of a PIR to activate security lighting would be at an entrance to a building door, overhead door, etc. When someone approaches the entrance, the PIR will activate a floodlight. The floodlight could be set to provide glare projection to blind the person approaching the entrance. A word of caution when setting the floodlight to provide glare projection. Make sure the approach is not used by vehicles, or an accident may occur if the person driving the vehicle is blinded by the glare.

MAINTENANCE OF LIGHTING SYSTEMS

Lighting systems require mechanical maintenance to keep the system at its optimal performance level. Maintenance includes not only repair of damaged equipment, but also preventive maintenance. Light levels will decrease over time. Aging lamps and dirt on fixtures and lamps can reduce the total illumination by 50 percent. This is especially true for lamps and fixtures exposed to the elements. A preventive maintenance and inspection program includes:

1. Inspect all electrical circuits

2. Replace or repair worn parts

3. Tighten connections

4. Check to make sure the insulation is not worn or frayed, which may cause a short circuit if the wires become exposed

5. Check that the fixtures are aimed properly

6. Clean fixtures every six to twenty-four months to ensure optimal illumination

7. Take measurements with a light meter periodically to see if there is proper illumination according to the design criteria for the system. The information should be included in a report of the findings and kept on file. The foot-candle requirements listed in Table 5-1 should still be available from the lighting system. If not, recommendations for redesign must be considered and added to the report.

SECURITY LIGHTING DESIGN CONSIDERATIONS

The steps to designing the most effective and efficient security lighting system are:

1. Perform a risk analysis and a threat assessment for the project.

2. Look at the minimum lighting requirement in Table 5-1 for the foot-candle power, and select the one the meets the requirement for the area.

3. Select the type of lighting system (lamps) that will provide the proper illumination based on the requirements for the area. Usually more than one system is used for a project, since different areas will require different lighting.

4. Review and comply with the jurisdiction's security lighting requirements, since the security lighting plan will be part of the overall lighting master plan submitted to the building department for approval.

5. Layout the lamps and fixtures on a site plan and ensure that the illumination overlaps to ensure effective illumination of the area. This will prevent dark areas for intruders to hide.

6. If a CCTV system is part of the security plan, the lighting must be compatible with the CCTV camera lens. Remember, the lighting spectra must be compatible with the camera lens spectra, or the camera will not provide the best image. Knowing what the lighting will be will enable a more informed decision about the CCTV system.

7. When designing the security lighting system, make sure the lights do not create a nuisance to surrounding neighbors. A properly designed security lighting system will illuminate both sides of the perimeter boundary but not extend too far outside the perimeter and into the neighbors' perimeters.

8. Parking lot light design and layout also should provide adequate illumination for the CCTV system to capture good images. Will the lights produce dark spaces for intruders to hide?

The following outline can be used to detail the specifications for the security lighting system. The information provided in the specification outline below can be modified to fit the needs of the project. The specification document is an important part of the bid package and is necessary for obtaining bids that will reflect the cost of the purchase and installation of the security lighting system will be for the project within the scope and design of the project.

PART 1 GENERAL

1.1 Related Documents

1.2 General Requirements

1.3 Submittals

1.4 Quality Assurance

1.5 Delivery, Storage, and Handling – when and where the materials are to be delivered to, how they will be stored until needed and any special handling requirements of the materials to prevent damage.

1.6 Warranty – the length of the warranty and what is covered and how to request work to be done under the warranty for replacement of defective parts.

PART 2 PRODUCTS

This part outlines the type of protective lighting, the materials, the luminaries, locations, emergency power, etc. This section also outlines finishes, lighting installation methods, pole mounted, building and the electrical wiring, etc. that is specific to the project.

PART 3 EXECUTION

3.1 Examination

3.2 Installation

3.3 Field Quality Control

Related Documents, Section 1.1, outlines what other sections or documents are related to this document or are included in other sections of the document in the sections that follow and any related sections. General Requirements, Section 1.2, outlines what is required for the project. Submittals, Section 1.3, outlines what is expected to be presented:

- Drawings and how many copies
- Type of lighting, locations schedule
- Copies of approved lighting and luminaries for the subcontractors (electrical contractor)
- Installation instructions if any such as locations of the light fixtures, distances, angles, etc. to provide the coverage needed for lighting the perimeter of the site
- Other

Quality Assurance, Section 1.4, addresses such things as:
- The length of time the installer has been in business
- Contractor's license number
- Attend a pre-installation meeting
- Ensure fence fabric and material meets the standards set forth in the submittals

CONCLUSION

As you can see there are various security lighting systems and luminaries to enhance perimeter security. The lighting scheme for security should enhance any other lighting that is planned for the site and should be used in the design of the perimeter security lighting plan as an element of the site physical security plan. Integrating security lighting into the site perimeter security plan will enhance security as well as aesthetics.

CHAPTER 6

Electronic Access Control

Electronic access control enhances the other physical security safeguards, such as the perimeter fence, barriers, and intrusion detection devices. An access control system minimizes pilfering, loss of assets like personal and company property, and the loss of intellectual property. An effective access control system also minimizes the introduction of harmful materials, devices, and compounds to the site. The administration and procedures of the access control system -l ike access control lists, personnel recognition, ID cards, badges, and personal escorts - all contribute to an effective access control system. An important component of the access control system is the hardware that reads the badges and permits access to the site by unlocking the entry doors and operating the perimeter fence gates, etc. This chapter will focus on the hardware of the access control system as well the types of systems. An access control system can be a simple lock on a door or a sophisticated electronic system. The focus will be on the electronic access control systems.

Electronic access control is based on physical IDs. It could be a PIN (personal identification number) for a keypad for a cipher lock, an ID access card with or without a picture, or a key fob. The ID card is the size of a credit card. When the card is inserted or placed near the electronic reader, the information on the card is verified in the access control system's database. Then the system sends a signal to operate an electric strike or magnetic lock to release the door for entry. The keypad is similar and, except in most cases, the system is connected to a main or head end part of the system. The right combination releases the lock on the door and allows entry. Sometimes the keypad operates an electric or magnetic strike, but the majority work a mechanical lock.

BIOMETRIC SYSTEMS

The other type of physical ID is biometrics. It is a good idea to combine a biometric device with a card system as a backup. Before access is granted, an access card and reader pulls the template from storage and the biometric reader or scanner verifies identity.

There is difference between identification and verification. Positive identification answers the question, "Who am I?" The system matches the person's identity from a number of possible matches. Verification addresses the issue of, "Am I who I say I am?" In the verification system, the person is matched with a template enrolled in the system. The types of biometric systems in use today are:

1. Hand geometry reader
2. Fingerprint reader
3. Iris scanner
4. Retina scanner
5. Voice recognition
6. Signature recognition
7. Facial recognition

Hand Geometry

A hand geometry reader analyzes more than 31,000 points and records more than 90 separate measurements of the hand. These measurements include the width of the hand, the thickness, the length of the hand and the surface area, including the person's grip on the palm reader. When a person places his or her hand on the reader, it matches the information with a template stored in the access control database. To activate the hand geometry reader, the person swipes an access control badge at a card reader, which activates the person's template for the match. If the person does not have access to the door upon presenting their access card then the card reader light will blink red.

Fingerprint Reader

The fingerprint reader analyzes the fingerprint from the tip of the finger to the first knuckle. The enrollment procedure is the same as for the hand geometry reader, creating a template that is stored in the database. The access control badge triggers the reader to pull up the template and to verify whether the person has access. If the person does not have access upon presenting their access card, then the card reader will blink red.

Iris Scanner

The iris recognition reader or pattern scan measures the unique patterns of striations, pits, freckles, rifts, fibers, filaments, rings, coronas, furrows, and vasculature of the iris. The person is enrolled by looking into the camera to record the iris measurements to make a template. An access control badge and card reader is used the same way as the hand geometry and fingerprint reader systems.

Retina Scan

A retina scanner measures the elements of the blood vessel patterns of the retina. The retina is the rear portion of the eyeball. A camera captures the image and makes a template for verification. A card reader is used in conjuction, as with the other forms of biometric readers. Unfortunately, iris and retina scanners have not really caught on as biometric devices for access control on a large scale.

Voice Recognition

Voice recognition analyzes the distinctive features of the voice to verify an individual. The voice can be captured a number ways, including PC microphones, cellular phones, and land lines. Since the medium where a voice is recorded can vary in quality, it is best to record the voice on the medium that will be used to identify it later. To enroll, a person usually is instructed to say a pass phrase or a series of numbers that will be long enough to record 1 to 1 1/2 seconds of speech, and the enrollee should repeat the pass phrase or numbers several times. Enrollment for this device takes longer than for the other devices.

Signature Recognition

Signature recognition analyzes the strokes, speed, and pressure a person uses to sign their name, rather than comparing signatures. The weakness with the signature scan is if the person is not consistent when signing their name. These people will have a tough time enrolling in the system. When enrolling, signing only initials is not acceptable. There are too many false positives with initials because it does not provide enough of a writing sample to compare the physical process of signing. An access control card can be used to pull up the signature template.

Facial Recognition

Facial recognition systems compare the features of the face, including the lines around the eye sockets, the cheekbones, the sides of the mouth, and the location of the nose and eyes. The lines near the hair lines are not used, since they can be altered easily.

Enrollment in the facial recognition system is easy. Several pictures which are taken by security personnel show the face from different sides and the images form a template. The system can be used in conjunction with an access card. The person swipes their access card and then sits or stands in front of a camera for a few seconds to scan an image to match to the template. As in all the other systems, if the person does not have access, the card reader blinks red.

Error Rates

False positives and negatives are an issue and need to be considered. A false positive occurs when the reader reads an unenrolled person's hand, fingerprint, iris, or retina scan as matching a valid template. A false negative occurs when the reader rejects a valid person's hand, fingerprint, iris or retina scan as being invalid. Error rates of the devices are disputed, depending on what type of testing was done and by whom. So it is important to perform a thorough threat assessment and analysis before selecting a biometric system. (See Chapter 2 for details on threat assessments.)

COMBINATION SYSTEMS

Combinations of biometric devices integrate two systems, such as facial recognition and fingerprint scanning. Then there is a multimodal biometric system, which combines at least three systems for verification. The more systems used, the more accurate the system. Combined systems are expensive and probably would be used only in high-security applications like government facilities.

There is plenty of information about biometrics on the Internet. One good Web site is www.biometricsinfo.org. This site provides information about the various biometric devices and applications, and the information comes from the site www.ibgweb.com. Table 6-1 summarizes the biometric system's strengths, weaknesses, and applications, and it lists the possible applications for each system.

ACCESS CONTROL SYSTEM CARDS

The types of electronic access control cards are:

- Magnetic stripe
- Proximity
- Smart cards
- Dual technology

Magnetic Strip

Magnetic strip cards have a magnetic strip on the back of the card that contains information about the person, his or her name, and access level. The magnetic strip card is the most common card technology. Credit cards, hotel keys, driver's licenses, and ATM cards use magnetic strip technology. The cards are swiped through specially designed readers that process the information embedded on the magnetic strip.

The type of information on the strip depends on the card type. For example, a hotel key contains the room number, the guest's name, and dates of stay.

TABLE 6-1   Biometric Systems' Strengths and Weaknesses

TYPE OF SYSTEM	STRENGTHS	WEAKNESSES	APPLICATION
Hand Geometry	Resistant to fraud	Injury to hands will require re-enrollment of other hand	Data center Used with access control card
	Easy to enroll	Cost	
	Not an issue for end user	Limited to 1 to 1 match	
Finger Print	Not easily defeated	High false negatives	Data center Used with access control card
	Differentiates between latex print and real	Injury to finger will case false negative	
Iris Recognition	Unique in each individual	People are afraid to use it. Negative perception	Sensitive government operations
	Easy to enroll		
Retina Scan	Unique in each individual	Same as for the Iris scan.... people are afraid to use it. Negative perception	Sensitive government facilities
	Easy to enroll		
Voice Recognition	Highly resistant to imposter attacks	Need to enroll on the system that will be used to identify the voice later	Data center Used with access control card
	No perception of invasiveness		
Signature Recognition	Difficult to forge since it is not the signature by the way it is signed	Enrollment can be a problem, if the person does not sign their names consistently will be rejected	Data centers Used with access control card
	People are accustomed to providing signatures	People who sign only their initials will be rejected	
Facial Recognition	Easy to enroll...person sits or stands in front of a camera	High rates of false positives and false negatives	Airports
	No negative public perception like Iris and Retina scans	Lighting can be a problem	

A credit card has the card (account) number, expiration date, and the name of the card holder.

Proximity Cards

Proximity cards are based on Wiegand technology. Wiegand technology uses small-diameter wire in short pieces embedded into a code strip in two rows. The number of codes the card contains depends on the number of wires. The wire is a special alloy with magnetic properties. The code strip is embedded into an access control or other type of identification card the size of a credit card. The code strip embedded in the card produces a small, strong electronic signal that is picked up by the coil in the reader.

Smart Cards

Smart card technology is a computer chip embedded into the card. The chip is programmable, and the information from the access control system database provides information to the chip. The type of information may vary, but should definitely have access codes (levels) and the card holder's name. Other information could include things like credit for use at a company cafeteria or store.

Dual Technology Cards

Dual technology cards have two types of technologies on the same card. For example, a proximity card for access to the buildings as well as a magnetic strip on the back of the card can be used as part of the company's property pass system when employees remove company property.

DESIGNING THE ACCESS CONTROL SYSTEM

The first step of designing an access control system is to designate restricted zones. The zones can be defined as part of the threat and vulnerability assessment outlined in Chapter 2. For government facilities, the design specifications for the access control system-like the rest of the physical security-is spelled out in the bid documents for the job. These are restricted areas, such as access to the elevators in the lobby of a large office building, or the office and other areas of a company's research facility. Sometimes access is restricted beyond the lobby or waiting area or the parking lot for employee use.

The first step in designing an electronic access control system is to decide what your needs are by designating the layers of access. Define each restricted area as either controlled, limited, or exclusion.

In a controlled area, access is controlled to those who need access. This is the first level of access and may include the parking lot or lobby. A limited area is a more secure area and access is limited to those that need access. This would include work areas like laboratories. Exclusion zones are those areas where access is restricted, such as a data center or the telephone and data cabling rooms.

The next step in the design process is to determine what type of system will best meet the needs and protect the facility in accordance with the layers of access and the control zones. This phase will be used to decide what the operational features the system will encompass.

The next step is to determine the system requirements and traffic flow (transactions) through a portal. This is the amount of people that will pass through the entry way and the times of day for the most transactions. To minimize problems, address the following questions:

- Does the system meet the requirements for life safety for exiting in an emergency? In most jurisdictions the fire marshal will need to approve the system before it is installed to ensure it meets the NFPA 101, the Life Safety Code. Essentially, the Life Safety Code says any doors used for emergency exits as well as entry must allow for exiting without any special clearance during an emergency. Also, if the power fails, you must still be able to exit. Failing safe means you can exit but not enter.

- Will the system handle the number of transactions at peak times at an entry portal without causing undo delay? For example, during morning rush hour, will the access control system cause a delay?

- How many entrances will be controlled?

- Is the system expandable?

- Is servicing available locally if the system malfunctions?

- What other systems will be integrated into the access control system? For example, CCTV and alarm monitoring.

The fourth step is to select a card technology. Choose the one that meets the needs of the project. Proximity access cards have a bit format on the card. The bit format is used for the parity, facility code, and card number. For example, if you have a 34-bit card, 2 bits are for parity bits, 16 for the facility code, and 16 for the card number range. The number of card bits is important, as is the facility code. More bits on the card allow more information to be put on the card. The number of bits and/or the card number for one facility can be identical to another, so the facility code permits access to the facility. This is an important consideration when determining the specifications of the cards. If the system is being designed to protect sensitive information, the card should have a minimum of 34 bits, so the facility code for the facility will be unique. These are known as custom cards. Not every location needs custom cards.

- Magnetic strip cards

- Proximity (Wiegand) cards

- Smart cards

- Dual technology

For details on the technologies listed below, refer to the section on cards in this chapter. The fifth step is to develop the design specifications for the system. The design specifications outline what the system will do, the amount of traffic it will need to handle, the type of locks (magnetic or electric strike) to be used, the type of portals (turnstiles, mantraps, etc.), the type of card/reader technology, backup power, integration with other systems (CCTV, alarms, etc.).

The sixth step is to design the system based on the design criteria outlined in Step 5. The design will include the system layout with drawings. The drawings will include all the locations that have readers for access control, the alarm devices and locations, CCTV camera locations, and the locations of the access control system panels. Access control system panels control and monitor a specified number of doors. Some panels are capable of monitoring up to 32 doors. The panels store the transactions and operate on battery backup if power is lost. Under normal conditions, the transactions are sent to the head end of the system at least once a day. See Table 6-2 for a checklist of design steps.

TYPES OF ACCESS CONTROL SYSTEM LOCKS

There are two main types of locks used with electronic access control systems. We will cover locks in more detail in a later chapter. The two discussed in this section are related to electronic access control systems:

1. Magnetic lock

2. Electric strike

The magnetic lock also referred to as a maglock. The electromagnetic lock is operated by 12 or 24 VDC (volts of direct current). The locks also have a bridge to allow AC operation. The lock operates on low voltage, between 1/4 and 1 amp. The two parts to an electromagnetic lock are the electromagnet and the armature. The electromagnet is the larger of the two, with the armature being the strike plate. The armature locks the door when the electromagnet comes in contact with it when it is energized with 12 or 24 VDC.

Maglocks usually are found on glass storefront-type doors. The lock and strike plate are at the top of the door. The strike plate is mounted on the bottom of the top frame, and the electromagnetic lock is mounted on the top of the door. The strike plate hangs down enough for the electromagnetic lock to

TABLE 6-2 Access Control Design Steps

STEPS	YES/NO

1. Determine restricted zones
   Controlled Area
   Limited
   Exclusion	

2. Select operational features
   Choose the number of card bits 32, 64, etc.
   Biometric
   Dual technology	

3. Traffic flow analysis
   Meet Life Safety Code
   Handle amount of transactions
   Number of doors to be controlled
   System expandable
   Local system service available
   Integration with other systems CCTV, alarms, etc.	

4. Select card type
   Magnetic
   Proximity
   Biometric
   Dual technology (Biometric and card swipe)	

5. Develop design specifications for the system
   What will the system do?
   Amount of traffic to handle
   Magnetic or electric strike locks?
   Portal type, turnstile, mantrap, etc.
   Card/reader technology
   Back up power
   Integration with CCTV, alarms	

6. Design system	

make contact, securing the door. This makes it easy to retrofit because the lock does not need to be built into the door handle. The electromagnetic lock is for both indoor and outdoor use. As with other locks used on doors for emergency exiting, check with the NFPA 101 Life Safety Code's section on electromagnetic locks. The local fire marshal will make the final approval before installing the lock. The fire marshal's office will test the lock to make sure it meets the requirements set forth in the Life Safety Code. Electromagnetic locks listed by the Underwriters Laboratories (UL) can be used on a rated door. The electromagnetic lock, however, cannot replace the positive latching hardware for the door.

Magnetic locks come in a wide variety of finishes to match the door-frame finishes. When preparing the specifications for the door hardware, make sure to include the color that will match the door.

The other type of lock used commonly is the electric strike. An electric strike lock operates on 12 or 24 VDC, as well as AC power. The electric strike lock looks like any other door handle lock, except in this case the lock is operated electrically. The lock will draw from 1/4 amp on 24 VDC to 45 amps on 12 VDC. The electric strike lock will remain locked if there is a power failure, so it fails secure. The lock will still allow exit from inside the building but will be locked on the outside and not allow entry during a power failure. With AC power used to electrify the lock, you will hear a buzzing sound when someone on the inside initiates access. DC power will not have the buzzing sound when the door is released from inside.

The electric strike lock is installed in the door handle and frame. The wires that control the lock need to be run through the frame. The door handle contains the latch, and the door frame will have the strike mounted into it. The strike is where the bolt slides in, just like any non-electric lock bolt. With the electric lock, the keeper will release the bolt when it is activated, allowing entry through the door.

There also are electric strike locks built into the handle of glass lobby- and storefront-type doors. The lock engages by having the bolt at the top of the handle slide into position in the frame. To exit from the inside the request to exit device will shunt the alarm, and the handle is pushed to exit.

REQUEST TO EXIT DEVICE (REX)

A request to exit device, also known as a REX, is important. Most access control systems do not require the use of a card reader to exit. The REX permits exiting through the door without triggering the alarm as a forced door. The REX shunts the alarm through the use of a motion sensor. The REX is mounted at the ceiling near the door or the top of the exit door's frame. When you walk by, you can hear the REX click or see the green light come on. The clicking sound and the green light lets you know the REX working to allow exit without causing a forced-door alarm. As a person walks up to the door, the passive infrared device or other motion sensor sends the signal to the door to shunt the alarm. The forced-door alarm is a feature of the access control system to record when doors are forced open or left open too long. The access control system computer receives the alarm, and the security officer or other designated person will need to respond. The alarm does not sound at the door that is forced open. In most cases, it sounds only at the security console on the access control system computer. The REX does not release the lock unless the access control system is programmed for this. So be careful when programming the access control system's head end, and make sure the REXs for the doors in the system will not unlock the door but only shunt the forced-door alarm when someone exits the door using the door

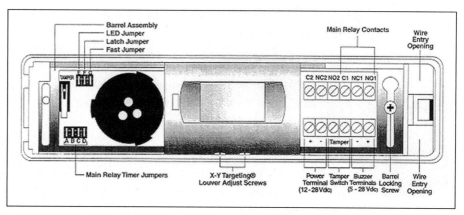

FIGURE 6-1   REX Device

hardware. Otherwise, every time someone on the inside of the perimeter walks passed the door, the REX will unlock the door. This will allow someone outside the perimeter to enter without an access card, negating the purpose of the access control system. See Figure 6-1 to view a cutaway of a REX.

DOOR CONTACTS

Electronically controlled doors also have contacts installed on them. The purpose of the contacts is to provide the alarm points for monitoring the status of the door. For example, the contacts monitor the position of the door, open or closed, and also if the door is held open too long. When programming the system, the doors can be programmed to be held open for a set time to allow a person to enter. The reason for setting the time is so the door alarm will not be activated during a normal entry. If the door is held open longer, an alarm will be sent to the console, alerting security officers that the door has not been closed, and the event is recorded. The last valid access card before the door was propped open also is recorded, so it is easy to discover which employee propped the door open. This feature keeps the door from being propped open, especially exterior doors, so people can re-enter without using their access control badge.

The door contacts are mounted either on the top of the door frame or on the side of the door frame. The important thing is that they a make contact when the door is closed.

AUTOMATIC DOOR CLOSER

Another important piece of door hardware is the automatic door closer. There are various types of closers, but the purpose of each is the same: to close the door automatically after entry. Without the automatic closer, the door would likely remain open. Self-closers are used on most exterior doors and can be adjusted to close quickly or slowly. All access controlled doors must have an automatic door closer, even interior doors.

ACCESS CONTROL SYSTEM PANELS

Access control system panels monitor a number of doors in the system. Some panels can monitor up to 32 doors. It is important to know the capacity of the system and plan for expansion.

The panel also will communicate with the system head end, which is the main system computer. Information is stored on the panel and will continue to allow access to doors, even if communications with the main computer are lost. Battery packs are installed in the panel in case power is lost. Most battery packs are good for four hours, and the access control system should have an emergency power supply like a generator. The panel stores information on the doors it controls and the recent transactions of the access card holders. Also, the panel will monitor the alarm points in the area, such as door alarms.

SAMPLE DESIGN SPECIFICATIONS

What follows is an abbreviated sample of design specifications to guide you so you can write your own design specifications for your project.

SECTION 17000 – ELECTRONIC SECURITY SYSTEM
    PART 1 GENERAL
        1.1 RELATED DOCUMENTS
            A. All drawings and the General Provisions of the Contract including the General and Supplementary Conditions and Division 1 Specification Sections, apply to this Section.
        1.2 PROJECT SCOPE
            A. The system being developed under this design is an electronic intrusion detection, egress control system that incorporates the technologies shown below. For the purpose of clarification, the following parties will be referenced in this document in the following manner:

1. The ABCD Corporation 5667 Gibraltar Drive Livermore, CA. 94588 925-224-7955 Tel 925-224-7964 Fax www.abcd.com	The Client
2. The XYZ Consultants Inc. 4847 S. Orange Blossom Trail Orlando, Florida, 32835 407-851-8734 Tel 407-851-1215 Fax www.xyzconsult.com	The Consultants

3. The ABCD Corporation   The Facility(s)
   Livermore, California
   Toronto, Canada
   Paris, France
   Amsterdam, Holland
   London, England

B. In all new facilities, the system is being installed for the purpose of controlling traffic in the Client's facility. The systems within the United States are being retro-fitted however the contractor must still comply with this specification and the bidder instructions. It is a requirement of the system that all technologies be integrated into one system to allow for instantaneous alert and response to any alarm condition that may be activated in the secured area. The system will be controlled through one central processor located in the facility. Archived information is to be sent via the "NET" to the remote server located in the Client's offices in Livermore, California. The system must be compatible from the standpoint of the ability to read existing access control cards and to provide the same report formats to allow for standardization of a global network.

C. It is also a requirement of the system to monitor all building management services as they relate to the facility. The operations manager shall have the ability to both monitor and control building management equipment through the access control screen located at the systems management console (SMC).

D. This Section calls for the contractor of choice to provide all labor, materials, equipment, and service necessary for the completion of the integrated electronic security system and subsystem(s), as indicated on the drawings and as described herein. The internal "NET" shall be supplied by the Owner however it is the responsibility of the contractor to verify that communication pathways are open and compatible with all components within the global system. The Owner reserves the right to supply other components if they are needed for this project. The system technologies called for within this Scope of Work are:

1. Access Control cards, readers, and field panels;
2. Closed Circuit Television camera and monitors;
3. Intrusion Detection Devices;
4. Duress Reporting Devices;
5. Video digital recording devices; and
6. Components required for installation

E. The Contractor shall provide all labor, materials, equipment, software, and programming required to provide the Client with an integrated security system that is compatible with existing components in other offices operated by the Client.

F. Contractor shall ensure the system meets the operational and functional needs of the Client as specified herein, and as indicated on the drawings. The drawings are diagrammatic only. Equipment and labor not specifically referred to herein, or on the plans, that are required to meet the functional and operational intent, shall be provided without additional cost to the Client.

G. Contractor shall be responsible for coordinating with other trades and contractors to provide a system that is totally integrated and operational as required for this project.

H. The Contractor shall be responsible for providing with their Submittal, a one year spare parts list with single component (itemized) and quantity pricing. Should any particular component be in redesign stage that would possibly cause it to be a non-production item within the 1 year period, this component shall be identified as such and the substitute or new component be identified on this spare parts list.

1.3 RELATED SECTIONS

A. The contractor shall review the following sections of the total project to ensure compliance with:
1. Division 2   Site Work
2. Division 7   Fire stopping
3. Division 8   Doors and Door Hardware
4. Division 16 Electrical
   All specification divisions are identified by The Construction Specification Institute Master Format

1.4 SUBMITTALS

A. Contractor shall submit bid data containing original catalog cut sheets that provide complete technical data as required by the Owner to allow evaluation of the material and equipment proposed. The information should include component dimensions, wiring and block diagrams, wire/cable sizes, conduit sizes, performance data, ratings, operational characteristics, control sequences, and other descriptive data to describe the items proposed.

B. The Contractor's submittal shall include a complete list of equipment, materials, and installation instructions. All prices shall be itemized in single component prices as well as quantity pricing with any discounts so indicated. Alternative proposals are acceptable under this specification and shall comply with all standard requirements for the bid package submittal.

C. The Contractor receiving the award shall submit within two weeks (14 days) of the award date a complete set of shop drawings. These drawings shall contain complete wiring and schematic diagrams, software descriptions, calculations, and any other details required to demonstrate that the system has been properly coordinated and installed to function as described within the specifications.

D. The Contractor shall upon the completion of the project, provide to the Client or their designated representative, a complete and accurate set of As–Built drawings. The submittal shall be in AutoCAD V2000 and supplied on a disk along with five copies of system(s) manuals and drawings. The submittal shall be completed and delivered to the Client and/or their designated representative at least two weeks prior to final acceptance testing. Punch item corrections will require a re-submittal if the list is substantial.

1.5 QUALITY ASSURANCE

A. Manufacturer's Qualifications:

The Contractor shall only represent a Company that specializes in the business of having provided Electronic Integrated Security Systems for a period of at least five (5) years. The supporting documentation supplied by the Contractor shall demonstrate the Manufacturer's as well as the Contractor's experience by including:

1. Installations for at least five (5) facilities of equal size and comparable technical requirements utilizing the equipment submitted.
2. For each facility, the information should include:
   a. Name and address of facility;
   b. Date of the Installation and System Acceptance;
   c. A point of contact for either the Owner or the Owner's designated representative;
   d. The name of the project or construction manager, if applicable; and
   e. The name of the Architect of Record, if applicable.
3. A description of the technical aspects of the system describing how the system functions in comparison to the System described within this specification.

B. References and Regulatory Requirements.

1. All workmanship and materials supplied under this Section shall comply with the requirements of the following agencies and authorities:
   a. International Electrical Engineers (IEE)
   b. European Committee for Electrotechnical Standardization (CENELEC)
   c. International Electrotechnical Commission (IEC)
   d. National Fire Protection Association (NFPA) US Standard
   e. National Electric Manufacturers Association (NEMA) US Standard
   f. Life Safety Code (NFPA 101) (1999) US Standard
   g. National Burglar and Fire Alarm Association (NBFAA) -Standards of Application - US Standard

    h. Closed Circuit Television Manufacturers Association (CCTMA)
      – US Standard

    i. Underwriters Laboratories (UL) – European Equivalent

1.6 REQUIREMENTS OF THE DESIGN

A. THE SYSTEM – The design for this system consists of several components. The intent is to allow full monitoring of all security and security related activities, including building management services (HVAC, Fire, Power, etc.) at the systems management console (SMC). The monitored functions shall consist of but not be limited to:

1. All access control devices for access and egress to and from the facility;

2. Intrusion detection equipment as it relates to fire doors, duress buttons, and other similar devices;

3. Delayed Egress Locking Devices;

4. Closed circuit surveillance cameras with a processor integrated into the overall system to provide reactive design functions and a digital recording device; and

5. Any additional components required for a complete installation but not identified within this specification.

B. THE INSTALLATION – The Contractor shall provide, install, terminate, and submit for final acceptance testing the electronic system required for this design. All work will be inspected during the installation process and final acceptance testing will be conducted prior to the system being accepted by the Client. The contractor shall advise the Client at each point of substantial completion to allow periodic inspections. Final acceptance testing shall be conducted when contractor advises the system is ready. Punch list corrections shall be completed within two weeks after list development. The testing process is on all items prior to acceptance of the system by the Client. The Client reserves the right to require complete system testing a second time if the punch list is of considerable size.

1. CENTRALIZED MONITORING – This design of this system is such that monitoring will be required in two locations. The primary monitoring of CCTV and all alarms will be at the systems monitoring console (SMC) located in the main console room. A second monitoring station at the Security Command Center (SCC) may be required for each site. This workstation will be monitored by security officers and shall mirror the information being sent to the SMC. This station will be a workstation with all security and security related functions reporting to this location as well as the SCM. The system shall archive all access control, intrusion detection alarms, BMS functions, and CCTV video storage information

at the main system server located in Livermore, California. The information shall be sent via the owner provided "NET" on a preprogrammed basis established by the Client and programmed by the Contractor.

2. The system shall provide for automatic display of alarm point locations at the SMC and SCC. The components of the integrated system shall include but not be limited to:

A. The Front-end processor for each site complete with software license;

B. One workstation, complete with software license;

C. One (1) Net-controller unit;

D. Power supply with battery backup;

E. Software to accommodate 32 card readers;

F. Software to accommodate up to 4 biometric readers (hand-geometry);

G. Field panels as required to monitor all points identified within this specification and on the drawings;

H. Building management systems (BMS) monitoring and control capability for up to 100 points;

I. Four (4) card reader units with locking and egress devices;

J. One (1) Hand Geometry reader unit;

K. Door position switches for each access control door leaf and other egress points within the facility;

L. Duress reporting devices (3) to be located at a later date;

M. Four (4) emergency break glass release units;

N. One (1) intercom master with 1 external slave unit;

O. Twelve (12) dual technology volumetric protection devices with adjustable lens units;

F. Training, manuals, service, and maintenance as specified; and,

G. Any additional components required, but not specifically mentioned within this or other sections.

E. CLOSED CIRCUIT SURVEILLANCE – The Contractor shall provide, install, terminate, program, and submit for final acceptance testing, a processor based Closed Circuit Television Surveillance system (CCTV). This system shall be integrated through the matrix switcher and the access control front end central processor to provide video coverage of each alarm point and/or surveillance locations identified for this project. Monitoring shall be required at the SMC and SCC with video storage both on site and at the Livermore, CA server. The system shall be reactive in design with all programming being done in accordance with this specification and the accompanying drawings. Each location shall be supplied with a 32 channel digital recorder that will serve as the video signal processor and shall be installed in such a manner as to allow it to integrate with other system components. The CCTV system shall consist of the following components:

1. Cameras – Fixed & Autodome
2. Monitors for SMC and SCC;
3. Video Matrix processor capable of handling up to 32 cameras with 8 outputs;
4. Digital Video Recording Unit;
5. Housings as required;
6. Power supplies as specified;
7. Training, manuals, service, and maintenance as specified; and,
8. Any additional components required, but not specifically mentioned within this or other sections.

F. INTRUSION DETECTION: The Contractor shall provide, install, terminate, and submit for final acceptance testing, door position switches as indicated on the drawings accompanying this specification. Each door position switch shall be interfaced into the system in order that either intrusion or egress alarms through secured doors are reported to both the SMC and SCC. The IDS also shall interface with the camera controller unit to activate the camera system for the purposes of alerting the personnel in the monitoring areas and also to activate the recording functions of the system. This system shall be integrated through the Contractor provided cabling for the purpose of activating the video and security response techniques required for both interior as well as limited exterior areas. The system shall consist of the following components:

1. Door Position Switches; and
2. Any additional components required, but not specifically mentioned within this or other sections.

G. DURESS REPORTING – The contractor shall provide, install, terminate, program, and submit for final acceptance testing, duress buttons at the locations indicated on the drawings accompanying this specification. The duress system shall, when activated, report to the SMC as well as the SCC. Additionally, the cameras selected by the Client and programmed by the Contractor shall be activated for the purpose of viewing the controlled area and recording all events that take place during the alarm. The components required for this portion of the system shall consist of:

1. Duress buttons – desk mounted
2. Any additional components required, but not specifically mentioned within this or other sections.

H. STRIKE PLATES – All access control doors and all egress points from within the controlled space to the outside of the facility shall have strike plates installed to protect against direct attacks against the lock bolt of the door.

G. DELAYED EGRESS LOCKING UNITS – Certain of the facilities covered under this specification may require the use of delayed egress locking devices. The contractor shall provide, install, terminate, service and submit for final acceptance testing, delayed egress locking devices at the locations indicated on the drawings accompanying this specification. The locking system shall be integrated with the fire alarm system to ensure compliance with all codes relative to the use of this device. Signage and other required components such as power supplies, etc., will the responsibility of the contractor to provide, install, terminate, service and maintain. The locking system, when activated, shall report to the SMC as well as the SCC. Additionally, the cameras selected by the Client and programmed by the Contractor shall be activated for the purpose of viewing the areas of egress and recording any events that take place during the alarm. The components required for this portion of the system shall consist of:

1. Delayed Egress Locking Units – mortise locking units;
2. Key cylinders;
3. Strike plates to fit each individual application;
4. Power supplies and transformers; and
5. Any additional components required, but not specifically mentioned within this or other sections.

1.7 WARRANTY

A. Warrant material and workmanship for a period of one year from the date of system final acceptance.
B. Warranty shall include the repair, replacement, and upgrade of defective security components and/or materials including the correction of defective work when given notice by the Client during the warranty period.
C. Warranty response time shall be within 8 hours upon receipt of request from Client or their designated representative during normal working hours. Weekend response shall be extended to a period not to exceed 12 hours.

1.8 RECORD DOCUMENTS

A. The Contractor shall provide project record drawings identifying the system architecture and rack/component distribution.
B. The "document package" shall include three sets of system manuals for the overall system concept as well as individual components within the system. Manuals shall consist of:
   1. Operations manual – provide all information for operation of the system, including but not limited to, trouble shooting information, as well as software operational information;

2. Installation manual – provide drawings describing all circuits, power distribution, equipment placement, and cable routing, in an As-Built drawings (C size) format. This manual shall also include reference to any conduit routing;

3. Maintenance/Service Manual – Provide all trouble shooting information, data that is applicable to on-site software manipulation, programming information, and service/maintenance records.

C. The "drawing package" shall include three (3) sets of As-built drawings. These drawings shall be supplied to the Client or the Client's designated representative for final acceptance testing, punch list development, and system acceptance. The drawings shall be corrected as required for final system acceptance. The As-Built drawings shall not be considered complete until accepted by the Client.

1.9 OPERATION TRAINING AND MAINTENANCE DATA

A. Included with the shop drawing submittal should be a syllabus outlining the training program that will be provided to the Client or their designated representative with reference to the operation of this system. This syllabus should include a minimum of 16 hours training with demonstrations of the features and functions of the primary system and integrated subsystems.

B. The training classes should be conducted with competent supervisors or factory trained technicians and shall be conducted on site. The Client shall designate which individuals from their organization shall receive the training.

1.10. OPERATION AND MAINTENANCE DATA MANUAL

A. Assemble a set of three (3) manuals in hard bound covers, presenting for the Client's guidance, full details for care and maintenance of visible surfaces, and of equipment included in the work.

B. Include manufacturer's literature relating to components and other equipment, catalog cut sheets, parts list, wiring diagrams, instruction sheets, and other pertinent information which will be useful to the Client in overall system operation and maintenance.

C. Include a list of installers and service representatives with company names and addresses, names of individuals to contact, and telephone numbers.

D. Prepare operating instructions, complete and explicit, including, but not limited to, instructions for start-up, operating, and stopping.

1.11 MAINTENANCE SERVICE

A. The contractor shall test and service system on a quarterly basis during the warranty period. Each quarterly inspection shall "cover" up to 30% of the installed components.

B. After each quarterly maintenance inspection the Contractor shall provide written notification to the Client of the system's condition before and after service, exact components that were tested and serviced, and overall status of the system. All notices shall be sent to Mr. Mike Arata, ABCD Corporation, 5667 Gibraltar Drive, Livermore, California, 94588.

PART 2 PRODUCTS

2.1 INTEGRATED ELECTRONIC SECURITY SYSTEM (IESS):

A. Refer to individual Integrated Electronic Security System Specification section for selected equipment and operational requirements.

2.1.1 Delayed Egress Locking Devices:

A. Required Performance Features:

1. The contractor shall provide, install, terminate, and submit for final acceptance testing, a delayed egress locking device that provides the following features:

   a. A request to exit switch shall be built into the device to detect attempts to use the door for unauthorized egress;

   b. Each unit shall be supplied with a lamp that indicates the disposition of the locking device. The lamp shall be protected by a masked bezel design that provide wide angle viewing along with the capability of providing three signals to indicate the armed status of the unit. The three signals shall be as follows:

      1. A continuously lighted lamp indicates the device has just been armed and as soon as the rearm timer expires the unit will be fully armed;

      2. A slow flashing light shall indicate the device being armed with no re-arm timing activation; and,

      3. A flashing indicator shall indicate the unit is in an alarm condition.

   c. The application of less than 15 pounds of pressure to the push pad shall cause an internal switch to start an irreversible alarm cycle;

   d. Activation of the internal switch shall cause an internal horn to sound at a minimum volume of 85 db at 6ft. The internal horn shall be supplied with the ability to select activation or non-activation during a fire alarm condition;

   e. The unit supplied shall also be capable of controlling nuisance alarms by being equipped with firmware that will provide a non-activation time of at least two seconds should the push pad be pushed by mistake;

   f. If the push pad is held for two seconds or more, the unit will revert to normal operating conditions, thereby activating the timing sequence as well as the internal sounding device causing the unit to release as designed for delayed egress requirements;

g. Each unit supplied shall have a set of relay contacts rated at 1 ampere, 24 VDC, for external alarm indication and remote monitoring. The contacts should be designed to close when the device goes into the irreversible alarm condition. The internal relay contacts shall also be capable of driving a horn, lamp, or other indicative devices in accordance with the design;

h. The contractor shall provide, install and terminate with each delayed egress device, a surface mounted door position switch to provide added monitoring capabilities to the secured door. The delayed egress locking device supplied shall have the ability to interface with this door position switch to allow activation of the alarm system should the door not close when the system is armed, the door is forced open when the system is armed, or to monitor anti-pass back activities through the shortening of re-arming times;

i. The unit shall be capable of being re-armed from the security console (SMC or SCC);

j. Each unit supplied shall be integrated into the fire alarm system to allow immediate disabling of the timing sequence and unlocking of the device in the event of a fire evacuation need. The unit shall be interfaced with the building's fire alarm system that should provide a set of normally closed contacts which open on alarm;

k. Each unit supplied shall be capable of accepting console "override" by being supplied with an external inhibit input device to allow interfacing capability with card readers, wall mounted key switches, and/or remote security console controls. The override feature shall be controlled by a normally closed switch that in an open position disarms the unit;

l. The firmware supplied with the unit shall have the ability to accommodate an adjustable re-arm time of from 2 to 28 seconds based on two second intervals or an infinite re-arm setting based on the status of the external door position switch. This adjustable time shall be changeable at the unit;

m. Each unit shall be capable of being adjusted to meet the requirements of the local AHJ (authority having jurisdiction, i.e., Fire Marshal) by providing up to 15 or 30 seconds of time delay as standard with adjustable capabilities of from 0 to 60 seconds based on 2 second increments. The contractor shall, for any delay adjusted longer than 15 seconds, receive and provide to the Client a letter of acceptance from the local AHJ confirming acceptance of the extended time delay;

n. The delayed egress devices shall also be supplied with an internal auxiliary locking device that is designed to engage when the unit is armed. This locking device shall be capable of withstanding forceful blows as well as pressures of more than 75 pounds on the push pad;

o. Each unit shall be supplied with a key switch designed to allow manual arming, disarming, and resetting of the unit. The contractor is responsible for verifying the need for the keyed unit with the Client prior to the units being supplied. If the key is not required, the unit shall be supplied with a blank cylinder; and,

p. The units supplied shall have been tested and accepted in accordance to ANSI A156.3, 1984, Grade 1, and shall meet all requirements for NFPA 101, Special Locking Arrangements.

2. The acceptable manufacturers for the delayed egress locking devices are as follows:

a. Von Duprin

b. Security Door Controls

c. Locknetics

2.1.2 Closed Circuit Television Surveillance Devices:

A. Required Performance Features

1. The contractor shall provide, install, terminate, and submit for final acceptance testing, a delayed egress locking device that provides the following features:

Closed Circuit Television Camera(s)

a. The camera supplied for this project shall have an imager consisting of a 1/4" DSP Color CCD (domed unit) and provide active picture elements of 512H X 492V thereby equaling a horizontal resolution of not less than 330 TVL.

b. The camera shall provide a usable picture under the conditions of scene illumination being 0.3 fc @ f1.4 and a 6.0 mm micro lens with Linear Electronic Iris.

c. Each camera shall be positioned accordingly to provide the best view of each controlled area.

d. DSP shall control back-light compensation, white balance, shutter speed and more.

e. Each camera shall be synchronized when powered by DC. Synchronization shall be adjusted to power line zero crossing for roll-free vertical interval switching with the vertical phase delay being adjustable externally to allow vertical synchronization in multiphase power installations.

f. Camera and dome housing size shall not exceed 3.09"H x 3.02W.

g. Each camera shall be capable of operating in an environment that does not exceed –10 degrees C to +45 degrees C.

h. Each unit shall be UL listed for safety

i. Each camera unit shall be supplied with the appropriate transformer and power supply needed to meet the intent of this specification.

j. Stand–by power packs shall be installed to provide a minimum of 4 hours of viewing should the building's primary power be lost.

k. Each camera shall be the WATEC DSP LCL–125D or equivalent.

2. Closed Circuit Television Monitors

a. Monitors supplied at the SCM and SCC shall be 17" inch color units manufactured by Sanyo. The unit shall be configured for desktop or rack style mounting.

3. Acceptable Manufacturers – Closed Circuit Television Cameras, Lens, & Housings

a. Watec America Corp.

b. Opticom Technologies

c. Sanyo

d. Kalatel Inc

4. Digital Recording/Camera Controller units

The contractor shall provide, install, terminate, and submit for final acceptance testing, a delayed egress locking device that provides the following features:

a. One master control digital recording unit capable of 32 camera inputs and 16 alarm outputs

b. 30 day recording speeds at 60 images per second

c. 5 analog outputs

d. Supplied with real time playback

e. Searching capability based on activity detection

f. Looping video for up to 32 cameras.

5. Acceptable Manufacturers – Digital Recording/Camera Controller

a. Integral Technologies (DVX–32000)

b. Sensormatic/Robot (Intellex)

c. Loronix Corporation

d. Nice Inc

2.1.3 Intrusion Detection Systems:

A. Required Performance Features

The contractor shall provide, install, terminate, and submit for final acceptance testing an intrusion detection system consisting of the following equipment:

a. Door Position Indicator Switches
b. Door Monitoring System
c. Power Supplies
d. Other components not identified within this specification but required to provide a complete installation.

1. The door position indicator switches shall be provided with the following features:
   a. manufactured for use on steel without insulating brackets;
   b. concealed terminal screws;
   c. easy claiming terminals for expedited installation;
   d. mounting screws;
   e. biased for high security applications;
   f. capable of providing detection over a 3/8" to 1 1/4" gap; and
   g. color – natural.

The door position switch supplied for this project shall be the Sentrol 1047 series with the 1933 magnet, biased for high security applications, or equivalent.

2.14 Duress Reporting System:
   A. Required Performance Features:
      1. The contractor shall supply, install, terminate, and submit for final acceptance testing, a duress reporting system that will be monitored at the SMC and SCC. The equipment required for this design shall be Sentrol 3040 Surface Mounted Panic Switch or equivalent and shall have the following performance features:
         a. the unit shall be UL listed for duress reporting;
         b. the unit shall be single pole/double throw;
         c. the unit shall be capable of mounting under or on the side of desks, counters, or any other area thereby making it hard to detect by outsiders;
         d. the unit shall be supplied in a housing that is smooth to prevent accidental damage to clothing;
         e. an actuating lever designed to accommodate only the tip of a finger for activation, shall be a feature of the unit;
         f. each unit shall have reed contacts that reset when the lever is in a closed position;
         g. a latching LED shall "lock-in" when the unit is activated and be powered by 12 VDC;
         h. the unit shall have single pole/double throw output for electrical compatibility; and
         i. the unit shall be supplied in white.

2.15 FIRE STANDARDS COMPLIANCE

The contractor shall ensure that all equipment supplied for this project is in compliance with the United States Standard NFPA 101 including delayed egress locking devices, door hardware, emergency lighting, signal transmissions, and signage.

PART 3 EXECUTION

3.1 EXAMINATION

A. Examine all surfaces, anchors, and "grounds" that are to receive materials, fixtures, assemblies, components, and equipment. Immediately report all unsatisfactory conditions in writing to project manager.

3.2 CLEANING AND ADJUSTING

A. Remove paint splatters and other spots, dirt, and debris. Touch up scratches and marred finish to match original finish. Clean all units internally using methods and materials recommended by manufacturer prior to final acceptance testing.

3.3 DEMONSTRATION

A. The Contractor shall demonstrate to the Client and/or the designated representatives of the Client, the features and functions of the system and subsystems as well as instruct and train the designated personnel in the proper operation and maintenance of the system.

B. The contractor shall provide, on high quality VHS formatted videotape, documentation of the training sessions and maintenance procedures. Each video shall be clearly identified for Client's future reference.

3.4 INSTALLATION

A. The contractor is required to install all equipment and/or devices in accordance with recommendations and/or instructions supplied by the Manufacturer. Where systems integration is required, the system shall work "as one" to provide the client an operational system as per specifications.

3.5 ELECTRICAL

A. Power will be available at the site. The contractor is responsible for wiring from the source of power to the individual components. The contractor shall be responsible for providing to the Client, a complete set of shop drawings indicating the wiring and power requirements of their individual system and conduct a review of the electrical drawings as they pertain to Section 17. It shall be the responsibility of the contractor to provide additions, corrections, or modifications to the electrical design as they relate to the installation of the security equipment called for under this specification.

Alarms (Intrusion Detection Systems)

CHAPTER 7

As a part of an overall security system, intrusion detection systems must be considered. Alarms and sensors have been around for a long time. In the early days, most of them were burglar alarms with door contacts and window tape. Today there is a variety of intrusion detection systems. The alarm points can be integrated into the electronic access control system for monitoring purposes. Alarms are one of the three elements of physical security, detection delay, and response. The detection is an important aspect because, without detection, there could not be a timely response, or any response at all, to an intruder or intruders. There is a factor known as "Probability of Detection" (PD) which is used to determine whether an intruder will be picked up by the sensor device before entry to the perimeter or structure is made. The PD is important for choosing the right detector to meet the application. The use of intrusion detection systems and alarms help make the work of security officers more efficient and can reduce the number of officers needed if the system is properly deployed and covers the critical areas. Today intrusion detection systems and alarms are integrated into the access control system and CCTV is used to view and record what is going on at the alarm point.

All alarm systems have three main parts: a sensor, monitoring station, and a warning device. The sensor is what detects the intruder or fire and sends a signal to the monitoring station. The sensors use various technologies such electrical circuits or infrared. More detail about the technologies used by sensors will be presented later in the chapter.

The monitoring station can be a panel in the lobby of the building, as is commonly used for fire systems, or an alarm notification screen through the access control system software. The alarm panel or console can be located at the security officer station as well an offsite monitoring station.

All alarm systems have some type of audible and visual devices so the alarm can be acknowledged and appropriate action can be taken. For example, a fire alarm system will have audible and visual devices that alert people in the building to evacuate. Intrusion detection alarms have audible and visual devices that alert the security force monitoring or offsite station that an alarm sensor has been tripped so the alarm can be acknowledged and the appropriate action can be taken.

We will focus on intrusion alarms in this chapter. Fire alarms will be discussed in a later chapter. Other alarms are explained below and they can be monitored by the access control system since most of the alarms in the other category are used to monitor critical building systems.

Intrusion alarms are used to detect intrusion into a building or restricted area. Motion sensors are the most widely used type of alarm sensor today. These are known as the burglar alarms.

Fire alarms, according to fire codes, need a separate panel for monitoring purposes. They can also be monitored through the access control system. However this does not negate the need for its own panel to meet the fire code. Fire alarms can be smoke or heat detectors, manual pull stations, and fire suppression systems like sprinklers and gaseous systems. Fire alarms not only detect the signatures of a fire but they also provide an audible and visual alarm for evacuation.

Other types of alarms can be used to monitor critical building systems like HVAC. For example they can detect a sudden temperature increase in a computer server room which could cause the servers to shut down due to excessive heat build up. Still other alarms are used to monitor process systems for temperature and flow. Most of the electronic access control systems' software allows for monitoring of building alarms and they will even send a page to the appropriate personnel in the event of an alarm.

ALARM CATEGORIES

Alarms are categorized by the technology used in the sensors. They are a variety of sensor technologies being used in today's alarms. The two main types of sensor categories are as follows:

- Exterior
- Interior

In most cases the sensors are not interchangeable due to the elements they may exposed to so, when designing the intrusion detection system, consideration must be given to the location of the alarm sensors.

Exterior Intrusion Detection Sensors

Exterior intrusion detection sensors are used to detect intruders that are attempting to enter the protected area. The sensors are placed in the clear zones, around buildings, along the perimeter fence line, or on the perimeter fence. The exterior sensor is designed to stand up to the elements such as heat cold, rain, dust, snow, and sleet and still be able to function and detect intruders.

As you might have already guessed, the false alarm rate for exterior sensors is high. This is due to uncontrollable elements such as wind-caused blowing debris, snow and ice build up, or animals brushing up or crossing through the sensor field. For example, sensors on fences are notorious for false alarms during wind storms just from the movement of the fence by the wind as well as blowing debris.

Interior Intrusion Detection Sensors

Interior intrusion detection sensors are used to detect intrusion into a building or into a restricted area of a building. For example, motion sensors are used to detect the movement of an intruder.

The functions performed by interior sensors are as follows:

- Detect an intruder penetrating a boundary like a door, wall, roof, floor, vent, and window
- Tracking the movement of an intruder inside the building
- Detecting the movement or touching of an object such as a portable safe by an intruder

The false alarm rate for interior sensors is not as high as for the outdoor sensors but still they are susceptible to nuisance alarms. The most common cause of interior false alarms is an authorized person not deactivating the alarm after entry.

SENSOR TECHNOLOGY

The sensor technology is based on the following types:

- Switches
  - Magnetic
  - Balanced magnetic
  - Mechanical
- Volumetric sensors
- Ultrasonic
  - Passive
  - Active
  - Infrared
  - Passive
  - Interior active
  - Exterior active

- Glass breaks

- Microwave

- Vibration
    - Fence
    - Wall

- Fiber optic

- Electric field

- Capacitance

- Taut wire

- Photo electric beam

- Video motion detection

SWITCHES

There are several types of switches in use today for intrusion detection systems. The switch technologies include, magnetic, balanced magnetic, and mechanical.

Magnetic Switches

The magnetic switch is a magnet contact switch used to detect the opening of a door or window. The switch is a two-position switch and designed to be normally open or normally closed. The switch is in the normal position when the door or window is closed. A magnetic field is produced and the magnetic field pulls the switch to the non-alarmed position. If the window or door is opened, the contact is broken and the alarm is activated. The magnetic switches are usually mounted on window and door frames and are used in conjunction with motion sensors to detect that an entry has been made.

Some of the conditions that will cause unreliable detection and nuisance alarms in magnetic switches follow:

- Excessive door or window movement will cause too much "play" in the door or window and its frame. So if the door is shaken, the contact will be broken and an alarm will be sent. The wind can rattle doors and windows causing false alarms because the contact is broken.

- Improper alignment of the switch on the door or window with the switch on the frame will cause false alarms. Improper alignment can be caused by a bent or warped frame.

- The fluctuations in the frame due to seasonal conditions such as heating and cold can cause the magnetic switch to lose contact and send an alarm.

The main method for defeating a magnetic switch is to use a stronger magnet and keep the contact, allowing the door or window to be opened without activating the alarm. This is accomplished because the location of the switch is observable to the intruder allowing the proper placement of the stronger outside magnet to jump the terminal.

Balanced Magnetic Switches

Balanced magnetic switches contain two parts like the magnetic switches however one magnet is mounted on the door or window frame and a balancing magnet is mounted on the door or window. The magnet mounted on the frame is known as the internal magnet and the magnet mounted on the door or window is known as the external magnet.

The balancing of the switch is accomplished by the magnetic field of the magnets in the open position. When the magnetic field is disturbed by movement of the external magnet, the switch closes. While the door or window in the normal closed position, the magnetic field will cause the switch to be stable. If the door or window is opened, the magnetic field is disturbed and the switch becomes unstable activating an alarm. Balanced magnetic switches provide a higher level of security than do the magnetic switches. The switches are used on doors and windows and are used with other devices such as motion sensors.

Some conditions that cause unreliable detection and nuisance alarms in balanced magnetic switches follow:

• As in the case of the magnetic switches, excessive door or window movement will cause too much "play" in the door or window and its frame. So if the door is shaken the contact will be broken and an alarm will be sent. The wind can rattle doors and windows causing false alarms because the contact is broken.

• Improper alignment of the switch on the door or window with the switch on the frame will cause false alarms. Improper alignment can be caused by a bent or warped frame.

• The fluctuations in the frame due to seasonal conditions such as heating and cold can cause the magnetic switch to lose contact and send an alarm.

The balanced magnetic switch cannot be defeated by using a stronger external magnet and placing it on the switch when the door or window is open. Balanced magnetic switches are widely used today because they cannot be easily defeated by using a stringer external magnet or taping over one of the magnets. Figure 7–1 shows the mounting of a balanced magnetic switch. The magnetic switch is the same as the balanced magnetic switch mounting.

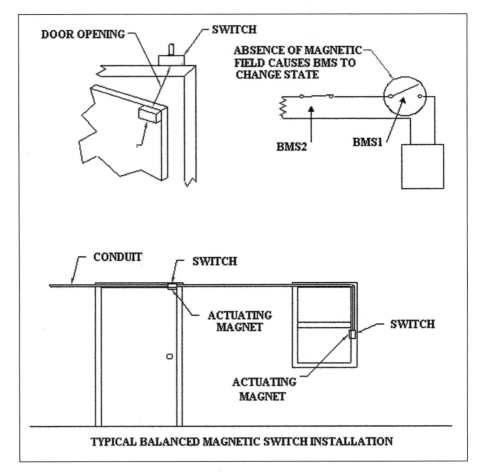

FIGURE 7-1   Balanced Magnetic Switch

Mechanical Switches

Mechanical switches are contact switches used to detect the opening of a door or window. Mechanical switches are spring-loaded plungers that are triggered when the door or window is opened. The switches send an alarm when there is physical disturbance to the sensor. Mechanical switches, like the magnetic switches, are mounted on doors and windows and are used in conjunction with a motion sensor to compensate for the failed alarm if is compromised.

Some conditions that cause unreliable detection and nuisance alarms in mechanical switches are:

• As with all of the switches, excessive door or window movement will cause too much "play" in the door or window and its frame. The alarm will be triggered if there is enough movement in the door or window. The wind can rattle doors and windows causing false alarms because the contact is broken.

* Improper alignment of the switch on the door or window with the switch on the frame will cause false alarms. Improper alignment can be caused by a bent or warped frame.

* The fluctuations in the frame due to seasonal conditions such as heating and cold can cause the magnetic switch to lose contact and send an alarm.

The mechanical switch can be defeated by holding the switch in the open position and taping it when the door or window is open. A small piece of metal will also hold the switch in the open position. Both of these methods will bypass the alarm and permit undetected entry when the switch is supposed to be in the closed position.

VOLUMETRIC SENSORS

Volumetric sensors are used to detect intrusion and motion in an interior space. Even though microwave is considered a volumetric sensor, it will be discussed later in the chapter under its own heading since it is used mainly for exterior use. There are two types of volumetric sensors, ultrasonic and infrared.

Ultrasonic Sensors

There are two types of ultrasonic sensors, passive and active. A passive ultrasonic sensor is a motion sensor that is listening for ultrasonic sound. The device reacts to high frequency sounds associated with an intrusion attempts. It listens for frequencies that are from 20 to 30 KHz. The range of 20 to 30 KHz is chosen because it is the sound range at which metal striking metal, the hissing of an acetylene torch, and the sound of that shattering concrete or brick makes. The sound travels the air in a wave-type motion. When it reaches the passive ultrasonic sensor, the frequency is determined and, if it meets the criteria characteristic of an intrusion attempt, an alarm is sent.

The ultrasonic sensors are mounted on a wall or ceiling and are used in a tandem with another type of sensor like a passive infrared sensor to increase the probability of detection (PD). The pitfall to using the sensor in tandem is that it increases the rate of false alarms and this will depend on the environment and how much control there is over what happens in the space.

Ultrasonic sensors are not affected by heat, so any changes in temperature either up or down will not make any difference in the sensor capability. Since ultrasonic energy does not pass through walls, roofs, or other partitions, it is easy to contain the detection to a defined area. On the other hand a big disadvantage is that ultrasonic energy does not pass through furniture, boxes, or other such obstructions and therefore creates "dead zones" where there is not any detection. To overcome this shortcoming, an additional detector can be added to cover the "dead zones".

Some conditions that cause unreliable detection and nuisance alarms in passive ultrasonic sensors follow:

- The sensors are susceptible to extreme changes in temperature and humidity from those conditions encountered during the initial installation and calibration and may cause detector reliability problems. The sensors need to be recalibrated periodically to maintain reliability. This should be done at the change of seasons.

- When installed on walls and ceilings in sensitive areas, detectors are effective when used in combination with passive infrared sensors.

- The most common false alarms from ultrasonic sensors are triggered by changes in air movement caused by the HVAC system, hissing from pipes, drafts from windows and doors, and the ring of a telephone. All of these stimuli can create noise near or at the ultrasonic range, triggering the alarm.

Since ultrasonic sensors have a narrow frequency range, intrusion methods, such as drilling, that fall into the frequency range will not trigger an alarm to be sent. This is why it is strongly recommended that the ultrasonic sensors be used in conjunction with another technology such as passive infrared sensors. Figure 7-2 shows an example of the wall and ceiling mount ultrasonic detectors.

The active ultrasonic sensor is a motion sensor. It emits ultrasonic energy rather than listening like the passive sensor does. The sensor reacts to the change in the reflected ultrasonic energy in the area that sensor is monitoring.

The principle of the active ultrasonic sensor is based on a frequency shift in reflected energy to detect intruders. This is similar to the sonar used to detect submarines and surface ships, except in that case the passive ultrasonic senor does emit a sound. The principle is based on the fact that sound uses air and travels in waves like motions. The sound wave is reflected back from the surroundings and the sensor hears the pitch characteristics of the protected environment. An intruder is detected upon entering the room because the wave pattern is disturbed and reflected back more quickly and sends an alarm.

Some conditions that cause unreliable detection and nuisance alarms in active ultrasonic sensors are the same as for the passive ultrasonic sensors. The only exception is that, since the active sensors are in motion, anything that causes movement will trigger an alarm, such as animals passing through the protected area.

The typical way to defeat active ultrasonic sensors is to move slowly in a horizontal direction. The detector will probably not detect the movement. To rem-

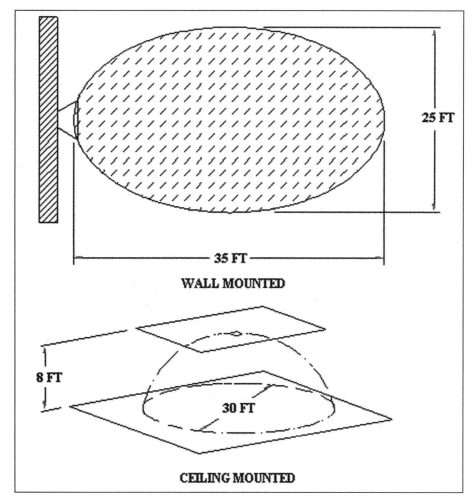

FIGURE 7-2   Wall-mounted and ceiling-mounted ultrasonic detectors

edy this shortcoming proper calibration is necessary to detect slow movement. Another way a knowledgeable intruder can defeat the system is to use a special test light to detect the coverage patterns and then avoid these areas. Figure 7–3 shows the active ultrasonic detector.

Infrared

There are two types of infrared sensors, passive and active. The passive infrared (PIR) sensors are divided into zones or sectors with each being defined with specific boundaries. Passive infrared sensors detect electromagnetic radiated energy

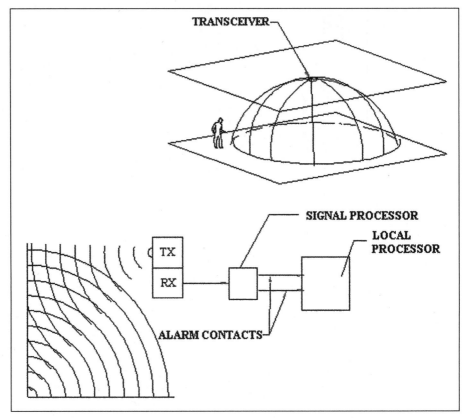

FIGURE 7-3 Active ultrasonic detector

that is generated by sources that produce temperatures below that of visible light. The sensors measure the change in thermal radiation. Passive sensors do not emit any signal. Instead the radiation of any movement in the room is checked against the environment of the room and changes that are hot images as contrasted between the hot image and the cooler background are detected as an intruder and an alarm is sent. This occurs because the room is at a certain temperature, usually below what a human emits so the image appears as "hot" to the sensor. The infrared energy is measured in microns and for humans the micron range is 7–14 with PIR sensors being focused on this narrow band.

Passive infrared, like the ultrasonic sensors, are mounted on the wall or ceiling and are used in conjunction with ultrasonic sensors, balance magnetic switches, glass break sensors, and time-delayed CCTV cameras.

A condition that can cause nuisance alarms is the radiation produced by small animals and/or rodents. Time-activated space heaters, ovens, and hot water pipes also will produce false alarms if they are in the field of view of the sensors. Room temperatures that are between 80 to 100 degrees will make the sensors less effective.

Passive infrared sensors can be defeated by cloaking, masking, or shadowing the intruding heat source from the field of view and this will decrease the probability of detection (PD) since it reduces the possibility of sufficient radiant heat being focused on the thermal sensor. Knowing the dead spots of the detection pattern can permit an intruder to bypass active regions. Also walking into the sensor rather than across the sensor's field of view will also reduce the detection capability by not allowing the boundaries of the detection beams to be broken.

Figure 7-4 shows the number ranges and projection angles of the detection beams vary depending upon design. Figure 7-5 is a ceiling-mounted PIR detector. Figure 7-6 is a wall-mounted PIR with a curtain-detection pattern. Figure 7-7 is a PIR wall mount showing the most sensitive area field of view. Figure 7-8 shows PIR placement and coverage patterns.

Active infrared, on the other hand, generates a curtain pattern of modulated infrared energy. The sensor then reacts to a change in the modulation of the frequency or an interruption in the received energy. These occurrences happen when an intruder passes through the area being protected by the sensor.

Active infrared sensors have a transmitter and a receiver within a single unit. The transmitter uses a laser to create the protection zone and the laser is projected onto a special retro-reflective tape that is used to define the protection zones outline. The energy is reflected off the tape back to the receiver located in the same housing as the laser projector. The energy is converted to an electrical signal and when the signal drops below a preset threshold for a specific period of time, an alarm is sent.

The coverage patterns are dependant upon the type of reflective tape used. The range can be between 15-25 feet wide by 17-30 feet long. The laser plane can be adjusted from 37 to 180 degrees. The system has a high probability of detection (PD) of an intruder and the speed, direction, and the temperature of the intruder have no effect on the detection characteristics.

Some conditions can cause unreliable detection and nuisance alarms. Dust or other particles that are deposited on the surface of the reflective tape will hinder the detection capabilities. Gaps in the reflective tape will cause unreliable detection. The tape must be continuous. The angle from the sensor to the ends or corners of the tape must not exceed 45 degrees.

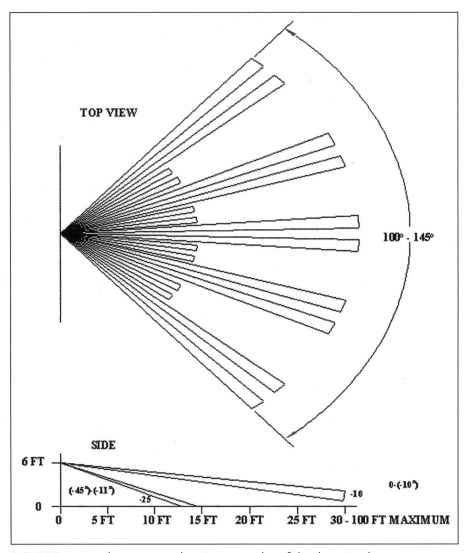

TOP VIEW

100° - 145°

SIDE

6 FT

0

0 5 FT 10 FT 15 FT 20 FT 25 FT 30 - 100 FT MAXIMUM

(-45°)-(-11°)   -25   -10   0-(-10°)

FIGURE 7-4   Number ranges and projection angles of the detection beams

An incandescent light that shines directly into the sensor will generate an alarm. Any incandescent light greater than 100 watts and sunlight falling directly in line with the tape to be reflected back to the receiver will cause an alarm.

The active infrared detector can be defeated by avoiding the projected laser plane. Also a knowledgeable intruder can deduce the field of the potential detection pattern from the location of the reflective tape and plan his movements to avoid detection.

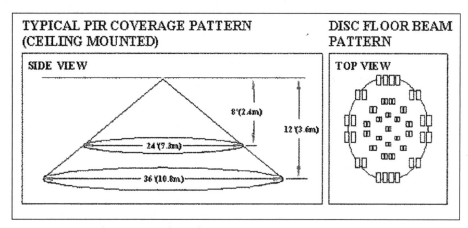

FIGURE 7-5 Ceiling-mounted PIR detector

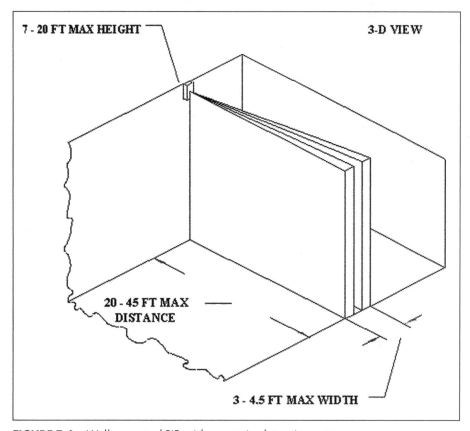

FIGURE 7-6 Wall-mounted PIR with a curtain-detection pattern

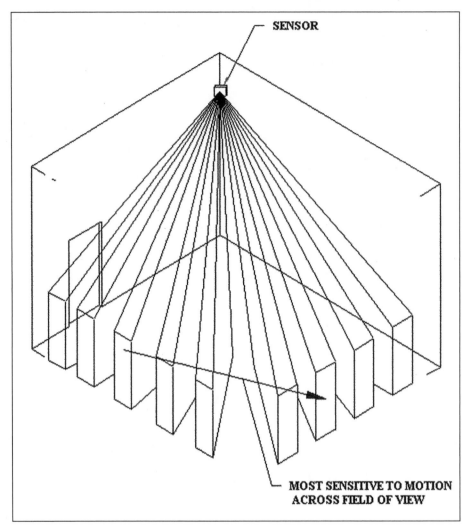

SENSOR

MOST SENSITIVE TO MOTION ACROSS FIELD OF VIEW

FIGURE 7-7 PIR wall mount showing the most sensitive area field of view

The exterior active sensor in Figure 7-9 produces a multiple-beam pattern. Exterior sensors are susceptible to nuisance alarms from animals and vegetation that grows to a size that, when blown by the wind, causes detection.

Since the sensors are outdoors, weather such as fog, heavy rain, and winds blowing sand and dust can affect the reliability of the sensors and may attenuate the infrared energy. The sensors can be defeated by tunneling underneath the sensors' beams.

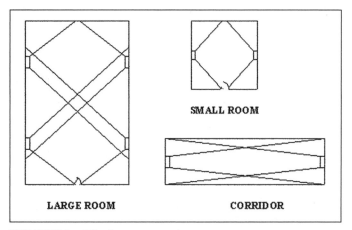

FIGURE 7-8 PIR placement and coverage patterns

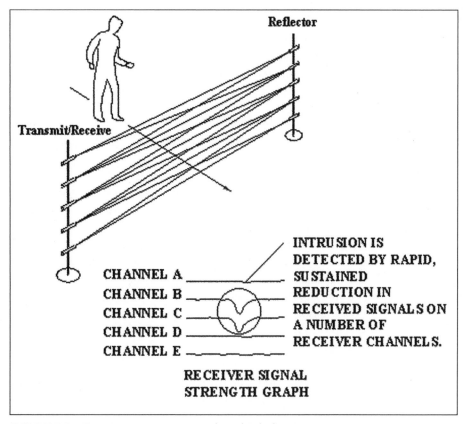

FIGURE 7-9 Exterior active sensor with multiple-beam pattern

GLASS BREAKS

Glass break sensors are used to monitor glass that can be broken during an intrusion for entry. The glass breaks use a microphone to listen for frequencies associated with breaking glass. The sensor has a processor that will filter frequencies not associated with glass breaking and allow only a certain range of frequencies to be analyzed.

Glass breaks come in three different types:

1. Acoustic

2. Shock

3. Dual technology acoustic/shock

Acoustic sensors are designed to listen for and detect the high frequency created when an initial shattering of the window occurs. This is the impact of hitting and shattering the glass. After the initial impact high frequencies will travel from the point of impact toward the outer edges of the glass. These are the vibrations that are picked up by the acoustic processor which passes them through the filter. A comparison is made to determine if there is a match and, if there is, an alarm is sent.

Shock sensors will "feel and sense" the 5 KHz frequency associated with the breaking of glass. Two types of shock sensors are available:

• Electric piezo transducers have electricity present.

• Non-electric piezo transducers do not have electricity present until the 5 KHz signal hits the transducer causing it to bend. This reduces false alarms.

Dual technology acoustic/shock sensors link the acoustic sensor with a shock sensor. The combination reduces the false alarm rate. The two sensors are located in the same unit and are connected electronically through the use of "AND" logic function. When one sensor, either the acoustic or shock, senses a break, each sends it to an "AND" gate. Once both signals are received by the "AND" gate, an alarm is sent.

Some conditions can cause unreliable detection and nuisance alarms in glass break sensors. The sensors should be mounted according to the manufacturer's specifications as some acoustic sensors are to be mounted on the window, window frame, wall, or ceiling. Sensors mounted on the glass should be placed in the corner about two inches from the edge of the frame. Sensors mounted on the ceiling or wall should be mounted opposite the window it is protecting. For best results glass break sensors should be used in conjunction with magnetic switches, balanced magnetic switches, or contacts.

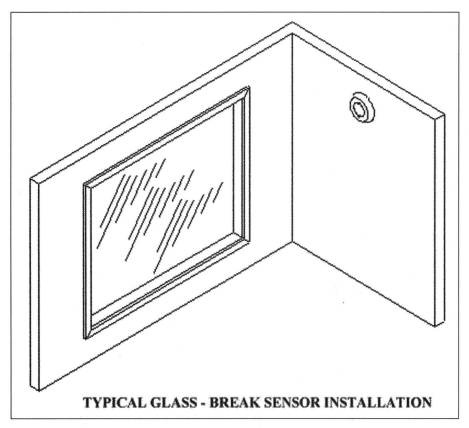

FIGURE 7-10 Wall-mounted installation of a glass break sensor

Inappropriate sensor matching of range capacity to window size and poorly locating the sensor may cause the sensor to be out of range and therefore not detect a glass-break intrusion. If the acoustic sensor is improperly calibrated or installed, it will be a cause of nuisance alarms. Any RF interference or sharp impact noises will cause false alarms.

The sensor is defeated by removing a window pane or cutting a hole in the window rather than breaking it. This is why it is important to use the sensor with another technology like motion sensors. Figure 7-10 shows a wall mounted installation of a glass break sensor.

MICROWAVE

Microwave sensors are motion sensors that use microwaves to detect intruders. They transmit and flood an area or zone with an electronic field. Microwave

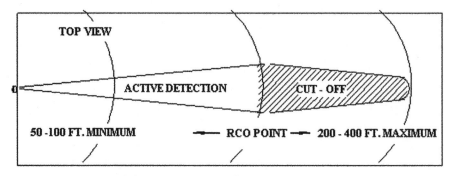

FIGURE 7-11   Typical detection pattern of a monostatic sensor

sensors use the Doppler frequency shift to detect intrusions. Human movements cause a frequency shift of 20Hz to 120 Hz so most microwave sensors are tuned to measure the Doppler shift of these frequencies.

There are two types of microwave sensors. Monostatic sensors have the transmitter and the receiver in the same unit. The antenna is mounted with in the microwave cavity and flexible enough to be configured and shaped to cover a specified area or zone. The beam can be a short oval or a long slender one. Figure 7-11 shows a typical detection pattern of a monostatic sensor. Figure 7-12 shows a short range monostatic sensor detection pattern.

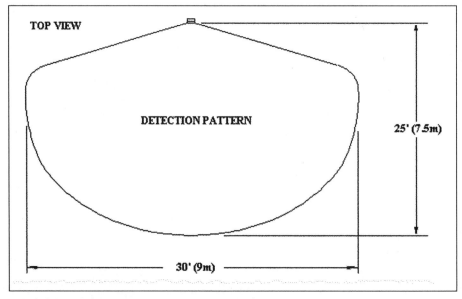

FIGURE 7-12   Short-range monostatic sensor detection pattern

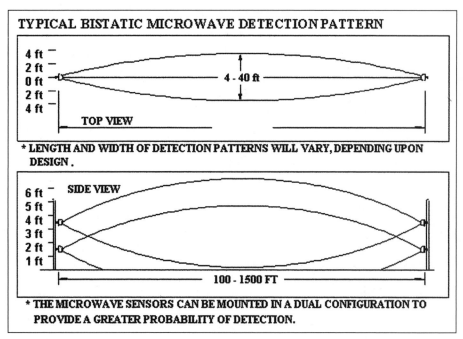

FIGURE 7-13   Bistatic detection pattern

Bistatic sensors have separate units for the transmitter and the receiver. A detection zone is created between the two units. The antenna is flexible enough to be configured to alter the signal field width and height to create different detection zones. Figure 7-13 shows a bistatic detection pattern. Figure 7-14 shows microwave detector zones. Figure 7-15 shows a stacked microwave sensor pattern. Figure 7-16 shows bistatic microwave layout configurations.

Some conditions can cause unreliable detection and nuisance alarms in microwave sensors. If the detectors are placed in close proximity to other high frequency spectrum bands, the signal can be adversely affected. The sensors should not be used near large electric generators or radio transmitters. Fluorescent lights also can be a problem because the ionization cycle created by the bulbs can be detected as motion by the sensor. Any large metal objects that can reflect or block the signal should be kept out of the detection zone.

The high frequency waves produced by the detectors can travel through walls, glass, sheetrock, and wood adjacent to the protection zone. This can be a source of false alarms. Tests should be conducted for dead zones to prevent them from being a source of intrusion attempts. Any objects that could reflect the signals should be removed from the protection zone because they can extend the coverage to areas not intended to be covered and be a source of false alarms.

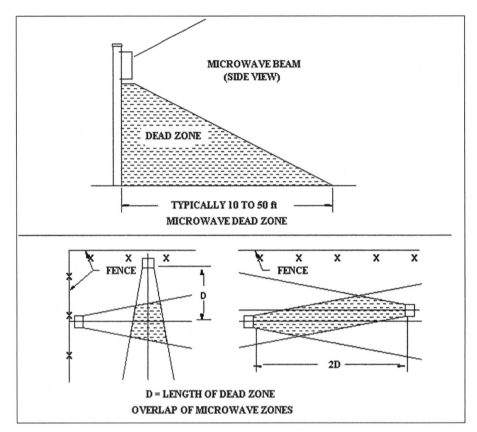

FIGURE 7-14   Microwave detector zones

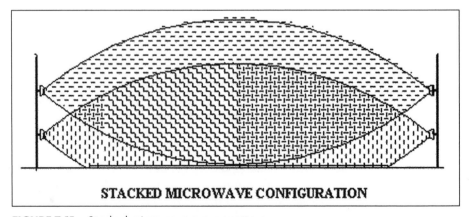

FIGURE 7-15   Stacked microwave sensor pattern

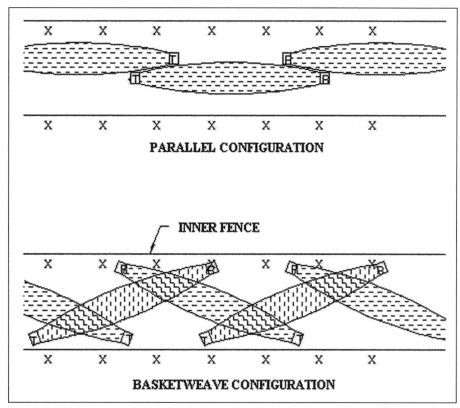

FIGURE 7-16 Bistatic microwave layout configurations

The system can be defeated by an intruder that has access to the area and periodically performs walk tests to determine the sensor patterns. He may be able to identify low detection points. An intruder that approaches in a slow deliberate manner using obstructions that may block or absorb the signal may avoid detection.

VIBRATION SENSORS

The vibration sensors are mounted on walls, ceilings, floors, and fences. The sensors are designed to detect mechanical vibrations caused by chopping, drilling, ramming, sawing, and any other physical intrusion attempt that would penetrate the protected structure.

The vibration sensor has transducers that detect low frequency energy like those found in vibrations generated by a physical intrusion attempt. There are two types of transducers, piezo electric and mechanical with both converting the seismic vibrations to electrical signals.

Vibration sensors need to be firmly mounted about 8 to 10 feet apart on a wall or ceiling where the intrusion is expected. When placing the sensor, be cognizant of whether the sheetrock, plywood, or thin metal wall is connected to a main support or the sensor will be prone to false alarms. The vibration sensor should be used in conjunction with a volumetric sensor such as a PIR or ultrasonic detector.

Some conditions can cause unreliable detection and nuisance alarms in wall vibration sensors. The main reason for nuisance alarms is poor placement. The unstable or improper placement of the sensors will cause detection issues. Mounting the sensors on rugs, fabric, or heavy wall coverings will also diminish the detector's effectiveness. If the vibration detector is placed on a wall that is prone

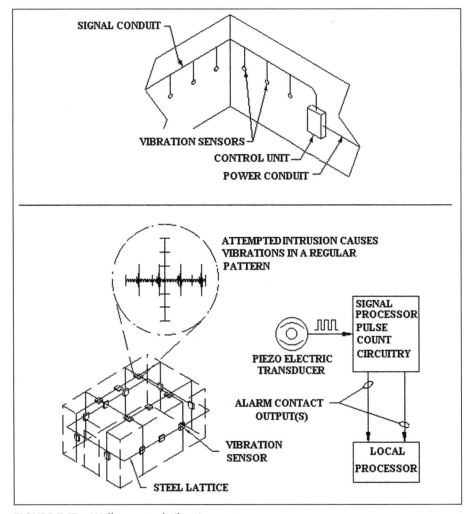

FIGURE 7-17   Wall-mounted vibration sensor

to external vibrations, such as planes or heavy truck traffic, false nuisance alarms may happen.

The sensor can be defeated by avoiding entry through an area or zone that is protected by vibration sensors. Another method is to produce random persistent false alarms over a period of time so the alarms will be ignored. Figure 7-17 shows a wall–mounted vibration sensor.

Fence Vibration Sensors

Fence vibration sensors are mounted on perimeter fence fabric to detect intrusion attempts to the fence. The detectors will sense cutting, climbing, sawing, or lifting of the fence fabric. There are two types of fence vibration sensors. Electromechanical sensors use mechanical inertia switches or mercury switches to detect vibration. Mechanical inertia switches consist of a vibration–sensitive mass that rests on two or three electric contacts so as to create a closed circuit. When an intrusion attempt is made, the vibration disturbs one or more of the contact points thereby opening the circuit and causing an alarm.

A mercury switch is a glass vial that contains a small amount of mercury with a set of normally open electrical contacts located in close proximity, but not touching the mercury. When an intrusion attempt is made, the mercury is displaced from its normal resting position causing contact with one of the electric contacts and creating an alarm.

Piezo electric sensors convert mechanical impact forces into electrical signals and operate similar to the wall piezo electric sensors using a filter processor to check the signal before an alarm is sent.

Some conditions can cause unreliable detection and nuisance alarms in fence vibration sensors. Improper spacing and installation are critical to the operation of the sensors. Fences with loose fabric that sags, sways, and flexes will cause false alarms.

When shrubbery, tree branches, or animals come in contact with the fence fabric, it will cause an alarm. In areas where the perimeter fence line is subjected to frequent animal interactions, fence vibration sensors can cause nuisance alarms.

Vehicles, containers, and structures should not be parked next to a fence that is protected using a fence vibration sensor because they can be used to bridge the fence. Finally, fence corners are an area that can be defeated due to the bracing of fence posts and more solid foundations used at a corner or turn point.

The system can be defeated by an intruder that deep tunnels under the fence and does come into contact with the fence. Figure 7-18 shows a fence vibration system.

Fiber Optic

There are two types of fiber sensors used in perimeter security. One is the in-wall fiber optic and the other is fence fiber optic. Rather than electricity for

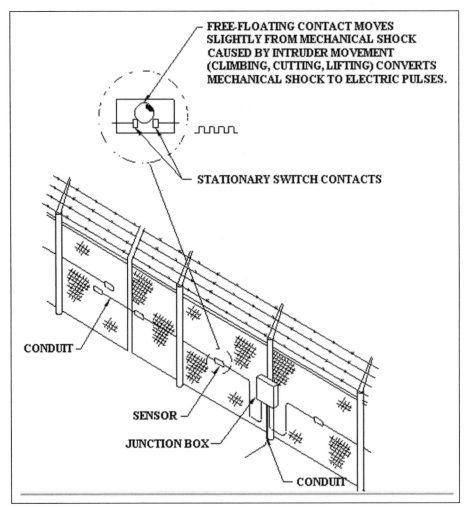

FREE-FLOATING CONTACT MOVES SLIGHTLY FROM MECHANICAL SHOCK CAUSED BY INTRUDER MOVEMENT (CLIMBING, CUTTING, LIFTING) CONVERTS MECHANICAL SHOCK TO ELECTRIC PULSES.

STATIONARY SWITCH CONTACTS

CONDUIT

SENSOR

JUNCTION BOX

CONDUIT

FIGURE 7-18   Fence vibration system

transmission and detection, fiber optic sensors use light in the form of a Light Emitting Diode (LED) as the light source. The fiber optic is used as a line sensor and uses an LED as the light source that travels through the fiber optic network and is picked up by a detector. The detector is very sensitive to changes in the light transmission and will send an alarm even if slight changes occur. The fiber optic sensors are very sensitive and analysis must be done to determine their suitability for a wall, roof, or fence.

There are two types of fiber optic sensors. Fiber optic continuity is where the fiber strand needs to be broken to initiate an intrusion alarm. Fiber optic microbending is the detection of alterations in the light pattern caused by movement of the fiber optic cable.

Some conditions can cause unreliable detection and nuisance alarms with in-wall fiber optic sensors. Improper calibration or installation will cause problems. They are not to be used on walls of lesser structural integrity such as sheet rock, plywood, or thin metal because they are susceptible to vibrations and will cause nuisance false alarms. Fiber optics should not be on walls near any machinery that causes vibrations as well as walls that are subjected to exterior airplane, train, and heavy truck vibrations.

The fiber optic wall sensor can be defeated by bypassing it altogether and making entry away from the area protected by the sensors. Figure 7-19 shows a wall fiber optic sensor.

Some conditions can cause unreliable detection and nuisance alarms in the fence fiber optic sensors. Radio frequencies, electro-magnetic interference, extreme changes in temperatures, and blowing debris can cause problems for the fence fiber optics. Poor fence quality is the most common cause of nuisance

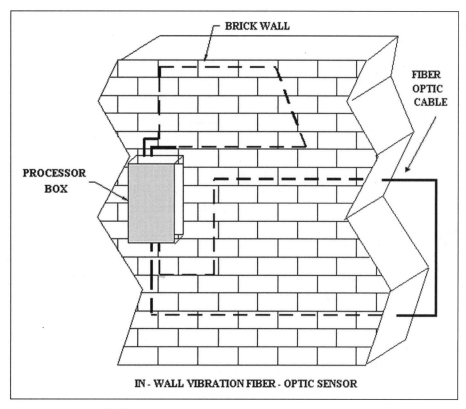

FIGURE 7-19 Wall fiber optic sensor

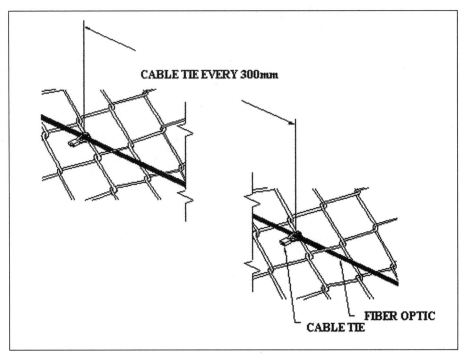

FIGURE 7-20   Fence optic sensor

alarms because the fence has too much movement. To compensate for the poor fence quality the calibration of the sensors is set lower than proffered. When properly installed on a stable fence, the wire will be taut. Extreme weather that causes damage to the fiber optic cable will cause nuisance alarms.

The fence fiber optic sensor can be defeated by tunneling under the fence and not contacting the fence during entry. Figure 7-20 shows a fence optic sensor.

Electric Field

Electric field sensors produce an electrostatic field between an array of wire conductors and electric ground. The sensors are designed to detect distortions or changes in the electric field. The distortions or changes are probably caused by someone approaching the fence.

The components of the electric field sensor include an alternating current generator to excite a field wire which consists of two or more sensing wires and creating an electrostatic field which amplifies to detect changes in the signal amplitude of the sensing wires. The changes in amplitude are caused when an intruder enters the field because large amounts of the electric charge flow from the intruder disrupting the field and thereby initiating an alarm.

Electric field wires are mounted on free standing posts or chain link fences. The wires are all mounted parallel to each other and to the ground which helps ensure uniform sensitivity along the entire fence length. Since the electric field sensor has a self adjusting circuit located in the processor, false alarms from wind and ambient noise are not an issue as they are with other fence sensors.

Some conditions can cause unreliable detection and nuisance alarms in the electric field fence sensors. The nuisance alarm rate for the electric field sensor is extremely low. Weather conditions such as rain, snow, and lightning can create problems for the sensor. Animals and vegetation along the fence line can also cause false alarms. During installation, large spaces between the wires should be avoided since they may make it possible to move between the wires without detection.

The electric field fence sensor can be defeated by deep tunneling under or bridging over the protected fence. Figure 7-21 shows the electric field sensor configuration patterns. Figure 7-22 shows a three-wire and a four-wire sensor.

Capacitance

The purpose of capacitance sensors is to detect a change in an electrostatic field. The electrostatic field is produced by an array of wires, usually three wires spaced close together. A low-voltage signal is used to create an electrical field in the fence and serves as the ground. The differential capacitance between the sensor wires and the ground is continually measured. Any change in the signal that is detected is sent to the process filter to determine if it is in the accepted range. If the signal is not in the accepted range, it will initiate an alarm.

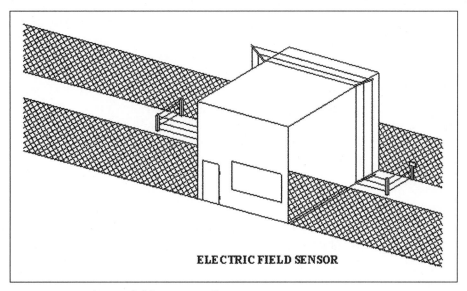

ELECTRIC FIELD SENSOR

FIGURE 7-21 Electric field sensor configuration patterns

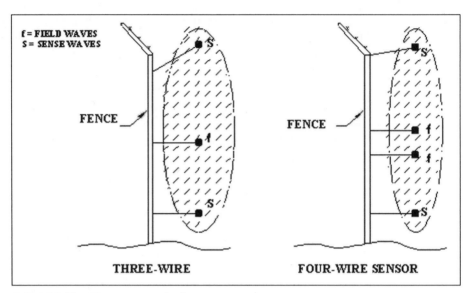

FIGURE 7-22   Three-wire and a four-wire sensor

The strands of wire used are 16-gauge and consist of three strands spaced closely together. The capacitance sensors are mounted the existing fence fabric. Capacitance sensors can also be used around other objects like safes and file cabinets inside a building.

The capacitance sensor is not affected by weather or EMI/RFI interference. The system does require a high degree of maintenance to keep the capacitance at the optimal settings. Some conditions can cause unreliable detection and nuisance alarms in the capacitance fence sensors. Vibration caused by weather (winds), animals, or vegetation coming into contact with the fence will cause nuisance false alarms. Birds landing on the fence will also cause nuisance alarms as will blowing debris that hits the fence.

The sensors can be defeated by bridging or tunneling under the fence. Figure 7-23 shows a capacitance system. Figure 7-24 shows the capacitance sensor used around a file cabinet and a safe.

Taut Wire

Taut wire sensors are micro-switches used to detect changes in tension on the fence fabric rather vibration. The taut wire is installed to the barbed wire on the top of the chain-link fence. The micro-switch consists of a movable center rod that is suspended inside a cylindrical conductor. The open position of the switch is when the center rod is in the middle of the cylinder and does not touch the outer cylinder. The switches are installed about 6 inches apart in a vertical line

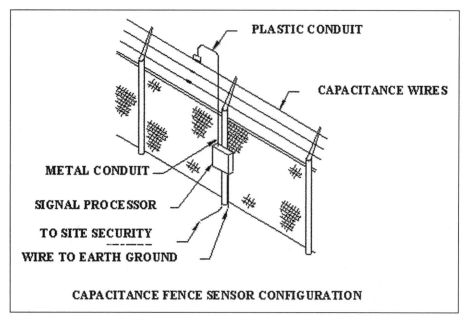

FIGURE 7-23 Capacitance system

on the inside of the tamperproof case and mounted on a fence post near the middle of the sensor zone.

When the taut wire sensors are used on the outriggers of the barbed wire at the top of the fence, they are designed to detect climbing. Sensors at the top of the fence on the outriggers have no detection capability for fence cutting at the lower part of the fence.

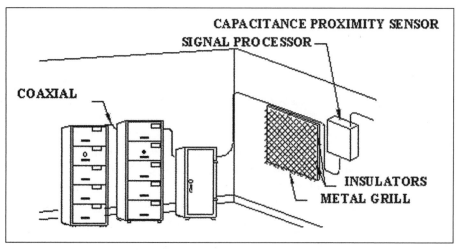

FIGURE 7-24 Capacitance sensor used around a file cabinet and a safe

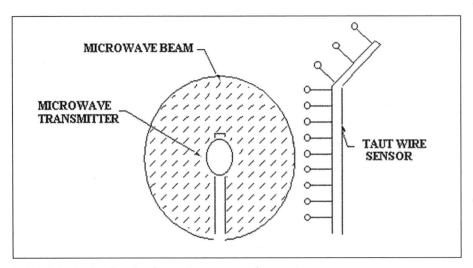

FIGURE 7-25   Dual technology microwave and taut wire system.

The taut wire sensor system is one of the most reliable fence sensor systems since it less likely to create nuisance alarms due to weather or small animals. However, some conditions can cause unreliable detection and nuisance alarms in the taut wire fence sensors. Improper or no maintenance will cause sensor sensitivity issues, especially if the tension on the wire is loose. Large animals that brush up against the fence will cause false alarms especially grazing animals such as cattle. As with all of the other fence sensors they can be defeated by bridging and tunneling to avoid detection. Figure 7-25 shows a dual technology microwave and taut wire system.

Photo Electric Beam

Photo electric beam sensors transmit a beam of infrared light to a remote receiver. The process of projecting the beam to a remote receiver sets up an "electronic fence". There are two components in the beam, a transmitter and a receiver. An LED is used as the light source to transmit a consistent beam of light to the receiver. The receiver is a photo electric cell that detects the whether the beam is present. The photo cell must receive at least 90 percent of the beam. If the beam is disrupted for 75 milliseconds, an alarm is initiated. The 75 milliseconds is the time it takes for an intruder to cross the beam.

The photo electric beam can be used to protect doorways, long wall surfaces, and hallways. The beam can be projected for a receiver up to 1,000 feet away. The beam's path can be altered by mirrors so a less predictable path can be created, but it will reduce the signal strength and lessen the distance the beam can be projected.

The false alarm rate is high with the photo electric beam sensor. Following are some conditions that can cause unreliable detection and nuisance alarms. Weather conditions such as fog, mist, or dust will cause the beam to be refracted or scattered and will initiate an alarm if there is a 10 percent reduction in the light signal. Birds, animals, blowing leaves, or paper can cause nuisance alarms because the signal will be interrupted. If the transmitter is out-of-line with the receiver, it will cause nuisance alarms.

To defeat the beam an intruder can step over or go under the beam signal path. Mirrors can be used to mitigate the risk of stepping over or going under the beam by causing a zig-zag effect to the beam's pattern.

Video Motion Detection

Video motion sensors use Closed Circuit Television (CCTV) with low-light capabilities and infrared to detect and provide a visual of an intrusion. CCTV systems also record the event for documentation purposes using digital or VHS recorders.

The video motion sensors detect changes in the monitored area by comparing the current scene to the pre-recorded stable scene. The motion sensors monitor the video signal being transmitted from the camera. A signal change indicates that there is some movement in the camera's field of "view" and an alarm is initiated. More about CCTV will be presented in another chapter.

Some conditions can cause unreliable detection and nuisance alarms in the video motion sensors. Poor lighting will produce unreliable detection. If the lighting is not adequate, a low-light camera and infrared detection is recommended. It is better to attempt to increase the lighting as much as possible. The infrared detector does not use light to detect an intruder. It uses the heat from the intruder so low or poor lighting is not a problem for the infrared sensor.

Remember, camera placement in critical when installing the CCTV cameras. The field of view can be adversely affected by direct sunlight such as a sunrise or sunset that looks directly into the camera iris. Clouds and wind- blown debris can cause false alarms. Manmade light sources such as vehicle headlights, changes in parking lot parking patterns, or security light patterns will also cause false alarms. Insects flying close to the lens will initiate an alarm. An intruder can defeat the system if they are aware of it and know the layout. They may be able to avoid detection by moving around "blind" spots.

INTRUSION DETECTION SYSTEM DESIGN SPECIFICATIONS

The following is a sample design specification for an intrusion detection system. an abbreviated sample of design specifications to guide you so you can write your own design specifications for your project.

SECTION 17000 – INTRUCTION DETECTION SYSTEM
PART 1 – GENERAL
1.1 RELATED DOCUMENTS
A. All drawings and the General Provisions of the Contract including the General and Supplementary Conditions and Division 1 Specification Sections, apply to this Section.
1.2 PROJECT SCOPE:
A. The system being developed under this design is an electronic intrusion detection, egress control system that incorporates the technologies shown below. For the purpose of clarification, the following parties will be referenced in this document in the following manner:

1. The ABCD Corporation   The Client
5667 Gibraltar Drive
Livermore, CA. 94588
925-224-7955 Tel
925-224-7964 Fax
www.abcd.com

2. The XYZ Consultants Inc.   The Consultants
4847 S. Orange Blossom Trail
Orlando, Florida, 32835
407-851-8734 Tel
407-851-1215 Fax
www.xyzconsult.com

3. The ABCD Corporation   The Facility(s)
Livermore, California
Toronto, Canada
Paris, France
Amsterdam, Holland
London, England

B. In all new facilities, the system is being installed for the purpose of detecting an intruder entering the Client's facility. The systems within the United States are being retro-fitted however the contractor must still comply with this specification and the bidder instructions. It is a requirement of the system that all technologies be integrated into one system to allow for instantaneous alert and response to any alarm condition that may be activated in the secured area. The system will be integrated through the access control system installed in the facility if applicable.

C. It is also a requirement of the system to monitor all building management services as they relate to the facility. The operations manager shall have the ability to both monitor and control building management equipment through the access control system or building management system, the only exception is the fire alarm, smoke detection systems will still have their own annunciation panels to meet the requirements of the fire codes.

D. This Section calls for the contractor of choice to provide all labor, materials, equipment, and service necessary for the completion of the integrated intrusion detection system and as indicated on the drawings and as described herein. The internal "NET" shall be supplied by the Owner however it is the responsibility of the contractor to verify that communication pathways are open and compatible with all components within the global system. The Owner reserves the right to supply other components if they are needed for this project. The system technologies called for within this Scope of Work are:

1. Intrusion Detection Devices
2. Duress Reporting Devices

E. The Contractor shall provide all labor, materials, equipment, software, and programming required to provide the Client with an integrated security system that is compatible with existing components in other offices operated by the Client.

F. Contractor shall ensure the system meets the operational and functional needs of the Client as specified herein, and as indicated on the drawings. The drawings are diagrammatic only. Equipment and labor not specifically referred to herein, or on the plans, that are required to meet the functional and operational intent, shall be provided without additional cost to the Client.

G. Contractor shall be responsible for coordinating with other trades and contractors to provide a system that is totally integrated and operational as required for this project.

H. The Contractor shall be responsible for providing with their Submittal, a one year spare parts list with single component (itemized) and quantity pricing. Should any particular component be in redesign stage that would possibly cause it to be a non-production item within the 1 year period, this component shall be identified as such and the substitute or new component be identified on this spare parts list.

1.3 RELATED SECTIONS

A. The contractor shall review the following sections of the total project to ensure compliance with:

1. Division 2   Site Work
2. Division 7   Alarm detection Devices
3. Division 8   Door Contacts for other than access controlled doors
4. Division 16 Electrical

All specification divisions are identified by The Construction Specification Institute Master Format

1.4 SUBMITTALS

A. Contractor shall submit bid data containing original catalog cut sheets that provide complete technical data as required by the Owner to allow evaluation of the material and equipment proposed. The information should include component dimensions, wiring and block diagrams, wire/cable sizes, conduit sizes, performance data, ratings, operational characteristics, control sequences, and other descriptive data to describe the items proposed.

B. The Contractor's submittal shall include a complete list of equipment, materials, and installation instructions. All prices shall be itemized in single component prices as well as quantity pricing with any discounts so indicated. Alternative proposals are acceptable under this specification and shall comply with all standard requirements for the bid package submittal.

C. The Contractor receiving the award shall submit within two weeks (14 days) of the award date a complete set of shop drawings. These drawings shall contain complete wiring and schematic diagrams, software descriptions, calculations, and any other details required to demonstrate that the system has been properly coordinated and installed to function as described within the specifications.

D. The Contractor shall upon the completion of the project, provide to the Client or their designated representative, a complete and accurate set of As-Built drawings. The submittal shall be in AutoCAD V2000 and supplied on a disk along with five copies of system(s) manuals and drawings. The submittal shall be completed and delivered to the Client and/or their designated representative at least two weeks prior to final acceptance testing. Punch item corrections will require a re-submittal if the list is substantial.

1.5 QUALITY ASSURANCE

A. Manufacturer's Qualifications:

The Contractor shall only represent a Company that specializes in the business of having provided Electronic Integrated Security Systems for a period of at least five (5) years. The supporting documentation supplied by the Contractor shall demonstrate the Manufacturer's as well as the Contractor's experience by including:

1. Installations for at least five (5) facilities of equal size and comparable technical requirements utilizing the equipment submitted.
2. For each facility, the information should include:
   a. Name and address of facility;
   b. Date of the Installation and System Acceptance;
   c. A point of contact for either the Owner or the Owner's designated representative;

        d. The name of the project or construction manager, if applicable; and

        e. The name of the Architect of Record, if applicable.

    3. A description of the technical aspects of the system describing how the system functions in comparison to the System described within this specification.

  B. References and Regulatory Requirements.

    1. All workmanship and materials supplied under this Section shall comply with the requirements of the following agencies and authorities:

        a. International Electrical Engineers (IEE)

        b. European Committee for Electrotechnical Standardization (CENELEC)

        c. International Electrotechnical Commission (IEC)

        d. National Fire Protection Association (NFPA) US Standard

        e. National Electric Manufacturers Association (NEMA) US Standard

        f. Life Safety Code (NFPA 101) (1999) US Standard

        g. National Burglar and Fire Alarm Association (NBFAA) – Standards of Application – US Standard

        h. Closed Circuit Television Manufacturers Association (CCTMA) – US Standard

        i. Underwriters Laboratories (UL) – European Equivalent

1.6 REQUIREMENTS OF THE DESIGN

  A. THE SYSTEM – The design for this system consists of several components. The intent is to allow full monitoring of all security and security related activities, including building management services (HVAC, Fire, Power, etc.) at the systems management console (SMC). The monitored functions shall consist of but not be limited to:

    1. All access control devices for access and egress to and from the facility;

    2. Intrusion detection equipment as it relates to fire doors, duress buttons, and other similar devices;

    3. Delayed Egress Locking Devices;

    4. Closed circuit surveillance cameras with a processor integrated into the overall system to provide reactive design functions and a digital recording device; and

    6. Any additional components required for a complete installation but not identified within this specification.

  B. THE INSTALLATION – The Contractor shall provide, install, terminate, and submit for final acceptance testing the electronic system required for this design. All work will be inspected during the installation process and final acceptance testing will be conducted prior to the system being accepted by the Client. The contractor shall advise the Client at each point of substantial completion to allow periodic inspections. Final acceptance testing shall be conducted when contractor advises the system is ready. Punch list corrections shall be completed within two weeks after list development. The testing process is on all items prior to acceptance of the system by the Client. The Client reserves the right to require complete system testing a second time if the punch list is of considerable size.

1. CENTRALIZED MONITORING - This design of this system is such that monitoring will be required in two locations. The primary monitoring of CCTV and all alarms will be at the systems monitoring console (SMC) located in the main console room. A second monitoring station at the Security Command Center (SCC) may be required for each site. This workstation will be monitored by security officers and shall mirror the information being sent to the SMC. This station will be a workstation with all security and security related functions reporting to this location as well as the SCM. The system shall archive all access control, intrusion detection alarms, BMS functions, and CCTV video storage information at the main system server located in Livermore, California. The information shall be sent via the owner provided "NET" on a pre-programmed basis established by the Client and programmed by the Contractor.

2. The system shall provide for automatic display of alarm point locations at the SMC and SCC. The components of the integrated system shall include but not be limited to:

A. Forty five (45) balanced magnetic switches for door contacts for non-access controlled doors;

B. Forty (40) Dual technology glass breaks;

C. Thirty six (36) dual technology volumetric protection devices with adjustable lens units;

D. Power supply with battery backup;

E. Field panels as required to monitor all points identified within this specification and on the drawings;

F. Building management systems (BMS) monitoring and control capability for up to 100 points;

G. Duress reporting devices (6) to be located at a later date;

H. Training, manuals, service, and maintenance as specified; and,

I. Any additional components required, but not specifically mentioned within this or other sections.

E. INTRUSION DETECTION: The Contractor shall provide, install, terminate, and submit for final acceptance testing, door position switches as indicated on the drawings accompanying this specification. Each door position switch shall be interfaced into the system in order that either intrusion or egress alarms through secured doors are reported to both the SMC and SCC. The IDS also shall interface with the camera controller unit to activate the camera system for the purposes of alerting the personnel in the monitoring areas and also to activate the recording functions of the system. This system shall be integrated through the Contractor provided cabling for the purpose of activating the video and security response techniques required for both interior as well as limited exterior areas. The system shall consist of the following components:

1. Door Position Switches; and
2. Any additional components required, but not specifically mentioned within this or other sections.

F. DURESS REPORTING – The contractor shall provide, install, terminate, program, and submit for final acceptance testing, duress buttons at the locations indicated on the drawings accompanying this specification. The duress system shall, when activated, report to the SMC as well as the SCC. Additionally, the cameras selected by the Client and programmed by the Contractor shall be activated for the purpose of viewing the controlled area and recording all events that take place during the alarm. The components required for this portion of the system shall consist of:

1. Duress buttons – desk mounted
2. Any additional components required, but not specifically mentioned within this or other sections.

1.7 WARRANTY

A. Warrant material and workmanship for a period of one year from the date of system final acceptance.

B. Warranty shall include the repair, replacement, and upgrade of defective security components and/or materials including the correction of defective work when given notice by the Client during the warranty period.

C. Warranty response time shall be within 8 hours upon receipt of request from Client or their designated representative during normal working hours. Weekend response shall be extended to a period not to exceed 12 hours.

1.8 RECORD DOCUMENTS

A. The Contractor shall provide project record drawings identifying the system architecture and rack/component distribution.

B. The "document package" shall include three sets of system manuals for the overall system concept as well as individual components within the system. Manuals shall consist of:

1. Operations manual – provide all information for operation of the system, including but not limited to, trouble shooting information, as well as software operational information;
2. Installation manual – provide drawings describing all circuits, power distribution, equipment placement, and cable routing, in an As–Built drawings (C size) format. This manual shall also include reference to any conduit routing;
3. Maintenance/Service Manual – Provide all trouble shooting information, data that is applicable to on–site software manipulation, programming information, and service/maintenance records.

C. The "drawing package" shall include three (3) sets of As-built drawings. These drawings shall be supplied to the Client or the Client's designated representative for final acceptance testing, punch list development, and system acceptance. The drawings shall be corrected as required for final system acceptance. The As-Built drawings shall not be considered complete until accepted by the Client.

1.9 OPERATION TRAINING AND MAINTENANCE DATA

A. Included with the shop drawing submittal should be a syllabus outlining the training program that will be provided to the Client or their designated representative with reference to the operation of this system. This syllabus should include a minimum of 16 hours training with demonstrations of the features and functions of the primary system and integrated subsystems.

B. The training classes should be conducted with competent supervisors or factory trained technicians and shall be conducted on site. The Client shall designate which individuals from their organization shall receive the training.

1.10. OPERATION AND MAINTENANCE DATA MANUAL

A. Assemble a set of three (3) manuals in hard bound covers, presenting for the Client's guidance, full details for care and maintenance of visible surfaces, and of equipment included in the work.

B. Include manufacturer's literature relating to components and other equipment, catalog cut sheets, parts list, wiring diagrams, instruction sheets, and other pertinent information which will be useful to the Client in overall system operation and maintenance.

C. Include a list of installers and service representatives with company names and addresses, names of individuals to contact, and telephone numbers.

D. Prepare operating instructions, complete and explicit, including, but not limited to, instructions for start-up, operating, and stopping.

1.11 MAINTENANCE SERVICE

A. The contractor shall test and service system on a quarterly basis during the warranty period. Each quarterly inspection shall "cover" up to 30% of the installed components.

B. After each quarterly maintenance inspection the Contractor shall provide written notification to the Client of the system's condition before and after service, exact components that were tested and serviced, and overall status of the system. All notices shall be sent to Mr. Mike Arata, ABCD Corporation, 5667 Gibraltar Drive, Livermore, California, 94588.

PART 2 - PRODUCTS

2.1 INTEGRATED ELECTRONIC SECURITY SYSTEM (IESS):

A. Refer to Intrusion detection system section for selected equipment and operational requirements.

2.1.2 Intrusion Detection Systems:

A. Required Performance Features

The contractor shall provide, install, terminate, and submit for final acceptance testing an intrusion detection system consisting of the following equipment:

1. Door contacts

2. Power Supplies

3. Other components not identified within this specification but required to provide a complete installation.

   a. The door contact switches shall be provided with the following features:

   b. manufactured for use on steel without insulating brackets;

   c. concealed terminal screws;

   d. easy claiming terminals for expedited installation;

   e. mounting screws;

   f. biased for high security applications;

   g. capable of providing detection over a 3/8" to 1 1/4" gap; and

   h. color – natural.

   The door balanced magnetic switch supplied for this project shall be the Sentrol 1047 series with the 1933 magnet, biased for high security applications, or equivalent.

2.1.3 Duress Reporting System:

A. Required Performance Features:

1. The contractor shall supply, install, terminate, and submit for final acceptance testing, a duress reporting system that will be monitored at the SMC and SCC. The equipment required for this design shall be Sentrol 3040 Surface Mounted Panic Switch or equivalent and shall have the following performance features:

   a. the unit shall be UL listed for duress reporting;

   b. the unit shall be single pole/double throw;

   c. the unit shall be capable of mounting under or on the side of desks, counters, or any other area thereby making it hard to detect by outsiders;

   d. the unit shall be supplied in a housing that is smooth to prevent accidental damage to clothing;

   e. an actuating lever designed to accommodate only the tip of a finger for activation, shall be a feature of the unit;

   f. each unit shall have reed contacts that reset when the lever is in a closed position;

   g. a latching LED shall "lock-in" when the unit is activated and be powered by 12 VDC;

   h. the unit shall have single pole/double throw output for electrical compatibility; and

   i. the unit shall be supplied in white.

2.1.4 FIRE STANDARDS COMPLIANCE

The contractor shall ensure that all equipment supplied for this project is in compliance with the United States Standard NFPA 101 including delayed egress locking devices, door hardware, emergency lighting, signal transmissions, and signage.

PART 3 – EXECUTION

3.1 EXAMINATION

A. Examine all surfaces, anchors, and "grounds" that are to receive materials, fixtures, assemblies, components, and equipment. Immediately report all unsatisfactory conditions in writing to project manager.

3.2 CLEANING AND ADJUSTING

A. Remove paint splatters and other spots, dirt, and debris. Touch up scratches and marred finish to match original finish. Clean all units internally using methods and materials recommended by manufacturer prior to final acceptance testing.

3.3 DEMONSTRATION

A. The Contractor shall demonstrate to the Client and/or the designated representatives of the Client, the features and functions of the system and subsystems as well as instruct and train the designated personnel in the proper operation and maintenance of the system.

B. The contractor shall provide, on high quality VHS formatted videotape, documentation of the training sessions and maintenance procedures. Each video shall be clearly identified for Client's future reference.

3.4 INSTALLATION

A. The contractor is required to install all equipment and/or devices in accordance with recommendations and/or instructions supplied by the Manufacturer. Where systems integration is required, the system shall work "as one" to provide the client an operational system as per specifications.

3.5 ELECTRICAL

A. Power will be available at the site. The contractor is responsible for wiring from the source of power to the individual components. The contractor shall be responsible for providing to the Client, a complete set of shop drawings indicating the wiring and power requirements of their individual system and conduct a review of the electrical drawings as they pertain to Section 17. It shall be the responsibility of the contractor to provide additions, corrections, or modifications to the electrical design as they relate to the installation of the security equipment called for under this specification.

CHAPTER 8

Parking Lots and Garages

Parking lots and garages are everywhere. Since space is limited in parking lots, there are more multi-story parking garages springing up. It wasn't long ago when parking garages were found only in the downtown areas of cities because of space limitations. In the suburbs, parking lots were the norm when garages ruled the cities. Now with the escalating price of land, even the malls are adding parking garages in suburban areas. Companies are building parking garages to accommodate the employees but still leave some room for expanding the office buildings or plant as the company grows.

Parking lots and garages have become a favorite target for criminals to commit their acts. Since parking lots and garages are often are not designed with security in mind, usually security is an afterthought in response to an incident or incidents that have occurred. The types of crimes that are committed in parking lots and garages range from crimes to persons to theft and burglary. Crimes to persons include rape, assault, and robbery. Thefts include vehicle theft and vehicle break-ins to steal laptop computers, purses, wallets, cameras, etc. from inside the vehicle.

Security at these parking facilities has received the attention of the courts in negligent security law suits. Juries have awarded large settlements to the plaintiffs in some of the cases for negligent security. The point is that parking lots and garages can either attract or discourage crime based on the design of the facility. Security can be designed into the facilities initially based on a survey of the proposed location.

In this chapter we will discuss the security factors to be considered when designing a parking lot or garage. There are things that can be done in the physical design that will help to enhance security. Crime Prevention Through Environmental Design (CPTED) is a process that uses the design of the building to help prevent crime by making the facility or space more user-friendly. The purpose is to deter those with criminal intent and to foster use by those who do not have such intent, the "normal" users. CPTED uses the approach of being proactive in preventing crime rather than reactive after an incident occurs. There are various training programs that teach the concepts of CPTED and some provide certification. A number of city police and planning departments have embraced the concept and require it in designs for new construction of parking garages and lots as well as other structures within their jurisdictions. One such training program is through the following link www.cpted-watch.com . Another source is the National Institute of Crime Prevention at www.nicp.net/cpted_conference.htm. The non-certified and certified CPTED training programs are open to all including architects. The American Crime Prevention Institute provides certification programs for CPTED and their web site is www.aegisprotect.com/acpi/basic%20CPTED.htm. The American Institute of Architects supports the use of CPTED as a method for designing security into projects including parking garages and lots.

PHYSICAL DESIGN FEATURES THAT ENHANCE SECURITY

Crime Prevention Through Environmental Design (CPTED) addresses these factors and presents some design features that can help improve security of the parking lot and garage. There are four key concepts in CPTED as listed below:

1. Natural surveillance

2. Territorial reinforcement

3. Natural access control

4. Target hardening

Natural Surveillance

The purpose of this concept is to keep intruders easily observable. For parking garages this means building exit stairs that are not hidden behind walls, but open and visible. There are not any blind corners where offenders can hide as well as dark areas because the lighting is not properly designed for the facility or lot.

Territorial Reinforcement

The purpose of this concept is that the sphere of influence can be extended which will have an impact on potential offenders by defining property lines and distinguishing private space from public space. This is accomplished through the use of landscape plants, pavement designs, gateways, and see-through wrought iron-type fences which are known as CPTED fences. CPTED fences are aesthetically pleasing and do not block the view into the site, but have the appearance of being formidable and hard-to-climb. The wrought iron fence is based on the design concept of openness, since you see through it on either side.

Natural Access Control

Natural access control is a way of denying access to offenders so they cannot perpetrate crimes and increasing the perception of a higher risk. Streets, sidewalks, building entrances, and neighborhood gateways are designed to clearly indicate public areas and discourage access to private areas using structural elements. This makes the offender's movement more difficult and they feel that detection is easier so they will think twice about attempting to commit crimes in the area.

Target Hardening

This is the goal of physical security - to harden the target. CPTED uses locks on windows, dead bolts for doors, and the hinges placed on the inside so they can't be removed. The proper physical design of the parking garage or lot can help improve security by making the locations less desirable for committing crimes. "Hardening the target" means that if it looks like it is a protected location then the potential offenders will move on to an "easy" target, one that is not protected at all or very minimally. This is based on the premise that, if a burglar cannot be in and out within a short period of time, they will go somewhere else because of the fear of being caught. So if the property appears to be hard to break into, the burglar will move on to an easier target. CPTED helps with the concept of the hard target without the fortress-like appearance.

PARKING GARAGES

Parking garages can be designed and built with security in mind and not just an afterthought or upgrade later which usually costs more. The CPTED process of building in security by including it the design phase is a modern concept and will vastly improve the security of parking garages as new ideas of using the structural features of the facility to enhance security.

Natural Access Control

The physical design features using natural access control that can enhance security for parking garages are as follows:

1. The stairwells should not be blocked by walls.

2. The use of reflective paint and materials should be used inside the garage to enhance the lighting.

3. Locate pedestrian entrances and exits next vehicle entrances

4. Locate elevators near the main entrance

5. The entire elevator should be seen from the outside when the doors are open.

6. There should be no more than two designated monitored entrances to the garage.

7. Post signs that the entire garage is monitored by CCTV with sound including the elevators.

Unobstructed Views

There should be an unobstructed view of the stairs from the garage floor near the stairwell. Where the code or weather conditions require closed stairwells, using a clear material will still provide visibility of the stairs. The bottom of the stairs in the lowest level should have an opening under the stairs closed off to eliminate any hiding places. Many garages have doors and walls that hide the stairwells from view creating a place for perpetrating crimes against persons since it will be easy to hide a surprise for an unsuspecting victim. The open stairwell provides more visibility and more of a safe feeling for the users so the potential offenders will feel less secure in committing a crime for fear of detection. Some communities will not permit open stairwells since the fire code calls for closed stairwells for emergency exits. This can possibly be overcome by making a case to local officials that the structure has fire sprinklers and is open to the outside so that smoke during a fire will be vented and allow occupants to escape. This strategy makes an enclosed stairwell not necessary.

Reflective Paint and Materials

Reflective paint and materials brighten up a garage and allow for better visibility by enhancing the lighting. The brightness provides an increased feeling of safety and is a deterrent to the potential offender for fear of being seen and detected. Also the CCTV will provide better images with more light.

Pedestrian Entrances

By locating the pedestrian exits near the vehicle entrances surveillance will be increased because of the traffic increase of vehicles coming and going as well as pedestrians. This will increase the possibility of detection so the potential offender will not attempt any acts for fear of being caught.

Elevator Visibility

Increasing the visibility of the elevators will decrease the potential offender's confidence in being able to commit a crime without detection. It also increases the garage users' feeling of safety because of the elevator visibility. The entire elevator should be seen from the outside when the doors are open.

This will increase the safety of the garage users because it will make it hard for potential offenders to hide in the corner of the elevator and attack an unsuspecting victim after they have entered the elevator.

Vehicle Entrances

By having only two entrances that are monitored, it's easier to track the comings and goings of garage users. Again the purpose is to present the feeling of being safe for the user and taking away the feeling of not being detected by the potential offender.

Signs

The posting of signs throughout the garage stating that it is monitored by CCTV with visible cameras and recorded sound adds to the feeling that being detected is a real possibility. The potential offender may go to a location where the target has not been hardened. It is important however that the signs do not say that the parking garage is protected by CCTV. CCTV does not protect anything and a sign stating that it is protected by CCTV could come back later to haunt you.

Natural Surveillance

The physical features that allow natural surveillance to take place in parking garages are follows:

1. CCTV

2. The garage should be visible by attendants monitoring by CCTV

3. Elevators should be located on the perimeter of the parking structure whenever possible.

4. Elevators should be made of a clear material on three sides

5. Reflective paints and materials should be used in construction to brighten the interior.

6. Elevators should not have a permanent stop button on any of the cars.

7. Solid retaining walls should be replaced with stretched cable railings that allow for better surveillance and lighting.

8. Lighting is important

9. Pedestrian walkways should be illuminated to a minimum of 6 foot-candles.

CCTV

CCTV should be monitoring all elevators, including sound that is voice–activated, in lieu of using cameras. The monitoring of elevators with CCTV and posting signs saying that the elevators are monitored is a deterrent to crime because of the strong possibility of being caught on tape. The garage should be visible by attendants monitoring by CCTV with visible cameras throughout the structure. Sound should be recorded as well. Designers should plan to post signs stating that the garage is monitored by CCTV. The use of CCTV should be substituted for CPTED, but should be seen as an enhancement. Do not use the word "protected" in place of monitored. CCTV does not protect anything; it only monitors. CCTV is a good tool if is properly designed and installed. More will be presented about CCTV systems in the next chapter.

Elevators

Elevators should be located on the perimeter of the parking structure whenever possible. Elevators that are constructed of a clear material on three sides are best so that the inside can be visible from the outside (the door side is not). This will create the feeling that detection is possible so a potential offender will probably be deterred for fear of being caught. This will add to the natural surveillance of the elevator. The elevators should usually be installed on the outside of the structure. The occupants can then see out on three sides as can those on the outside being able to see into the elevator on three sides.

Elevators should not have a permanent stop button on any of the cars. The button is not needed for the operation of the elevator and can be used by an offender to aid in committing crimes such as muggings, assaults, rape, and robbery.

Reflective Paint and Materials

Reflective paint and materials brighten up the garage and allow for better visibility by enhancing the lighting. The brightness provides an increased feeling of safety and is a deterrent to the potential offender for fear of being seen and detected. Also the CCTV will provide better images with more light.

Walls

Solid retaining walls should be replaced with stretched cable railings that allow for better surveillance and lighting. This will help give the feeling of openness and the area will be visible from the outside of the structure. Also it will aid in visibility be improving the illumination and enhance the perception that the garage is safe for the users.

Lighting

Lighting is important because most garages are dark and have places where the lighting is poor to non-existent. Lighting is also important to the CCTV system, especially if color cameras are used. Proper illumination will make the parking garage feel safer if it is brightly lit. To help with the illumination as previously stated, reflective paints and materials can aid the lighting and make the garage brighter. Pedestrian walkways should be illuminated to at a minimum of 6- foot candles.

Lighting for parking garages plays an important role in the overall security and using an incandescent lamp with wattage of 10-10,000 range that produces a warm white light will create the illumination needed to meet the lighting requirements. The foot-candles should be a minimum of 2 in most areas but install lighting with at least 5 foot-candles in pedestrian walkways, stairwells, and near the elevators. The more brightness that a garage has, the safer it will feel to the users and less enticing to the potential offenders.

When designing the lighting system the following must be taken into consideration:

1. The lighting must be uniform throughout the parking structure to eliminate light and dark areas so that the driver's eyes will not have problems adjusting. The parking stalls also need to be illuminated especially at the edges. The uniformity ratio is determined by dividing the maximum or average illumination by the minimum illumination. For example if the average to minimum ratio is 2:1 and the average illumination of 4-footcandles is the goal then the minimum illumination must be 2-footcandles.

2. Vertical illumination is important in parking garages to help drivers and pedestrians see vertical objects like signs.

3. Too much glare is a potential problem and can affect depth perception for all drivers in the parking structure. To eliminate glare, the lighting fixtures can be mounted in the parking space rather than above the drive aisles, according to Mary S. Smith in a report based on a study of grant awarded to the American Institute of Architects by the National Institute of Justice (NIJ) in 1996.

4. Staining the concrete walls and ceiling with non-graffiti coatings will help to improve the lighting as does the reflective material and paint in the pedestrian walkways.

Traditional Physical Security

Included with the CPTED are the traditional approaches to security, such as the use of and CCTV. Visual monitoring by attendants or security officers is also important. Another feature is inclusion of panic buttons and call boxes strategically located through out the structure. The call boxes and panic alarms will be received by the attendant station if the garage is used for public parking. The police would receive the call as a 911 emergency. The panic buttons/call boxes could also have a built-in CCTV camera that would record the video and audio of the person making the call, as well as the surrounding area. For parking garages that are private or company-only, the security console would receive the panic button/call box calls, video, and audio. As a part of the security procedures, there would be a response to the location of the caller and the police would called to respond as well depending on the nature of the call.

Panic buttons and emergency call boxes are by no means a substitute for CPTED but instead as an enhancement to CPTED in the overall security design. Figure 8-1 is a picture of a call and intercom box for parking structures called the Parking Sentry(tm). The box has an emergency button and an information button. Having the two buttons clearly marked, as they are in the picture, is important during an emergency situation.

The box in Figure 8-1 will allow customers of the garage to talk directly to roving security officer's radios so help can be there quickly. The location of the call boxes needs to be clearly marked so the locations can be readily identified. This can be done be using reflective paint on the floor and wall of the garage to mark the location of the box. Also a blue or red light is placed at the top of the box to mark its location.

To help maintain a clear zone and to minimize places for perpetrators to hide, landscaping should be kept low. Plant mainly ground cover or plants that grow no higher than 2 feet high.

FIGURE 8-1 Parking Sentry™

Access Control

Another way to help improve security in parking garages is the use of access control. All access points need to be surveyed and a determination made as to whether they are needed. If not, they should be fenced and provided with some type of access control to prevent anyone from entering the facility on foot. These access points should be monitored by roving security or the parking garage staff to make sure that the fence has not been breached. To shut the facility down when not in use, fences, gates, doors, etc should be used.

Side entrance doors of parking garages that are not open to the public, such as those on private property and that do not permit public use, can have access limited to those who have an access control card issued by the owner.

Exterior doors that are not near the attendant and open into non-secure areas in public garage should be used as emergency exits only and the doors should fitted with an alarm that sounds when opened. The doors should have panic hardware on them and a blank face (no hardware) on the exterior since it is not a designated entry door and not used by anyone for entry into the facility.

Vehicle access control in public garages is accomplished by making the driver take a ticket to open lift the gate for entering. The ticket area is usually monitored by CCTV. Upon exiting, the driver presents the ticket to an attendant and pays for the amount of time the garage was used. The attendant will release the gate for exiting. The process of paying is monitored by CCTV and all of this monitoring and controlled access and exiting can be a deterrent to those with criminal intent from entering the structure to commit crimes.

Vehicle access to private parking structures can be controlled using an access control card to operate the gates for entry and exiting. The entrances and exits should be monitored by CCTV.

Security Officers

The role of security officers in deterring crime has been proven and should be considered in all high-risk parking structures. Security officers making unscheduled rounds throughout the shift are effective. Routine rounds at scheduled times are too easy for those with criminal intent to work around. Some locations employ the use of watch stations to record the frequency of the rounds. The watch stations are a carryover from the watch clocks where there was a key and the security officer carried a clock and inserted the key into the clock to record the station and time. It is now done using a handheld bar code reader and the information can be downloaded to a computer. A later chapter will detail the role of the security officer to an overall security program.

Security Survey

As with any planned structure, to ensure that proper consideration is given to security, a survey and risk analysis needs to be done. Security surveys and risk analyses are discussed in detail in Chapter 2. Security has to meet the needs of the facility and what is appropriate for one may not be the right one for another. The security has to be customized to the facility and the location including the crime rates. To accomplish this task, the facility location needs to be ranked. The steps in the planning for security are as follows:

1. A good first step is to obtain a copy of the CAP Index for the proposed location of the parking garage. Remember, the CAP Index is a predictor of loss. The CAP Index uses crime information and other factors to predict what the risk of crime is for a given location.

2. The information is then used to determine if the location is a low, medium, or high risk. A low risk location is where the incidence of violent crimes against persons occurring is low. A medium risk location is where property crimes such as vehicle thefts will occur. A high risk location is where crimes against persons are likely to occur. The level of risk classification for the location will determine the level of security.

3. The parking garage's design and its relationship to security must be determined. Not all garages will need the same security. For example, a facility that is to be located in a low risk area may not initially need security measures such as panic buttons/call boxes, but the design should take this into account should allow for later installation like running conduit.

4. Security planning should be documented in the design phase and CPTED measures included since they fit all the risk levels and it makes sense to include them in the design.

PARKING LOTS

Parking lots are also a place for those with criminal intent to commit their acts. A large percentage (between 60%-80%) of the crimes committed at shopping centers, office complexes and strip malls occur in the parking lot. Parking lots are also the center of liability stemming from insufficient security or not taking "reasonable care" to protect customers, and employees from criminal acts.

Many of the same CPTED security features used in the parking garage are also applicable to the parking lot. The following are the CPTED techniques that apply to parking lots.

- Natural surveillance—Open and not blocking the view with landscaping on the parking lot that may obscure some spaces from view especially those lots with a parking attendant. To enhance natural surveillance a properly designed and installed CCTV system should be used.

- Territorial reinforcement—Clearly marking the boundaries of the lot with landscaping or a fence, wrought iron or chain link, with clear zone.

- Natural access control—Planting thick shrubbery with thorns or needles that grow to three feet high in areas where the lot is fenced off from an adjoining property.

As with the parking garage, a security survey should be part of the planning and design process. The proposed location for the project needs to be analyzed from a security perspective. The same approach that was used on the parking garage will be used for the parking lot.

1. Get the CAP Index for the location

2. Determine the risk level

3. The parking garage's design and its relationship to security must be determined. Not all garages will need the same security. For example, a facility that is to be located in a low risk area may not initially need security measures as panic buttons/call boxes but the design should take this into account and should allow for later installation like running conduit,.

4. Security planning should be documented in the design phase and CPTED measures included since they fit all the risk levels and it makes sense to include them in the design.

5. The level of risk is used to determine the security needed for the parking lot.

Lighting in Parking Lots

As with parking garages, lighting is important to the overall security and feeling of safety in the parking lot. Proper lighting for security is an important to project the feeling of safety for those using the parking lot. Nobody wants to enter an area that is dark and there are places that someone could hide in "plain sight". What is meant by plain sight is that, if the area was not dark the person could not hide from view. To help eliminate these "hiding" places the parking lot lighting should meet at a minimum the following:

- The parking spaces are to be illuminated to a minimum level of two (2) foot-candles during hours of darkness to height of 6 feet from the surface of parking lot.

- The aisles of the parking lot aisles are to be illuminated to a minimum level of one (1) foot-candle during hours of darkness to height of 6 feet from the surface of parking lot.

- The parking lot landscape areas are to be illuminated to a minimum level of 1/2 foot-candle during hours of darkness to height of 6 feet from the surface of parking lot.

- All parking lot lighting shall be illuminated during the hours or darkness by using a photocell sensor.

Landscaping in Parking Lots

The parking lot landscaping should be in accordance with the following to ensure that security is not compromised because of the landscaping creating hiding places for offenders:. Parking lot landscaping should not to grow to more than a maximum of 2 feet:

- Around parking-lot landscape islands
- Six feet from the curb to the parking lot border
- Around driveways that are entrances to parking lots to prevent visibility issues and provide hiding places

Some jurisdictions have lists of plants that can be used for landscaping. When submitting the plans for review the list will be provided by the officials that will review and approve the plan and issue the permits. The landscaping needs to be no higher than 2 feet maximum when fully grown because anything higher will provide a hiding place for offenders so they can spring out on unsuspecting users of the lot.

Landscaping used around perimeter fences in the back part of the parking lot should have thorns or needles and be very thick. These plants are known as barrier plants and they can grow to greater than 3 feet. The purpose of the plants is to discourage pedestrian traffic.

Landscaping needs to aid in natural surveillance and not hinder it. If the parking lot has an attendant booth, it needs to sit where the attendant can get the best view of the entire lot and not be blocked by landscaping that is higher than 2 feet high.

CCTV in Parking Lots

The addition of CCTV cameras on lighting poles throughout the parking lot and signs stating that the parking lot is monitored 24 hours a day by CCTV will also be a deterrent to crime. To have effective CCTV the lighting is important and the positioning of the cameras is important as well. Camera positioning will be discussed in more detail in the next chapter. When using CCTV there is something called the "field of view" based on the actual picture size, which is the width and height. In other words, "field of view" means the image area (picture) produced by the camera/lens combination. More will be presented about field of view and lens calculators in the next chapter. For our discussion here it is important to determine what you are trying to capture with the CCTV camera and knowing where to mount the cameras to provide the images you are looking for. There are things that affect the image from a camera lens and they include the following:

- Distance from the scene
- Focal length - length of the lens measured in mm

- Desired field of view

- Lighting

Camera lenses come in different sizes which are measured in mm. If the camera does not have the proper lens for the job, then the pictures being recorded are not going to be what you are expecting. The further the camera is away from the scene, the harder it will be to get a good image if the lens is not right for the job. So camera placement is important and one or two cameras to cover an entire lot are not going to provide the desired field of view.

Emergency Call Boxes

Emergency call boxes are mounted in some parking lots and are another tool that can deployed. The boxes can have cameras to help deter calls that are hoaxes as well as two intercoms with a security console for private parking lots. In public parking lots, the call boxes could connect to 911 operators and the camera can be used to help to deter calls that are hoaxes.

The boxes can be placed on the light poles and clearly marked with a red or blue light high on the pole to mark their location. This will allow the location of the boxes to be seen at night from anywhere in the lot. For daytime viewing lettering saying "Call Box" with an arrow pointing down on all sides of the pole could signify the location. All calls for help need to have an immediate response to assist the caller.

Security Officers

For private parking lots, security officers should make random patrols through the lot. These patrols, like those in the parking garages, should not be scheduled. Security officer watch stations can be strategically spaced throughout the lot so the officer doing the patrol can document the time of the patrol. Also the security officers can carry a radio that picks up the calls for the call boxes so the office can talk to the caller and respond to the request for help. A call box like the one in Figure 8-1 can be used in parking lots as well as parking garages. For public parking lots, if the call boxes connect the caller to the 911 operator, the police will be dispatched to the call. They also will patrol the street adjacent to the lot.

The following appendix to this chapter provides a sample design/build specification document from the Precast Concrete Association of New York, Inc and used with permission. Security design specifications can be added to all the appropriate sections and under the equipment section, CCTV and call boxes can be added under separate heading.

SAMPLE DESIGN SPECIFICATIONS FOR A PARKING GARAGE

What follows is an abbreviated sample of design specifications to guide you so you can write your own design specifications for your project.

DIVISION 01 – GENERAL REQUIREMENTS

01001 GENERAL

A. All facilities, labor, material, equipment, and design services that are typically required for the completion of the Work are included in this design/build proposal. All Work shall comply with the applicable federal, state and local requirements.

B. All sections in the Outline Specifications carry a one (1) year Standard Construction Warranty and Guarantee against labor and material defects including Work performed by subcontractors. All equipment warranties greater than one (1) year will be passed to the Owner at project completion.

01002 INSURANCE AND BONDS

Design/Builder's Liability Insurance:

A. Design/Builder shall purchase and maintain in a company or companies authorized to do business in the state in which the Work is located such insurance as will protect the Design/Builder from claims set forth below which may arise out of or result from operations under the Contract by the Design/Builder or a subcontractor of the Design Builder, or by anyone directly or indirectly employed by any of them, including:

1. Claims under workers' or workmen's compensation, disability benefit and other similar employee benefit laws which are applicable to the Work to be performed;

2. Claims for damages because of bodily injury, occupational sickness or disease, or death of the Design/Builder's employees under any applicable employer's liability law;

3. Claims for damages because of bodily injury, sickness or disease, or death of persons other than the Design/Builder's employees;

4. Claims for damages covered by usual personal injury liability coverage which are sustained by a person as a result of an offense directly or indirectly related to employment of such person by the Design/Builder;

5. Claims for damages, other than to the Work at the site, because of injury to or destruction of tangible property, and

6. Claims for damages for bodily injury of death of a person or property damage arising out of ownership, maintenance or use of a motor vehicle.

B. The insurance required by the above subparagraph shall be written for not less than limits of liability specified in the insurance certificates submitted with the bid of _____.

    C. The Design/Builder's liability insurance shall include contractual liability insurance applicable to the Design/Builder's obligations under AIA A191 Part 2, Paragraph 11.7.

    D. Certificates of Insurance shall be delivered to the Owner prior to commencement of design and construction. These Certificates, as well as insurance policies required by this Paragraph, shall contain a provision that coverage will not be canceled or allowed to expire until at least thirty day's prior written notice has been given to the Owner.

    E. Builder's Risk Insurance can be provided by the Design/Builder, but is not included in the bid.

    Design/Builder's Errors and Omissions Insurance:

    Design/Builder shall carry Architects and Engineers Professional Liability insurance with the following limits:

    $2,000,000 per Claim

    $2,000,000 Aggregate

    $100,000 S.I.R.

    Performance & Payment Bonds:

    Design/Builder shall provide a Payment and Performance Bond for the overall construction project value.

    Design/Builder's Surety will assume no responsibility for any design work performed in connection with this project.

01003 ALLOWANCES

Allowances refer to items of scope or cost which have not been sufficiently defined to date. The stipulated Allowance amount has been included in the base proposal price. Actual billings against these items will be supported by supplier and subcontractor invoices. Actual costs of less than the original Allowance will result in a reduction of base contract price. Actual costs greater than the original Allowance will be billed at cost plus a 15% General Contractor's Fee and result in an increase to the base contract price. Allowance items if anticipated are clearly noted in the Construction Budget Summary.

01004 DESIGN AND SUPERVISION

This proposal includes all required architectural, structural, plumbing, mechanical and electrical engineering design with stamped drawings and corresponding specifications for the garage structure. The cost associated with peer review by the State of _____ is also included.

Supervision:

   Design/Builder will assign a Project Manager to this job who will be responsible for all project activities from design through construction including coordination with the Owner, Regulatory Agencies, other Prime Contractors, etc.

Design/Builder will assign, on site, a full-time superintendent solely for this project.

01050 FIELD ENGINEERING

 A. Field engineering services required for proper completion of the Work including but not limited to:

  1. Extend base lines and elevations from initial site survey provided by owner.

  2. Locate and protect control points before starting work on the site.

  3. Layout of all foundations.

01310 PROJECT SCHEDULE

Design/Builder will provide an overall design and construction schedule. The schedule will be updated monthly.

01410 TESTING SERVICES

 A. Inspection Testing:

  1. Concrete testing with cylinder breaks for foundations and slabs-on-grade and on-site structural welding tests shall be performed by an independent agency paid by the Owner.

  2. The Owner is responsible for all geotechnical services and soil inspections to verify soil bearing capacity for the site. This includes inspection of excavations and footings prior to placement of concrete. Full time inspection if required will be provided by the Owner.

  3. Precast concrete manufacturing plant inspections and tests and field installation tolerances in accordance with standards established by the Precast Concrete Institute (PCI). The Owner may provide at his expense independent inspection of precast concrete operations.

  4. Additional independent testing required by the governing building codes shall be performed at the Owner's expense.

01500 TEMPORARY FACILITIES AND CONTROLS

 A. Temporary facilities and controls needed for the Work including but not limited to:

  1. Telephone service for the Design/Builder office trailer.

  2. Portable sanitary facilities located on the site for Design/Builder personnel only.

  3. Field offices/sheds for Design/Builder construction and office personnel.

  4. Temporary electric power and lighting connection to an existing supply within 25' of the site. Metered electricity usage is at Design/Builder's expense.

  5. Temporary construction water connection to an existing supply

within 25' of the site. Metered water usage is at Design/Builder's expense.

B. Temporary barricades:

1. Elevated deck edge fall protection and deck opening protection.
2. Safety barricades around major excavations in accordance with OSHA guidelines including warning tape and lighted flashers if required.
3. Temporary barricades, traffic barriers, safety lighting etc. if required for partial occupancy are not included in this proposal. The scope of services can be added at a future time when it is defined.

C. Temporary chain link fencing, 6'-0" high including construction safety signs and warnings for the parking garage site is included. Removal at project completion.

01700 CONTRACT CLOSEOUT

A. To provide an orderly and efficient transfer of the completed Work, upon substantial completion of all work:

1. The project will be inspected with representatives of the Owner and Design/Builder for the purpose of itemizing a final punch list.
2. The project will be turned over broom clean and ready for use.
3. Closeout submittal to include but not be limited to:
   a. Project record documents i.e. "as built" drawings, specifications, shop drawings, etc.
   b. Operation and maintenance manuals as available.
   c. Warranties and bonds.
   d. Keying and keying schedule.
   e. Spare parts and material extra stock.
   f. Release of liens.
   g. List of subcontractors, service organizations and principal vendors.

01710 CLEANING

A. Throughout the construction period, Design/Builder will maintain the building and site in a standard of cleanliness consistent with safe and efficient construction operations.

1. Design/Builder will provide dumpsters for the use of all trades under its contract on this project.
2. All storm drains will be protected from debris during construction.

B. Final cleaning of the structure.

1. Broom clean all decks.
2. Clean and wash all glass inside and out.
3. Clean and empty all sediment baskets on all drains.
4. Clean all flooring materials.

DIVISION 02 – SITE WORK

02110 SITE PREPARATION

A. The parking garage site will be cleared and graded to subgrade elevation by the Design/Builder. All known underground utilities will be relocated prior to excavation.

02220 EXCAVATING, BACKFILLING AND COMPACTION

A. Excavate and backfill foundations as follows:

1. Excavating, backfilling and compacting required to facilitate the installation of all parking structures foundations as stated in Section 03300.
2. Soil erosion control measures with hay bales and fabric mesh as required.
3. Filling and backfilling with on-site material to restore design rough grade elevations.
   a. Backfill materials free from organic matter and deleterious substances, containing no rock or lumps over 6" in greatest dimension.

B. Hauling of excess or unusable excavated material to an off-site disposal area chosen by the Design/Builder.

02710 STORM AND SANITARY DRAINAGE

A. Roof leaders and floor drains will be connected to the existing storm and/or sanitary sewer system outside the building perimeter.

02831 PERMANENT FENCING

A. Galvanized chain link fencing included as shown on schematic drawings:

1. Interior lite wall.
2. Security screening at building perimeter, if required.

02900 LANDSCAPING

A. Include landscaping and seeding allowance in the amount of $_____.

Closed Circuit Television (CCTV)

CHAPTER 9

Closed Circuit Television (CTV) means that the system is a closed system and is intended for use by a facility to monitor their premises. The idea of closed means that the system does not broadcast TV signals over the airwaves, as do the commercial TV stations, but transmits them over a closed circuit. There are some systems that use wireless cameras but the system is still monitored by a central location on the site or over the company's intranet.

CCTV systems have been around for a long time and were primarily used by the government and government contractors in the beginning. These early analog systems were large, expensive, and needed to be monitored by security personnel since there was no motion-sensing recording in the system. The camera images were recorded on reel-to-reel video tape recorders (VTR). Then came the VHS tape recorded on a video cassette recorder (VCR) and now digital video recorders (DVR) are common. The advent of CCTV allowed multiple locations to be viewed by one or two people and freed up security officers to perform other duties, like responding to alarms. CCTV is used by security officers to do a video tour of the area.

The system consists of a camera, monitor, and cable that ran from the camera to the monitor. More sophisticated systems with multiple cameras use other hardware like multiplexers which can transmit up to 16 cameras' signals through a single cable, microwave, or infrared line to a location for viewing and recording. It can transmit the images almost simultaneously to the central point. A multiplexer (MUX) is used to accept and record a number of camera inputs simultaneously.

In this chapter we will explore the various components of a CCTV system, how they work, and what information is needed to design a system. This chapter will cover the basics of CCTV and is not intended to make you an expert. The purpose of the chapter is to acquaint you with CCTV systems. There are

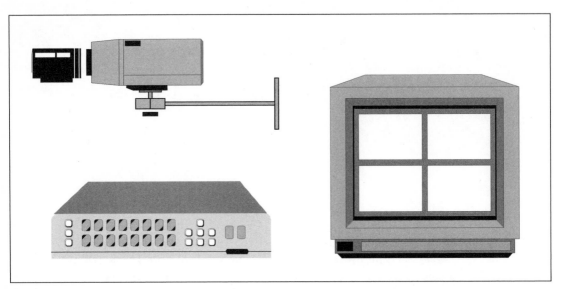

FIGURE 9-1   CCTV system with a MUX and monitor

entire books devoted to the subject of CCTV systems and one excellent book on the subject is called *Application & Design of CCTV* by Charlie Pierce. Remember, a CCTV system is not a security system in and of itself, but it is a part of an overall security system and is used to enhance security by documenting what is happening in critical areas. When the system is set to record on motion or in conjunction with another security system, they become powerful tools in the security industry's arsenal. There are different types of systems: wired, wireless, fixed cameras, and Pan Tilt Zoom (PTZ) cameras. Either black and white or color cameras can be chosen.

A word about dummy cameras – DO NOT USE THEM. You will be setting yourself up for a "False Sense of Security" claim. A dummy camera is made to look like a real camera except that there is nothing inside the housing, so nothing is viewed or recorded. If you feel the urge to use a dummy camera, then why not install the real camera instead? The money you think you are saving is not worth the potential lawsuit settlement when you can't produce a "tape" of the incident because the camera is a fake. When you place a camera in an area that the public perceives needs to be watched, the feeling of safety comes with it.

With that being said, let's now explore the basic components of a CCTV system. Figure 9-1 shows a CCTV system with a MUX and monitor.

CCTV SYSTEM COMPONENTS

The CCTV system is designed and installed with the cameras wired to a central location on the site for monitoring. It consists of cameras, multiplexers, monitors, and recorders depending the on the size and complexity of the system. Some even use a disk array for storing recordings.

Camera

The first piece of equipment is the camera. The camera is what captures the image and has two main components:

• Lens

• Housing

Cameras are either black and white or color. Black and white cameras need less light to produce a good quality picture. Color cameras, on the other hand, need more light. Today there are cameras that are color in the daytime and black and white at night or other times of low light. Figure 9-2 shows a camera lens and housing.

The lens is basically the "camera", what captures the images. The following are some of the lens sizes. The most common lens measurements are:

• 2.8 mm

• 3.2 mm

• 4.2 mm

• 6 mm

• 8 mm

• 12 mm

• 16 mm

There are three main types of lenses:

1. Fixed focus lens has a preset focal length and the lens calculator will help in choosing the angle of view. The lens has two main angles of view:
   a. 30 degree for a narrow view
   b. 60 degree for a wider view

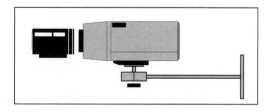

FIGURE 9-2 Camera lens and housing

2. Varifocal lens is more flexible than the fixed focus lens and can be adjusted manually to obtain the field of view desired.

3. Zoom lens, just as the name implies, can be adjusted to zoom in very close or to a wide-angle setting. The lens provides the widest variety of settings and is the most complex lens. It can be adjusted remotely by an operator in a central monitoring station.

Selecting the proper lens takes a little bit of work but, in the long run, it is worth the effort. By taking the guesswork out, the system you end up with will deliver what you expect. You won't need to wait until an event happens only to find out that the recording of the incident does not meet your objectives for the system - to identify the perpetrator and the activity being performed at the time of the recording.

The Charged Coupled Device (CCD) chip is the imaging device of the camera and the common sizes are listed below. The CCD is light sensitive and it is what forms the image in most cameras today. The size is measured diagonally:

• 1/3"

• 1/2"

• 1/4"

The first two listed are the most common on the market today and the 1/4" is starting to be more available. The 2/3" being used less frequently.

The lens is placed in the lens mounting and the mounting is placed in the body or housing of the camera. The housing is what protects the camera from the elements: rain, ice, snow, etc. and this is important especially for outdoor cameras. Another problem with outdoor cameras is the problem of having the lens fog from changes in temperature. To prevent this from occurring, the outdoor camera housing has a heating device installed to keep the temperature from fluctuating and causing fogging of the lens.

Cameras that are used in hostile, corrosive, or dusty environments inside as well as outside have special housings to protect them as well. The housing either comes equipped with a mounting bracket or a mounting bracket can be installed after purchase. The housing can be large like those that are sometimes seen around shopping malls like in Figure 9-3 which is known as the "weatherproof housing". There are also dome housings which are smoke-colored so the position of the camera and what it is pointing toward cannot be seen (see Figure 9-3). This is to try and prevent the intruder from knowing where the camera is pointing, especially a PTZ (pan tilt zoom) if the security officer monitoring the CCTV system at the console is following the intruder using the camera in the dome.

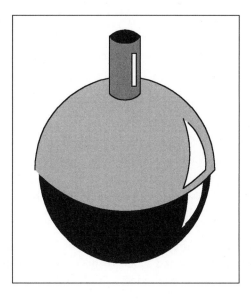

FIGURE 9-3 Weatherproof housing

The lens has an iris that regulates how much light passes through and is picked up on the image sensor. All cameras have an iris and the important thing to remember about the iris, since it light sensitive, is to not have it pointing directly into the sunlight. This will damage the lens and will also result in the images to be washed out in appearance by appearing too bright. Images may not be identifiable other than the recognition that it is a person.

The lens and the angle of the camera determine how much information is in the image that is sent to the monitor for review. The focal length is directly related to the angle of view depending on whether the length is short with a wide angle view or long with narrow angle of view. The focal length is measured in millimeters.

Coaxial Cable

The coaxial cable is used to connect the cameras to the monitor and recorder. Coaxial cable is shielded to prevent interference from other electrical cables. There are coaxial cable connectors that are used to make the connections to the back of the MUX and monitor. These are usually screw connections called coax patch cables similar to the ones you find on your own VHS or DVR player.

Fiber Optic Cable

Fiber optic cable is now being used to transmit CCTV video. The fiber optic cable turns the electronic video signal into laser light and injects into one of the glass rods, the fiber optic cable and transmits it to a receiver The receiver takes the laser light and coverts it back to an electronic video signal that can be displayed on a monitor. The fiber optic signal is not interrupted by water in the conduit or interference from high voltage being run the same conduit. The bandwidth of fiber optic is large.

Microwave

Microwave is another method for transmitting video from a CCTV system. The microwave turns the video signal into a high frequency radio signal and the signal is transmitted from one location to another via free air waves. The receiver converts the high frequency radio signal back into video signal so it can be displayed on a monitor. Microwave transmits by line of sight and also has large bandwidth. A big disadvantage of microwave being used for video transmission is that it can be affected by weather and other climatic conditions. A heavy rain will cause the microwave-transmitted video to have the video feed interrupted in transmission causing the loss of the video. This is not good when the video is critical because there may be gaps in the recorded video.

MUX

The MUX is a device that can accept a number of cameras and record them almost simultaneously. An example of MUX is in Figure 9-4. The MUX is used in multiple camera systems to display the images on the screen in multi-split screen displays. Another name for the MUX is the "Multiplexer" and it is the switch that allows multiple cameras to be seen on one monitor. The Multiplexer can be used to transmit a number of cameras over the same transmission medium i.e. coaxial cable, infrared, and microwave. This saves in the cost of the system since only one medium needs to be used. A good feature of the multiplexer is that, during playback, it allows for viewing only certain frames from the same camera or the camera can viewed in full screen which is duplexing.

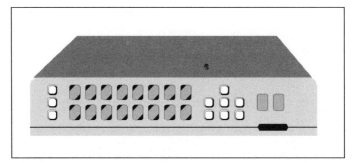

FIGURE 9-4   MUX

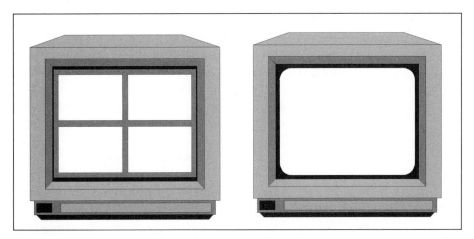

FIGURE 9-5   Monitors - split 4-camera view and single camera

Monitor

A TV that is used to display the video either in real time or playback of recorded video. The number of lines of resolution that the monitor can produce relates to the quality of the picture. For example, a monitor that produces 1,000 lines of resolution will have a much clearer, sharper picture than one that produces 300 lines of resolution. With some of the systems today the video can be displayed on a computer monitor. To display the video on a monitor the system coaxial cable is connected from the multiplexer to the video monitor. Monitors come in all shapes and sizes and any TV monitor can display the video using the video input jack.

The information that was presented above is the basics of a CCTV system. The intent of the presentation is not to make any CCTV "experts" but to acquaint those that will be preparing security design specifications for a project to understand enough about the systems to know what to look for in the design and to prepare some basic system design specifications based the needs of the project.

Figure 9-5 shows a typical monitor with a split 4 camera view and a single camera view.

Recorders

The recording of CCTV system images has evolved from VTR through VCR to digital recorders. The VCR recorders used time lapse recordings. Time lapse was used to slow down the recording rate by recording the tape in steps one frame at a time to extend the recording time of the tape. A frame is one complete TV picture and is made of two fields and there are 25 frames per second in a TV picture. For example a 3–hour tape can have the extended recording time of 960 hours using the time lapse format. The problem with time lapse recording is that if is done over a long period of time there is a great deal of activity that is lost and not recorded since the picture is made of 25 frames per second and since the recorder is recording one frame at a time there is likely going to be some frames that do not get recorded and they may have the image we are looking for. The reason for using time lapse was because the cameras would be recording everything that happened and, yes, that includes nothing, 24 hours a day seven days a week. When there was no one available to change the tapes the time lapse on a three day holiday weekend would last the entire time.

When it was necessary to review the tapes for an investigation without a time or at least an approximate time of the occurrence the investigator would spend hours upon hours going through the tapes without any luck of seeing and recording the event. Even with a time of occurrence there may not be an image because of the way the time lapse recording is done, frame by frame. The event may not show up on the recording.

Digital Video Recorders (DVR) do not use tape. The recording is done on a computer hard drive. No worry that the tape was not changed or none was in the recorder so there was no recording made or the tape was used too many times so the recordings are of poor quality. DVR also makes it easier to search the drive for the images you are looking for by showing the alarm points. The DVR works well with the cameras that are set to record on motion using infrared. The recorder can be programmed to record on motion everything that happens starting at 7:00 pm or 1900 hours until 7:00 am or 0700 everyday. So when you want to see an event you can go to the alarm point which detects movement or a change in the video motion on the hard drive to view the recording. Viewing the video you can look for changes in the scene to see what occurred. Frames per second (fps) are the number of frames that are recorded in one second. The recordings are done in real time which is approximately 30 frames per second (fps) per camera, not time lapse, so frames are not omitted that could contain the information you need.

The DVR takes the analog signal, converts to digital, and compresses it. The DVR is equipped to handle 4, 8, 16, or 32 camera inputs on the same recorder. So the system can grow with your needs. One camera will use approximately 2 gigs a day of drive space so if you have a 4-camera system then you will use 8 gigs a day of space. If you don't have any movement or change in the field of view then the system will not record so drive space will not be a problem. If on the other hand there is a great deal of movement then more recording will take place and more hard drive space will be used. When the hard drive is filled the recordings will start recording over what is already on the drive. For a very large system a disk array is used and can be cataloged into a juke box for searching and viewing at a later time. Very large CCTV systems utilize a juke box storage system for the recorded images. The information is kept in the juke box for a specified period of time and when the predetermined time limit has passed, the disks are reused to record new images.

The DVR can also be PC-based rather stand-alone. The PC based DVR records on the hard drive of the computer. PC-based systems can be unstable because the PC itself is unstable. An embedded DVR is designed to work as a DVR and is more stable and reliable since there are few moving parts.

Wireless Cameras

Most of the wireless cameras transmitters in use today only have a short range of between 300 to 700 feet distance. The systems operate on 900 GHz and 2.8 GHz. The 900 GHz systems have a range of 300 feet and the 2.8 GHz system has a range of 300 to 700 feet. There is a 5.8 GHz system that has a range of 7 miles but it is not widely used because of the high cost.

Like all radio transmissions the FCC regulates the wireless CTV systems which the manufacturers of the equipment obtain, but the systems cannot be modified without FCC approval. The FCC also limits the number of transmitters on a site to four channels. The number of receivers is not limited by the FCC.

The problems with wireless CCTV systems are that the signal may be blocked by microwave, high voltage power lines, and heavy metal walls. There are applications where wireless cameras will work well but remember the limitations on distances and know what will cause interference with the reception.

IP Addressable Cameras

A digital camera captures the image, digitizes the image and sends via the LAN to a server that manages the information received. The server can record the information, display it on a monitor, and retransmit it over the LAN to remote locations.

The IP cameras uses the CCD chip for digitizing the images and streams the video (sends) over the LAN using CAT 5 cable and the TCP/IP protocol. The video images use a great deal of bandwidth so the streaming of video may not be a good idea unless the pipe you have at your disposal is large enough to not be affected by the large video streaming over the LAN. Check with the IT person before planning the use of real time streaming video to make sure it will not affect the rest of the LAN users.

All devices that traverse the Internet need an address and the CCTV cameras, recorders, multiplexers, etc. all need addresses. The IT people will provide the necessary block of addresses to be used. Without an address the cameras and other equipment will not be reachable over the LAN.

The use of the LAN to send CCTV images to a server and remote locations has distinct advantages. The information can be shared quickly with remote sites so they can be provided with details of an incident. For investigative purposes the information can be analyzed quickly even from a remote location.

Monitoring of remote locations can be done more economically from one location as long a there are procedures for addressing incidents at the remote location such as emergency phone numbers. The recording of the video cannot be tampered with by destroying the local recorder.

The disadvantages of using the LAN for CCTV:

- The amount of bandwidth used is large.

- Sensitive video may need to be encrypted using more bandwidth.

- Like all computer information, it must be backed up in case of a server failure or hard drive crash.

BASIC SYSTEM DESIGN CONSIDERATIONS

The steps in preparing the design specifications for a CCTV system are as follows:

1. The first step is to do a site assessment or proposed site assessment based on the following. The CAP Index is a good tool to help assess the crime and the potential for crime at the location as well as the following:
   What is the threat?
   What types of things may occur. For example, in a parking garage is vehicle thefts or crimes against persons? (CAP Index)
   What assets are we trying to protect from the threat?
   What is the potential loss that could occur from the threat?

2. The second step is to do a vulnerability analysis.
   What is the likelihood of occurrence of the threat?
   What will be the consequences?
   What will be the loss?
   Is there a liability issue?

3. Do a complete survey of the location or proposed location as outlined in Chapter 2. This is important since the CCTV system is a part of the overall security system for the location.

4. Now do a threat assessment, this will help in the decision making of whether to install cameras, where to install the cameras, and how many. These are accomplished by taking all the information collected in the site assessment and using it to make an informed decision on the use of a CCTV system.

Why is it so important to do the tedious job of the site assessment, the threat and vulnerability analysis? Why not just place cameras around the perimeter, doors, windows, fence lines, etc.? The upfront work will be time well spent because the dividends of a well-designed CCTV system will yield good results in both deterring crime and catching and prosecuting those who commit crimes at the location. A number of CCTV systems are just thrown together. The camera locations are picked at random or with some idea of the expected outcome only to be disappointed when the images did not catch the perpetrators in the act. The money spent on the system coupled with the resulting loss was money wasted. To improve the use of CCTV as a tool, planning is the key.

Now you have the information needed to make a decision on the use of CCTV as one of the tools in the overall security plan for the location. To address the design considerations for the system, the following checklist will help guide you through the process. The information collected in the threat and vulnerability analysis and the site assessment will help you in completing the checklist below:

1. What is the objective of the CCTV system?
   a. To monitor
   b. To detect
   c. To recognize
   d. To identify
   e. Other, to deter

2. What targets are going to have surveillance?
   Persons
   Groups of individuals
   Objects/packages
   Vehicles
   Entrances
   Point of sale
   Other

3. What activities are important?
   Assaults, robberies
   Vehicle theft
   Damage to property
   Burglary
   Intruders
   Other

4. What is the purpose of the surveillance?
   Person
   Monitor
   Detect

Recognize
Identify
Other

5. How important is the clarity of the video image (recordings and real time)?
   Ability to identify a perpetrator
   Identify what the perpetrator is doing
   Identify a vehicle license plate
   Identify the clothes the perpetrator was wearing (color camera)
   Other

6. When is surveillance needed?
   After hours only (after normal business hours) and on weekends
   24 hours a day
   Every day
   Every night
   Walking tours for security officers
   Other

7. What actions will the video surveillance bring?
   Immediate response
   Investigation
   Other

8. Is the lighting adequate for the camera?
   Outside cameras
   Inside cameras
   Color vs. black and white

9. How will the system be monitored?
   By security officers
   Just for recording
   Other

By conscientiously completing the checklist answering the questions in all 7 sections you will now have a good ides of what the CCTV system is going to do to enhance the site security. It is important to know what images are important. For example, if you need to identify people, then designing a system that will only monitor the scene will not provide the level of CCTV quality you need and are expecting.

The checklist will help in camera, lens, and housing selection. The selection of the lens is based on the following. Just placing any lens on the camera will not get the job done and you will not have the optimal system producing the quality and detail you want. To help in choosing a camera lens there is a lens calculator that will help. Most of the CCTV vendors have an interactive lens calculator on their websites. To find a lens calculator, type in the words "lens calculator" in your browser search engine and the results of the search will yield all the lens calculators on the web. Since these calculators are interactive, when you enter your data, you will get the answers on the screen. The lens calculator will give you the field of view. To do this the lens calculator asks for and will provide the following information:

1. To select a lens of the correct size all you do is highlight the size.

2. Next select the CCD size by doing the same thing as you did for the lens size, highlight the selection.

3. The camera angle or reading direction selection for one of the following:
   horizontal
   vertical
   diagonal

4. Now fill in the distance to the target in feet or millimeters.

5. There is a calculate button and the following information is provided:
   angle in degrees
   height
   reading direction

You will notice that as you click on a different reading direction the degree of the angle changes. Also as you change the lens size the degree of the angle also changes. The results you obtained in step five above will help you place the cameras around the location. By using a scaled drawing you can site the cameras where they should be placed to meet your system's design objectives.

• Will the camera be an indoor or outdoor installation? It is recommended that if the camera is to be used in an indoor setting that color be selected since it will enhance identification of people.

• Will the camera be used for identifying a person or activity?

• At what distance will the person or activity be identified?

The selection of the housing is based on whether the camera will be an indoor or outdoor installation. For outdoor installation the camera housing needs to be weatherproof to protect it from the elements.

The use of PTZ cameras will need to be determined in the planning phase. There is no sense in paying for PTZ cameras if the system will not be monitored by security officers 24 hours a day. Fixed cameras will be installed if there are not security officers on the site or at remote station to monitor the CCTV system which will save money. Also consider dome housings versus the large weather proof housing like those in Figure 9–3. These housings give away where the camera is pointing, the domes on the other hand do not.

The next part of the design will be camera placement. Camera placement will depend on the answers to the above questions. This is the heart of the system and will be designed and installed to meet the desired goals. For example, if the recognition and identity of perpetrators and their activity are important, then the cameras need to be placed so that the objective is met. The following must be decided if the cameras are to meet the objective:

- The proper camera angle is also important because, along with the lens, this will determine what is captured by the camera.

- If the cameras will not be monitored by security officers, then fixed cameras will be installed.

- The fixed cameras must have the proper lens, be placed at the proper angle, and at the right distance so proper identification of the perpetrators and activities can be made.

To help with the camera placement you can use a drawing that has the layout of the area, site, etc. and mark the camera locations on the drawing so you a reference point to start from. The lens calculator will help with the placement of the cameras since you will know the distance and angle that is optimal for the most common lenses that are available and for the CCD sizes of the camera. The calculator will give the field of view for each of the lenses listed, and the CCD sizes based on the distance and angle of the camera.

TABLE 9-1   Light Reflectance Chart

LOCATION	REFLECTANCE VALUE
Empty asphalt	5%
Trees, grass	20%
Face Caucasian	25%
Red bricks	35%
Concrete unpainted	40%
Concrete with matt white paint	60%
Glass	70%
Snow	85%

LIGHTING

The lighting for the proposed location that the camera will be viewing needs to be the minimum required for the camera to be effective usually .2fc. Remember color cameras need more light. Table 9-1 provides come light reflectance percentages for common objects and things. The chart is important for determining the camera's sensitivity, which is the amount of reflective light sensitivity a camera would need to operate in the environment. To determine the sensitivity needed there is a simple equation that can be used.

Available light expressed in foot-candles × the reflectance value = the reflectance value. For example:

- You have 4fc of light and the camera is viewing a matt-painted concrete wall which has 60% reflectance for the background.

- Then, 4fc × .6 = .24fc reflective light so you need a camera that has a sensitivity of .24fc of reflective light. The light sensitivity of a camera is on the manufacturer's specifications sheet under the heading of camera sensitivity.

Locks and Keys

The original intent of locks was to keep out those that did not have a key and therefore did not have access out of certain areas, buildings, etc. It was not long after locks were used that they then became the target of those attempting to gain access. Locks can be compromised using special lock picking tools, drilled out using drills or using a duplicate key made from an impression or from a master key. These are all methods of gaining access to a locked area. Locks are the most widely used security device to help protect facilities and property. Locks are not going to keep the determined well-equipped thief out of the property. They are instead a delaying device similar to perimeter fences. The better the lock, the more delay there will be for the intruder. Remember, thieves do not want to spend a great deal of time working on the lock since time is important to them. The longer they spend on defeating the lock, the less time they have inside the property, building, etc. The approximate time limit thieves like to stick to is around ten minutes from entry to exit. Anything that adds to that time is a delaying tactic and may make the location less attractive as a target. By using high security locks in conjunction with other security devices such as instruction detection increases the odds that the thief will be caught. So the use of good locks will add to the hardening of the target.

Because all locks can be defeated with the proper tools and expertise make sure that the lock you choose is right for the job and will provide some level of security. Therefore locks are to be used as a stand-alone security device. Locks can be used as a delaying tactic especially if the lock is a lock that was designed to be pick resistant and impression resistant. The pick resistant and the impression resistant locks cost more than other locks but work well as a delaying tactic to slow down an intruder. Lock picking is not used that frequently because of the expertise and skill needed to successfully pick the lock. Lock picking is harder to do than it is portrayed in the movies on the television. Overall locks are the least costly security device made, especially the mechanical locks, and are a part of the first line of defense in security. The quality and strength of the lock the potential thief encounters will send the message that this is a hardened target or a soft target. If the effort was made to install a good security lock then probably here are other security devices that have been installed as well such as an intrusion detection system so the potential thief may think twice and will move on to a softer target to attack. Since locks are extension of the door or window into the wall the lock is only as good as the wall around it. If the wall is weak the lock will be bypassed by attacking the wall to gain entry.

In this chapter the types of locks and their uses will be presented. Also a look at some new innovations in locks that offer keyless entry. Keyless locks are gaining in popularity since they are no keys to lose or carry. Keyless entry has increased in recent years as in vehicle entry; some are even offering keyless ignition. This use of keyless entry locks has and will continue to affect residence locking systems and in fact there are locks on the market today that offer keyless entry.

TYPES OF LOCKS

There are different types of locks on the market today. These range from deadbolts to electric strikes to keypad and combinations locks. Some locks offer more security than others and require considerable time and expertise to open and other locks can be opened more easily without any special knowledge. Dead bolts are the most popular lock for residential use. All locks are operated by either a key, electronically using an access card, or numerical combination by entering pin numbers into a keypad to gain access. To enhance the use of locks they are usually used in conjunction with another security device such as an intrusion detection system.

The primary part of a lock is the latch or bolt and most key-operated locks use it except for combination and padlock locks. There are various types of locks and below are the most widely used locks:

1. Cylindrical locks are also known as key-in-knob or key-in-lever locks. Normally these locks are used to secure, offices, storage rooms, etc. The cylinder in the center of the doorknob identifies these locks. Some of the cylinder locks have a key way in both sides of the lock to unlock or lock the lock. These are used in a door that has a window above the doorknob and the potential exists that if the glass is broken, entry can be made by reaching in and turning the thumb turn or handle to open the door. Some cylindrical locks are also installed with lever handles with the cylinder in the center.

   The cylindrical lock has a cylinder or plug that is the key way. The grooves in the key are there so when the key is inserted into the lock they line up with the configuration of the pins in the plug. The pins cause the rotation of the plug as the key is turned moving the latch from the strike plate.

FIGURE 10-1   A picture of a cylindrical lock made by Sargent Locks, Inc.

The cylindrical lock is good for low security locations and applications. The lock is easily compromised by either removing the doorknob or lever or prying the latch from the strike plate. Figure 10-1 is a picture of a cylindrical lock made by Sargent Locks, Inc.

2. The dead bolt lock is also known as a tubular dead bolt. The lock is mounted on the door in a similar fashion to the cylindrical lock except that there is a bolt that slides into the strike plate. When locked the bolt extends into the frame at a minimum of 1 inch to prevent easy forcing of the lock out of the frame.

    The dead bolt lock is used on apartment doors, house doors, etc. The lock provides more protection than the cylindrical lock. To prevent unlocking the lock by breaking a window, it is recommended that dead bolt locks that are placed in doors with windows or next to windows have a double key cylinder which means that a key is needed to lock or unlock the lock on either side of the door.

    Deadbolt locks are used for residential and office security and provide an acceptable level of security. The lock can be defeated by prying the bolt back from the frame freeing the bolt from the strike plate. This is why a minimum of a one-inch throw on the bolt is important since it cannot be forced back by prying the bolt. The frame can be forced open by spreading the door frame using an old automobile jack. The jack is placed in between the door frame and is extended until the frame forces the bolt to open. Another way to defeat the deadbolt is to find a weak point to enter, like a window. Figure 10-2 is a typical deadbolt lock.

4. The mortise lock gets its name from the way that the lock case is "mortised" recessed into the edge of the door. The mortise lock that has a doorknob on the both sides of the door is the most common one. There is an exterior thumb latch on entrance doors rather than a doorknob on some models. To lock the lock there is a thumb turn or button. The button is usually in the

FIGURE 10-2   A typical deadbolt lock

side of the door above the latch and pushing the button in will lock the door. On some doors there is a very small lever instead of a button and moving the lever up or down, the lock is either locked or unlocked. To install the lock into the edge of the door by recessing it into the door, weakens the door and therefore the lock is considered to be low security and not to be used for areas requiring high security. Figure 10-3 shows a Sargent mortise lock.

5. Drop bolt locks also known as jimmy proof locks are used as auxiliary locks like the dead bolt. The strike and the lock body have interlocking leaves that are similar to a door hinge and when closed, the locking pins in the lock body drop down into the holes in the strike locking the lock. The lock is extremely difficult to separate since the lock body and strike are interconnected with locking pins and the lock becomes a single unit. The lock is used in residential and commercial locations.

FIGURE 10-3   A Sargent mortise lock

FIGURE 10-4   A Medeco drop bolt lock

The drop bolt lock is a deterrent to spreading the door frame since the strike does not extend into the door frame horizontally. Spreading the frame will not free the bolts from the strike since the bolts drop down into the strike. Figure 10-4 shows a Medeco drop bolt lock.

6. Rim cylinder locks are mounted by screwing to the inside surface of the door face. The rim cylinder lock is usually used in conjunction with the drop bolt lock or other surface-mounted lock. The lock consists of an outer barrel, a cylinder and ring, tailpiece, back mounting plate, and two mounting screws. To help the lock fit varying door thicknesses, the tailpiece screws are scored. Figure 10-5 shows a Yale rim cylinder lock.

7. Disc tumbler locks were designed for automobile doors. The locks are now used for desks, file cabinets, and other uses because they are easy and cheap to produce. The lock however, has a limited life because they are produced using soft metal. The locks are not very effective as a security

FIGURE 10-5   A Yale rim cylinder lock

FIGURE 10-6   Several disc tumbler locks

device and do not have an extensive delaying since they are easily compromised. Figure 10-6 shows several disc tumbler locks.

8. Pin tumbler locks are widely used today in residential and industrial settings. The lock has a cylinder that rotates and is called a plug that is linked to the locking mechanism. The plug has a shell around it and the shell with the plug inside is fixed to the door. When a key is inserted, the cylinder will rotate and this rotation is what works the locking mechanism. The key for the pin tumbler lock is grooved on both sides. When in the locked position the plug cannot rotate because a set of pin stacks that are spring-loaded extend into the top of the plug to keep it in place. The pin tumbler locks can be mater keyed to a variety of patterns. The lock is not for high security applications since it can be compromised easily. Figure 10-7 shows an old Yale

FIGURE 10-7   An old Yale pin tumbler lock cut away with the key inserted

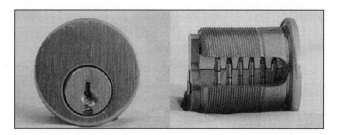

FIGURE 10-8 A front and side view of a pin tumbler lock

pin tumbler lock cut away with the key inserted. Figure 10-8 shows a front and side view of a pin tumbler lock.

9. Unit locks are used in areas that have heavy use like institutional buildings, hospitals, etc. The lock is installed into the door by cutting a notch at the door's edge. The lock is one piece and the lock has a standard size for the cutout which helps simplify the door in preparation for the lock installation.

10. Cipher locks are also known as keypad locks or mechanical push button locks. These locks have a key pad with numbers from 0-9 and anyone wanting to gain entry that has access inserts their assigned PIN into the keypad and the lock is released. The locks are similar to the unit lock since the lock and door handle is one piece. These locks are used in secure areas, to limit access, and provide access control.

11. Fingerprint locks are similar to the cipher lock in design and look, however instead of a keypad, there is a fingerprint reader installed. The lock also has a dual technology system that incorporates the fingerprint with a keypad. The lock is powered by 4 AA batteries and can get up to 5,000 operations before the batteries need to be replaced. Since the lock is standalone, it can hold up to 10 persons' fingerprint records. A key is needed to add or delete users. The lock can be used to replace an existing mechanical lock.

12. Padlocks are portable, detachable locks and are used in conjunction with a hasp. There are low and high security padlocks. The low security padlocks are made using hardened steel shackles. High security padlocks on the other hand are made of case hardened steel and are used with a security hasp.

13. Electric strike locks are used in conjunction with an access control system. The strike is electrified rather than the lock. The strike is the part of the lock that is installed into the door frame. When an access card is presented that has valid access, the electric strike moves and releases the latch from the lock allowing the door to open. Electric locks are also used in conjunction with

an access control system. The electric lock electrifies the lock which is the part of the lock that is attached to the door. When a valid access card is presented at the reader the electric lock releases the lock for the strike and the door opens.

14. Magnetic locks also known as Mag locks are an electronic magnet. The locks are used in conjunction with an access control system.

15. High security locks meet the following criteria:
    a. Resistant to being picked
    b. Resistant to forced entry
    c. Tamper-resistant
    d. Permit entry to those with special knowledge and tools
    e. Record access and entry using electronic locks.

All of the major lock manufacturers make a high security lock. For example, Schlage makes the Primus(tm) lock which is a high security lock. The Primus(tm) lock uses special keys. Special blanks are needed to make duplicate keys as well as a special machine to cut the key. To change the cores in these locks a special key is used and this allows for easy, rapid re-keying of the locks in the event a key is compromised or when someone leaves the company, etc.

Medeco has a high security lock called KeyMark™ that uses special keys and the cylinders are interchangeable as well. To make duplicate keys special machine duplicate blanks are needed so any keymaking machine cannot make duplicate keys.

Corbin Russwin has a high security lock called the Pyramid(tm). The lock's cylinder is 7 pin and is also interchangeable with other cylindrical locks that Corbin Russwin makes. The keys like the other high security locks cannot be duplicated without a special machine and special key blanks.

KEYING SYSTEMS

The cores of some locks are interchangeable allowing the same key to be used for a variety of locks. Padlocks, cabinet locks, electrical key switches, and door locks are capable of using the same key.

There are several different ways to key locks. The ways are identified by the keying system used. Below is a list of the various keying systems used:

- Grand master key is the one that will open all the locks in the system including two master groups.

- Master key will open one of the locks on the one or two submasters.

- Submaster key will open any locks within the submaster. This keying system can be used to have all the keys for the offices in one department opened by one key. The offices keys are keyed alike.

Master keying is done for convenience and not for security since it compromises security due to the loss of control. Some keys have do not duplicate stamped on them but this does not mean that the keys will not be duplicated. There are keys that cannot be duplicated without special equipment and tightly controlled special key blanks.

One such key works with a lock made by Schlage called Primus™ A regular key will not work a Primus™ lock and the Primus™ lock cylinders can be interchanged with almost any 6 pin cylinder that Schlage makes as well as most other brands of cylinders made by other manufacturer. Primus™ locks are resistant to drilling and almost pick proof and are therefore considered high security locks.

Medeco KeyMark™ locks have a special key that cannot be duplicated by just any keymaking machine even with an impression. The duplicate blanks are tightly controlled and an ordinary blank can not be used to make a duplicate key for the KeyMark™ lock. Medeco cylinders are interchangeable with Medeco cores and can be changed rapidly after employees leave to maintain the high security integrity of the lock.

Corbin Russwin Pyramid™ locks have special keys as well and the duplicate blanks are controlled. Each facility using Pyramid™ locks must complete a registration form. The form is used to order key blanks and cylinders as well as pin kits.

The advantages of the high security locks and keying systems are as follows:

1. The cylinders are interchangeable within their product line and most of the other product lines as well.

2. The cores can be changed rapidly so when someone leaves the company, lost keys, etc. the cylinders can be changed to keep the integrity of the system.

3. The keys cannot be duplicated by any keymaking machine even with an impression.

4. The key duplicate blanks are unique and are tightly controlled.

SPECIFICATIONS

Here are some general requirements for specifying locks for a project:

Choose type of lock

- Mortise

- Cylindrical

- Deadbolt

- Drop bolt

- Rim Cylinder

- Disc tumbler

- Pin tumbler

- Unit lock

- Cipher

- Fingerprint

- Electric strike

- Electric lock

- Magnetic

- High security

Choose color and style of lock

Prepare specification sheet for lock chosen

The general specifications are necessary for specifying the type of locks to be used and where. Sometimes the site will have more than one type of lock and the specifications will call out each type of lock. The manufacturers of the locks have cut sheets for their products. The cut sheets provide the specifications for the various locks. If the project is a part of an overall security design package, then you can add the sections on locks to the overall specifications as another section. The Instructions to Bidders is part of the document and will also have sections pertaining to the locks. By putting all the security related documents in one package it helps make the bidding process go more smoothly as well as the installation.

After the type of locks and where they are to be used on the project has been decided the next thing to do is to prepare the bid documents including the specifications. The more detailed you make the specification document the better off you will be in the long run. The details are important if you are going to get a good quote on the work of purchasing and installing the locks. The other part of the bid package preparation is the standard "Instructions to Bidders" document that will accompany the specification document. Also part of the bid package, it is helpful to provide a set of preliminary drawings showing what doors will have which locks. The drawings will be used to do the "job walk" for the pre-bid meeting.

Below is a sample bid specification for locks on a job for a fictitious company called ABCD Corporation:

PART 1 GENERAL

1.1 RELATED DOCUMENTS

A. Section Includes:
1. Finish hardware for doors as specified and as listed in "Hardware Groups" and required by actual conditions.
2. Include screws, special screws, bolts, special bolts, expansion shields, and other devices for proper application of hardware.

B. Related Sections:
1. Section XXXX: Carpentry 1. Section ZZZZ, Section WWWW, and Section YYYY – Certain hardware items installed with doors. Note: these sections are in another part of the construction design specifications so the letters are used rather than the section numbers since the design document is for illustrative purposes.
2. Division 16: Electrical.

1.2 GENERAL REQUIREMENTS

A. To purchase and install the locks listed in this document according to the schedule listed below. For the purpose of clarification, the following parties will be referenced in this document in the following manner:

1. The ABCD Corporation   The Client
   5667 First Street
   Livermore, CA. 94588
   925-224-7955 Tel
   925-224-7964 Fax
   www.abcd.com

2. The XYZ Consultants Inc.   The Consultants
   1200 Broadway
   Pleasanton, California
   925-555-1234 Tel
   925-555-1235 Fax
   www.xyzconsult.com

3. The ABCD Corporation   The Facility(s)
   Office construction project
   1700 Main Street
   Livermore, California

B. In all new facilities, the system is being installed for the purpose of securing the Client's facility. The locks will be installed on all the doors for the new office building for the corporation meeting this specification and the bidder instructions. The requirements for the locks to be used in conjunction with the access control system will be specified in the access control system part of the security requirements.

C. Provide items, articles, materials, operations and methods listed, mentioned or scheduled herein or on drawings, in the quantities necessary to complete the project. Provide hardware that functions properly and is good working order. Apprise the Architect of hardware items that will not operate properly, are improper for the conditions as specified, or will not remain permanently anchored as required by the installation instructions. "Change Orders" using the form supplied are to be submitted for any changes to hardware and the reason for such changes

D. This Section calls for the contractor of choice to provide all labor, materials, equipment, and service necessary for the completion of the installation of locks for all the doors for the office building as indicated on the drawings and as described herein. The Owner reserves the right to supply other components if they are needed for this project. The system technologies called for within this Scope of Work are:
   1. Install locks on all exterior and interior doors;
   2. Components required for installation

E. Contractor shall ensure the locks meet the operational and functional needs of the Client as specified herein, and as indicated on the drawings. The drawings are diagrammatic only. Equipment and labor not specifically referred to herein, or on the plans, that are required to meet the functional and operational intent, shall be provided without additional cost to the Client.

G. Contractor shall be responsible for coordinating with other trades and contractors to provide a system that is totally integrated and operational as required for this project.

H. The Contractor shall be responsible for providing with their Submittal, a one year spare parts list with single component (itemized) and quantity pricing. Should any particular component be in redesign stage that would possibly cause it to be a non-production item within the 1 year period, this component shall be identified as such and the substitute or new component be identified on this spare parts list.

1.3 RELATED SECTIONS

A. The contractor shall review the following sections of the total project to ensure compliance with:
   1. Division X Site Work
   2. Division X Doors and Door Hardware
   3. Division X Electrical

All specification divisions are identified by The Construction Specification Institute Master Format

1.4   SUBMITTALS

A. Hardware Schedule: Submit 5 copies of hardware schedule in vertical format as illustrated by the Sequence of Format for the Hardware Schedule as published by the Door and Hardware Institute. Schedules, which do not comply, will be returned for correction before checking. Hardware schedule shall clearly indicate architect's hardware group and manufacturer of each item proposed. The schedule shall be reviewed prior to submission by a certified Architectural Hardware Consultant, who shall affix his or her seal attesting to the completeness and correctness of the schedule.

1. Provide 2 copies of illustrations from manufacturer's catalogs and data in brochure form.

2. Check specified hardware for suitability and adaptability to details and surrounding conditions. Indicate unsuitable or incompatible items and proposed substitutions in hardware schedule.

3. Provide listing of manufacturer's template numbers for each item of hardware in hardware schedule.

4. Furnish other Contractors and Subcontractors concerned with copies of final approved hardware schedule. Submit necessary templates and schedules as soon as possible to hollow metal, wood door, and aluminum door fabricators in accordance with schedule they require for fabrication.

5. Samples: Lever design or finish sample: Provide 3 samples if requested by architect.

B. Wiring Diagrams: Provide complete and detailed system operation and elevation diagrams specially developed for each opening requiring electrified hardware, except openings where only magnetic hold-opens or door position switches are specified. Provide these diagrams with hardware schedule submittal for approval. Provide detailed wiring diagrams with hardware delivery to jobsite.

C. Installation Instructions: Provide manufacturer's written installation and adjustment instructions for finish hardware. Send installation instructions to site with hardware.

D. Templates: Submit templates and "reviewed Hardware Schedule" to door and frame supplier and others as applicable to enable proper and accurate sizing and locations of cutouts and reinforcing.

E. Contract Closeout Submittals: Comply with Sections 1.4 and 1.5 including any other specific requirements indicated.

1. Operating and maintenance manuals: Submit 3 sets containing the following:
   a. Complete information in care, maintenance, and adjustment, and data on repair and replacement parts, and information on preservation of finishes.
   b. Cut sheet for each product.
   c. Name, address, and phone number of local representative for each manufacturer.
   d. Parts list for each product.
2. Copy of final approved hardware schedule, edited to reflect "As installed".
3. Copy of final keying schedule.
4. As installed "Wiring Diagrams" for each opening connected to power, both low voltage and 110 volts.
5. One complete set of special tools required for maintenance and adjustment of hardware, including changing of cylinders.

F. The Contractor's submittal shall include a complete list of equipment, materials, and installation instructions. All prices shall be itemized in single component prices as well as quantity pricing with any discounts so indicated. Alternative proposals are acceptable under this specification and shall comply with all standard requirements for the bid package submittal.

1.5 QUALITY ASSURANCE

A. Manufacturer: Obtain each type of hardware (i.e. latch and locksets, hinges, closers) from single manufacturer, although several may be indicated as offering products complying with requirements.

B. Supplier: Recognized architectural finish hardware supplier, with warehousing facilities, who has been providing hardware for period of not less than 3 years. The supplier shall be, or employ, a certified Architectural Hardware Consultant (AHC), who is registered in the continuing education program as administered by the Door and Hardware Institute. The hardware schedule shall be prepared and signed by a certified AHC.

C. Installer: Firm with 3 years experience in installation of similar hardware to that required for this project, including specific requirements indicated.

D. Regulatory Label Requirements: Provide nationally recognized testing agency label or stamp on hardware for labeled openings. Where UL requirements conflict with drawings or specifications, hardware conforming to UL requirements shall be provided. Conflicts and proposed substitutions shall be clearly indicated in hardware schedule.

E. Handicapped Requirements: Doors to stairs (other than exit stairs), loading platforms, boiler rooms, stages and doors serving other hazardous locations shall have knurled or other similar approved marking of door lever handles or cross bars in accordance with local building codes.

F. Pre-Installation Conference: Prior to the installation of hardware, manufacturer's representatives for locksets, closers, and exit devices shall arrange and hold a jobsite meeting to instruct the installing contractor's personnel on the proper installation of their respective products. A letter of compliance, indicating when this meeting is held and who is in attendance, shall be sent to the Architect and Owner.

1.6 DELIVERY, STORAGE AND HANDLING

A. Deliver hardware to jobsite in manufacturer's original packaging, marked to correspond with approved hardware schedule. Do not deliver hardware until suitable locked storage space is available. Check hardware against reviewed hardware schedule. Store hardware to protect against loss, theft or damage.

B. Deliver hardware required to be installed during fabrication of hollow metal, aluminum, wood, or stainless steel doors prepaid to manufacturer.

1.7 WARRANTY

A. Guarantee workmanship and material provided against defective manufacture. Repair or replace defective workmanship and material appearing within period of one year after Substantial Completion.

B. Provide ten year factory warranty on door closer body against defects in material and workmanship from date of occupancy of Project.

C. Replace shortages and incorrect items with correct material at no additional cost to Owner.

D. At completion of project, qualified factory representative shall inspect closer installations. After this inspection, letter shall be sent to Architect reporting on conditions, verifying that closers have been properly installed and adjusted.

PART 2 PRODUCTS

This part outlines the type of lock and the materials of construction the dimensions, diameter, etc. This section also outlines finishes, etc. Electronic locks are also outlined in this section. Some examples follow:

2.1 LOCKSETS - MORTISE

A. Acceptable Manufacturer and Series:
Manufacturer

Series

Sargent

8200 x LNL

Yale

8700FL x AUR

Corbin Russwin

ML2200 x NSA

B. Provide lock functions specified in Hardware Groups, with following provisions:

1. Cylinders: Manufacturer's high security removable core 6-pin, meeting the requirements of UL437.

2. Backsets: 2-3/4 inches.

3. Strikes: Provide wrought boxes and strikes with proper lip length to protect trim but not to project more than 1/8 inch beyond trim, frame or inactive leaf. Where required, provide open back strike and protected to allow practical and secure operation.

2.2 LOCKSETS - CYLINDRICAL

A. Acceptable Manufacturer and Series:

Manufacturer

Series

Sargent

10-Line x LL

Yale

5400L x AU

Corbin Russwin

CL3400 x NZD

1. Cylinders: Manufacturer's high security removable core 6-pin, meeting the requirements of UL437.

2. Backsets: 2-3/4 inches.

3. Strikes: Provide wrought boxes and strikes with proper lip length to protect trim but not to project more than 1/8 inch beyond trim, frame or inactive leaf. Where required, provide open back strike and protected to allow practical and secure operation.

2.3 LOCKSETS - 11-LINE

A. Acceptable Manufacturer and Series (No Substitutions):

Manufacturer

Series

Sargent

11-Line x LL

1. Locksets shall be able to withstand 2400 inch pounds of torque applied to the locked lever without gaining access.

2. Locksets shall be cycle tested per ANSI A156.2, 1996, to two million cycles without any visible lever sag.

3. Locksets shall be able to fit a standard 2-1/8 inch (55 mm) bore without the use of thru-bolts. Standard rose size shall be 2-3/4 inches (70 mm) in diameter.

4. Lockset levers shall be made of solid material with no plastic fillers.

5. Latchbolt head shall be one piece stainless steel.

6. Latchbolt assemblies shall be encased within the lockbody.

7. Cylinders: Sargent Signature Series, UL437 listed, high security 6-pin cylinders.

8. Backsets: 2-3/4 inches.

9. Strikes: Provide wrought boxes and strikes with proper lip length to protect trim but not to project more than 1/8 inch beyond trim, frame or inactive leaf. Where required, provide open back strike and protected to allow practical and secure operation.

10. Locksets shall have a seven year limited warranty.

2.4 TYPICAL FINISHES AND MATERIALS

A. Finishes, unless otherwise specified:

1. Butts: Out-swinging Exterior Doors
   a. US32D (BHMA 630) on Stainless Steel

2. Butts: Interior Doors and In-swinging Exterior Doors
   a. US26D (BHMA 652) on Steel

3. Continuous Hinges:
   a. US28 (BHMA 628) on Aluminum

4. Flush Bolts:
   a. US26D (BHMA 626) on Brass or Bronze

5. Exit Devices:
   a. US32D (BHMA 630) on Stainless Steel

6. Locks and Latches:
   a. US26D (BHMA 626) on Brass or Bronze

7. Push Plates, Pulls and Push Bars:
   a. US32D (BHMA 630) on Stainless Steel

8. Coordinators:
   a. USP (BHMA 600) on Steel

9. Kick Plates, Armor Plates, and Edge Guards:
   a. US32D (BHMA 630) on Stainless Steel

10. Overhead Stops and Holders:
    a. US26D (BHMA 626) on Brass or Bronze

11. Closers: Surface mounted.
    a. Sprayed Aluminum Lacquer.

12. Latch Protectors:

a. US32D (BHMA 630) on Stainless Steel
13. Miscellaneous Hardware:
a. US26D (BHMA 626) on Brass or Bronze

PART 3 EXECUTION

3.1 EXAMINATION

A. Examine doors, frames, and related items for conditions that would prevent the proper application of finish hardware. Do not proceed until defects are corrected.

3.2 INSTALLATION

A. Install finish hardware in accordance with reviewed hardware schedule and manufacturer's printed instructions. Pre-fit hardware before finish is applied, remove and reinstall after finish is completed. Install hardware so that parts operate smoothly, close tightly and do not rattle.

B. Installation of hardware shall comply with NFPA 80 and NFPA 101 requirements.

C. Set units level, plumb and true to line and location. Adjust and reinforce attachment to substrate as necessary for proper installation and operation.

D. Drill and countersink units which are not factory-prepared for anchorage fasteners. Space fasteners and anchors in accordance with industry standards.

E. Set thresholds for exterior doors in full bed of butyl-rubber or poly-isobutylene mastic sealant, forming tight seal between threshold and surface to which set. Securely and permanently anchor thresholds, using countersunk non-ferrous screws to match color of thresholds (stainless steel screws at aluminum thresholds).

F. Lead Protection: Lead wrap hardware penetrating lead-lined doors. Levers and roses to be lead lined. Apply kick and armor plates with 3M adhesive #1357, as recommended by 3M Co., on lead-lined doors.

3.3 FIELD QUALITY CONTROL

A. After installation has been completed, provide services of qualified hardware consultant to check Project to determine proper application of finish hardware according to schedule. Also check operation and adjustment of hardware items.

3.4 ADJUSTING AND CLEANING

A. At final completion, hardware shall be left clean and free from disfigurement. Make final adjustment to door closers and other items of hardware. Where hardware is found defective repair or replace or otherwise correct as directed.

B. Adjust door closers to meet opening force requirements of Uniform Federal Accessibility Standards.

C. Final Adjustment: Wherever hardware installation is made more than one month prior to acceptance or occupancy of space or area, return to work during week prior to acceptance or occupancy, and make final check and adjustment of hardware items in such space or area. Clean operating items as necessary to restore proper function and finish of hardware and doors.

D. Instruct Owner's personnel in proper adjustment and maintenance of door hardware and hardware finishes.

E. Clean adjacent surfaces soiled by hardware installation.

CHAPTER 11

Doors and Windows

D oors and windows are the openings into a building. Windows provide light and, if the windows can be opened, fresh air. Doors provide a means of ingress and egress to a building, room, etc. Security of doors and windows is important to the overall security of the building or room. Window and door security is sometimes not emphasized in the overall security plan.

The chapter will address the types of vulnerabilities of each type of window and will explore how to secure them. The types of doors will be outlined as well as the vulnerabilities of each. Methods for better securing doors and windows will be explored.

Doors and windows are considered weak points in the perimeter since they are cut into the perimeter of the building, such as a wall, and can be compromised more easily than the wall to provide possible entry points for those attempting to enter the location without authorization.

Even though most windows in commercial and office buildings today cannot be opened. some type of glass sits in the frame as the main part of the structure. The glass lets the light from the outside enter the building.

TYPES OF WINDOW FRAMES

There are various types of window frames. The window frame is what holds the glass in place and is made of steel, aluminum, wood, or other material. Below are the types of window frames listed by the construction materials used:

1. **Aluminum window frames.** These frames are made from extruded aluminum and are used for residential, commercial, or light factory buildings to hold the glass in place. The frames come as either fixed or operational depending on the needs of the project.

2. **Steel window frames.** These frames are made from hot rolled steel or formed steel and are used in residential and commercial buildings. The frames are either fixed or operational.

3. **Wood window frames.** These frames are made from wood. Wood frames are commonly used in double-hung windows. The window frames can be fixed or operational (double-hung).

4. **Tubular plastic window frames.** Tubular plastic window frames are made from PVC (polyvinyl chloride) plastics. The frames are either fixed or operational (double hung). The windows are used in residential and commercial buildings.

5. **Fiberglass and composite window frames.** These frames have the advantage of expanding and contracting with temperature changes. The frames are made of fiberglass and composite materials such as plastics.

There are four main types of windows based on operation:

1. Fixed-pane windows are windows that are typically found in most buildings today. These windows cannot be opened. This is for energy efficiency. The fixed window comes in a variety of shapes:
   a. rectangular. like those found in picture windows
   b. oval tops
   c. circle tops
   d. triangular view

2. Casement or awning windows have hinges on the side and top and bottom so they can be opened. Some of the windows open from the side like a door. There is a handle that is also the lock and, when the handle is moved from one side, the window can then be pushed open. The handle is usually in the middle of the frame at the bottom.

3. Awning windows are usually used in residential applications. The window is opened by turning a crank that is located on the side of the window frame. The windows are hinged at the top, sides, and bottom and when the crank is turned the window juts outward to the open position.

4. Double-hung windows are constructed with a top and bottom sash which is the sliding section of the window. The window can be opened from either the top or bottom. The double-hung window is the most widely used in residential buildings.

5. Slider is similar to the double hung except instead of moving up and down the window slides from side to side to open. The slider is used on residential

and in commercial properties where there outside ventilation is acceptable to the building design.

Types of Window Glass

The term glazing is used to refer to the glass in a window or door. There are numerous types of glass and treatments available. The only types of glass we will explore are the safety and security glasses.

1. The first type of glass is the tempered safety glass. Tampered safety glass is made by using annealed glass and heating it. The purpose of the heating is to provide strength and when the glass is broken the shards produced by the shattering affect are small and the damage is minimal.

   Tempered glass is used in oven doors, computer monitors, storm doors, LCD (Liquid Crystal Display) displays, etc.

2. Laminated glass is two or more pieces of glass bonded together with a layer of clear PVB. Heat and pressure are used in the process to bond the layers of glass together. The laminated glass is used in high security areas because the glass has a good probability it will stay in the frame even when shattered. The glass also provides good sound reduction as the thickness increases. When shattered, the laminated glass will break into large shards like the annealed glass does but the PVB inner layer holds the shards together.

   Laminated glass is used in windows in office doors, shower doors, office partitions, etc.

3. Bullet resistant glass is another type glass that used to enhance security. Bullet resistant glass is made from laminates that are several layers of glass with a polycarbonate spall plate that is bonded together with layers of PVB (polyvinyl butyral). The bullet resistant glass can resist bullets fired from small arms such as pistols and rifles.

   The glass has different ratings dependant upon the thickness. There re two common ballistics standards for rating bullet resistance of glass are UL 752 and the National Institute of Justice Table NIJ 0108-01.

   The Underwriters Laboratory is the most widely used in the commercial sector and rates the glass using UL test 752. The UL ratings range from 1-8. The levels 1-3 usually are applied to the commercial sector and levels 4-8 usually apply to the government and military sectors. Table 11-1 below summarizes the ratings form 1-8 with the addition of two levels for shotgun, one with a slug and the other with 00 buckshot. As can be noted the tests are based on

TABLE 11-1   Underwriters Laboratory 752 Glass Rating Summary

THREAT LEVEL RATING	AMMUNITION TYPE	WEIGHT AND GRAINS	RANGE	NUMBER OF SHOTS
Level 1	9 mm copper jacket with lead core FMJ (full metal jacket) lead core	124 grains	15 feet	3
Level 2	.357 Magnum lead soft point	158 grains	15 feet	3
Level 3	.44 Magnum lead Semi-Wadcutter gas checked	240 grains	15 feet	3
Level 4	30 caliber rifle lead core soft point	180 grains	15 feet	1
Level 5	7.62 (.308 caliber) rifle FMJ copper jacket, military ball	150 grains	15 feet	1
Level 6	9 mm copper jacket with lead core FMJ		15 feet	5
Level 7	5.56 mm rifle (.223 caliber) copper jacket with lead core	55 grains	15 feet	5
Level 8	7.62 (.308 caliber) rifle FMJ copper jacket, military ball	150 grains	15 feet	5
Shotgun	12- gauge lead Slug	28 grains	15 feet	1
Shotgun	12- gauge 00 Buckshot	42 grains	15 feet	1

the caliber of the weapon being fired. There are other factors included in the testing process such as the weight and grains of powder of the bullet and the distance from the target in this case the glass.

The National Institute of Justice Table NIJ 0108-01 has ratings from I through IV. Table 11-2 below summarizes the levels. The NIJ ratings take into account the number of shots fired which are five except for the 30.06 rifle which is one shot. The amount of grains of powder in each load is the same as for the UL 752 tests.

4. Blast resistant glass is made from standard two-ply laminate that is 0.030-inch (0.76-mm) interlayer and is designed to perform within a wide range of blast threats. The new ASTM Standard for blast resistant glass is F2248-03. The standard outlines the bomb size and distance from the building with the requirements to withstand the blast and keep the glass shards from flying everywhere. The glass laminate is bonded to a steel frame. The laminate is used to hold the shards in place even after a catastrophic event as a bomb blast. The flying shards of glass account for a large amount of damage. To keep the shards from flying laminate is used to hold the glass in place even after a catastrophic event like the detonation of an explosive device. The affect is similar to what an automobile windshield does during an accident.

TABLE 11-2   National Institute of Justice Glass Rating Summary

ARMOR TYPE	AMMUNITION TYPE	NOMINAL BULLET MASS	NUMBER OF SHOTS	DISTANCE	PERMITTED PENETRATIONS
I	.22 LR and handgun lead	2.6 grains	5	6	0
	.38 Special RN lead	40 g			
		10.2 grains			
		158 g			
II and II-A	.357 Magnum	10.2 grains	5	6	0
	JSP	158 g			
	9 mm	8.0 grains			
	FMJ (full metal jacket)	124 g			
III-A	.44 Magnum	15.55 grains	5	6	0
	Lead SWC gas	240 g			
	Checked	8.0g			
	9 mm	124 grains			
	FMJ				
III	7.62 mm	9.7 grains	5	9	0
	308 Winchester	150 g			
	FMJ				
IV	30.06	10.8 grains	1	9	0
	AP	166 g			

The glass is shattered but it is held in place by laminate. This reduces the damage from flying shards of glass.

5. Lexan is a polycarbonate that is used to replace glass. It is durable and is not subject to shattering and therefore will not produce glass shards. Lexan is hard to penetrate as most tools bounce off when hitting the Lexan glass. Lexan is considered bullet proof.

   Lexan is used for making shower doors so they will not shatter causing injury if broken. It is also used as a bulletproof barrier for 24 hour gas station/convenience stores to protect the clerk form being shot during a robbery attempt. Sheets of Lexan are also used to protect taxi drivers from being shot in a hold up attempt from a passenger riding in the back seat of the taxi cab.

6. Plexiglass is not really glass but is used as a replacement for glass. Plexiglass is a transparent thermoplastic. The strength is equivalent to that of Lexan and used for the some applications.

Intrusion Detection for Windows

Intrusion detection for windows is discussed in Chapter 7 in more detail and we will summarize the systems here by listing them below. There are four methods for applying intrusion detection to windows. Glass breaks will not work for Lexan and Plexiglass but, since the windows cannot be shattered, is moot point.

1. Mechanical contact switches

2. Magnetic switches

3. Balanced magnetic switches

4. Glass break detectors

The switches will work for the Lexan and Plexiglass windows in the same way as they do for the glass windows since the position of the switch is what triggers the alarm and not the breaking the frequency of the breaking of the glass.

It is recommended to use dual technology sensors systems for intrusion detection for windows. A dual technology system would include for example, glass breaks and contact switches, or glass breaks and motion sensors, or contact switches and motion sensors for Plexiglass and Lexan windows. The reason that glass breaks are not effective for Plexiglass and Lexan windows is because they don't create the high frequency sound that shattering glass makes that the glass breaks are designed to "listen" for.

Windows are a potential entry point for intruders to the building. To minimize or at least delay the threat posed by the window there are steps you can take in the design of the windows. The following are some guidelines for increasing the security of windows.

1. Use protective coatings or a polycarbonate glass replacement material like Lexan or Plexiglass. This will minimize the threat of breaking the glass to enter the facility.

2. Incorporate the use of perimeter monitoring to detect potential intruders before they strike. This can be done by using outdoor motion sensors near the windows.

3. Install dual technology sensors to detect an intruder. Dual technology sensors include glass breaks and motion or wall vibration and motion sensors. Contact switches are also a good sensor to use with motion sensors.

4. The use of bars over the windows must meet local building and fire codes. Also bars are not aesthetically pleasing from an architectural perspective so they should be used as last resort.

5. Keep shrubbery from growing up around windows on the ground floor to a point that an intruder can use the cover to gain access to the window without being detected especially around the building that is visible from the street.

6. Install window locks on windows that can be opened. The locks can be thought of as a delaying device and will probably stop an intruder from gaining entry.

Doors

The construction and operation of a door will determine its function. For example an exterior door is usually constructed of more substantial material than an interior door. Doors are also further defined by how they operate, i.e. swing on hinges, slide, roll, fold, and unfold, etc.

Exterior doors are used as the main access points to a facility, office building, residence, etc. Doors are used on the interior to provide privacy and security. These doors are made of metal, metal frame and glass (store front), and wood. The exterior doors that are made from wood are usually solid core doors or wood covered with metal on both sides. Some exterior entry doors are made of a hollow wood core with a metal exterior to harden the door and these doors are usually used as entry doors for residences. Commercial doors are metal or steel and in some cases like stores and lobby doors glass doors are used. The frames of commercial doors are sometimes cast into the concrete of the walls. These frames are often metal and metal exterior doors are hung on the frames. The metal frames cast into the wall are resistant to spreading type attacks since there is very little if any "give" to the frame because of the rigid nature of the concrete walls. Most commercial doors are more substantial than doors used in residential buildings and have contact switches installed as a part of an intrusion detection system.

Types of Doors and Frames

There are various door types and frames. Some frames provide more security than others. The doorway is only as strong as the frame it is hung on. Some frames are wood are easily spread using nothing more than an automobile jack, others are more rigid. The door frame and door is called the doorway. Doorways have four main parts:

1. The first part of a doorway is the door. The primary purpose of the door is to block the entrance which is an opening in the exterior or interior wall structure.

2. The second part is the door frame. The frame holds the door in place by connecting it to the wall.

3. The third part of a doorway is the hinge. The hinge is used to connect the door to the frame.

4. Finally the fourth part is the lock. The lock is used to secure the door to the door frame and not permit unauthorized entry. Locks can be mechanical or electronic.

Each of the parts of the door are important to providing security to the door and changes to one part may affect the integrity and security of another part so careful planning needs to be done when considering changes to any door part.

A door is used to provide security to anything that is located behind the door. In order to provide any sense of security the door has to be able to resist physical damage from such things as physical force, fires, explosions, etc.

Door frames is the part of the door that connects the door to the wall. Doors are hung on a frame using some type of hinge. The frame is anchored to the wall and the frame provides a way for the lock to connect to the wall to secure the door from unauthorized entry. The anchoring method used to anchor the door frame to the wall is usually done by screwing it to the wall or by casting the frame especially metal frames into the concrete of the wall as it is being poured. Frames are also built into stud partitions and sometimes the frames are welded to a wall if the wall is metal or the concrete is end capped with steel channels.

The door hinge is used to hang the door in the frame and also allows for opening and closing of the door. The hinge allows for swinging motion of the door

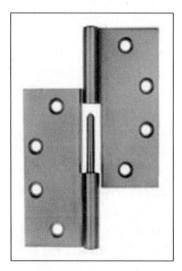

FIGURE 11-1 McKinney two knuckle door hinge

to take place. Hinges are made of two steel plates held together by a hinge pin. To hang the door one hinge plate is mounted on the door frame and the other hinge plate is mounted on the door. Figure 11-1 shows a hinge.

Intrusion Detection and Security for Doors

As discussed in Chapter 7 there are several types of door alarm switches used to detect an intruder. The list below is the types of door contact switches used to detect intruders. For details about how they work see Chapter 7.

1. Mechanical contact switches

2. Magnetic switches

3. Balanced magnetic switches

The door contact switches are usually used in conjunction with another intrusion technology such as motion sensors. The reason for using dual technologies when planning and installing intrusion detection is to make sure that there is a backup if one system fails to detect the intruder. For example, the intruder may be able to defeat the door contact switches but the motion sensors will detect the intruder as they move past the compromised door and contact switch.

Another sensor to use with the door contact switch is some type of pressure switch usually in the a mat concealed on the floor just inside the door so the intruder compromises the door switch and door the pressure switch will detect the intrusion.

Wall vibration sensors are sometimes used to detect the vibrations caused by someone forcing the door for entry. The vibration may caused by the tools used to spread the frame or pop the lock.

Hinges

Other security measures that can be taken to enhance the security of a door include the use of hinge pins or welded hinges to prevent easy removable of the exposed hinge pins. Hinges are considered adequate for security based on the materials of construction and their size. A larger hinge affords more protection since it requires more mass that must be bent or removed before entry is gained by forcing the hinge. Steel is the strongest of the materials that hinges are made from and is the preferred material for security. There are several other factors to be considered for increasing the security of hinges:

1. The hinge should be located on the inside of the door rather than on the exterior where is vulnerable to being removed to gain entry.

2. How the hinge plates are anchored to the frame and the door. To increase security the hinge plates should be secured to the frame and the door using

machine screws and in some cases the hinge can be welded to the door frame providing additional security.

3. Exposed exterior hinges should be pinned or spot welded to prevent easy removal. Non-removable hinge pins can also be used for exterior hinges. The non-removable hinge pin is held in place with a set screw that is screwed through the hinge plate and can only be removed when the door is opened. Another option is the safety stud which is a projection or stud that is built into one plate of the hinge an when the door is closed the safety stud fits into a cavity in the other hinge plate. Even the hinge pin is removed the stud will hold the door in place. Finally there is what is known as a fast riveted pin. The fast riveted pin is actually a pin that is longer than the hinge plates and is flattened so the pin is wider than the pin hole and cannot be removed without cutting the pin.

It is better to have the hinge pins on the inside of the door rather on the outside where they are vulnerable to attack and compromise. Pinning the hinges prevents separation of the two hinge plates which will allow for removing the door from the frame.

Spot welding the hinges to prevent the removal of the hinge pin is another method to secure exterior facing hinges. So the hinge pin plates need to be securely fastened to the door frame. Toe fastened the hinge plates to the door frame use steel hinges and machine screws which provide more strength than steel screws. Also a long screw can be inserted into the hinge plate and fastened to the door frame and then cut the head of the screw off to prevent easy removal.

Frames

Door frames should be anchored to the wall by screwing, welding, or casting the frame into the concrete as the walls are being poured. Since the frame is prone to prying the screws should be of sufficient length to prevent easy removal. This is usually 3 inches or more in length.

A common method for gaining entry through a door is to spread the frame. This works when there is sufficient "play" within the wall structure that the frame is anchored to. When the frame is spread enough the lock will be pulled from the strike plate and the door will be compromised. To prevent this from occurring it is advisable to strength the area around the frame by filling it in with a sturdy material to prevent the spreading of the frame. This not a problem when a metal frame is set in concrete.

Doors

The door should be a metal or solid core wood door. To increase the strength of a semi solid core metal or 1/2 inch sheet of plywood can be added to both sides of the door. Doors can also be reinforced by adding steel stiffeners into the core to add rigidity and strength. The added rigidity will increase the door's resistance to direct force by hitting the door with heavy blunt tools like a sledge hammer.

Doors with glass side panels should use a 1/2 inch piece of Lexan or Plexiglass instead of the glazed glass. This will add to the integrity of the door by making it harder to penetrate the "glass" side panels to gain entry.

Security doors are doors that are reinforced so that damage to them is prevented or minimal and will hinder easy entry by unauthorized people. By reinforcing exterior doors you add to the time factor of slowing an intruder down so that detection becomes more likely. Most security doors are metal or a wood door with a metal frame or core.

There are security doors that provide fire, blast, and bullet resistance. To receive the UL 752 rating for being bullet resistant, the door and frame are rated together so if you just replace the door with a security door and not the frame you will not meet the standards of UL 752. The same holds true for receiving a "labeled" fire door. The rating is applied to the door, frame, and anchoring of the door frame. The door and frame are tested and rated as one unit.

The fire resistance rating of doors typically goes from 20 minutes to 120 minutes or more. Most doors are rated for 20 minutes and that means it take 20 minutes for the door to fail during a fire. More about fire resistance ratings and tests is in Chapter 17.

The bullet resistance rating is based on the door's ability to absorb the impact of a bullet. A bullet unlike a blast exerts its pressure over a small area of the door's surface. Bullet resistant doors are similar in construction to blast resistant doors since both contain a hollow inner cavity under an exterior of heavy duty steel plates, or a solid wooden frame. The inner cavity contains impact-absorbing material such as fiberglass, polyurethane fiber, or Mylar to help maintain the integrity of the door when it is struck by a bullet. The test for rating doors for bullet resistance is done according to UL 752 weapons criteria. The rating is based on the doors ability to withstand bullets form different weapons and that includes handguns to rifles and high-powered weapons. See table 11-1 for the ratings. The lower the rating the lower the power of the weapon, for example, ratings 1–3 are for handguns. Ratings 1 and 2 are for .38 caliber handguns and rating 3 is for a .44 magnum handgun. The ratings from 4 and above are for high powered weapons.

The blast resistance doors are made of two metal plates enclosing a hallow cavity. There is an interior structure in the cavity that is made from reinforced steel ribbing or a steel frame. As in the case of the bullet resistant door void space is filled fire resistant material to give the door a fire resistance rating as well. The blast resistant door is installed as an entire doorway and this includes the steel frame, door and blast resistant hinges and blast resistant locking hardware.

Blast resistant doors are rated according to the strength of the blast they are designed to withstand. The blast is measured in pounds per square inch (psi) or pounds per square foot (psf). The rule of thumb is the thicker and heavier the door the higher the blast rating. With new materials of construction on the market today the rule of thumb is no longer true. There are materials that are stronger and offer greater blast resistance and they are not thicker or heavier.

DESIGN CONSIDERATIONS FOR DOORS AND WINDOWS

Depending on the doors and windows chosen for the project design specifications need to be outlined. The following outline can be used as a guide to help preparing the specifications for the doors and windows.

PART 1 GENERAL

1.1 RELATED DOCUMENTS

1.2 GENERAL REQUIREMENTS

1.3 SUBMITTALS

1.4 QUALITY ASSURANCE

1.5 DELIVERY, STORAGE AND HANDLING

1.6 WARRANTY

PART 2 PRODUCTS

This part outlines the type of windows and doors including the materials of construction the dimensions, diameter, etc. This section also outlines finishes, etc.

PART 3 EXECUTION

3.1 EXAMINATION

3.2 INSTALLATION

3.3 FIELD QUALITY CONTROL

The related documents section outlines what other sections or documents are related to this document or are included in other sections of the document in the sections that follow and any related sections. The general requirements section outlines what is required for the project.

The submittals section outlines what is expected to be presented:

• Drawings and how many copies

• Hardware (locks) and door and window schedule

- Copies of approved hardware, window and door material schedule for the subcontractors (windows and door installer)

- Installation instructions

- Other

The section on quality assurance addresses such things as:

- The length of time the installer has been in business

- Contractor's license number

- Attend a pre-installation meeting

- Ensure door and window material meets the standards set forth in the submittals.

Sample design specifications for window and door design/build installation are presented below:

DESIGN/BUILD - OUTLINE SPECIFICATIONS FOR DOORS AND WINDOWS

The Qualifications section provides specific clarification of scope issues not necessarily identified in the Outline Specifications.

If a specific material or brand name product has been referenced, it is only to show the quality of material being used. In the final specification and during construction of this project, "or equal" products may be installed.

DIVISION 01 - GENERAL REQUIREMENTS

01001 GENERAL

    A. All facilities, labor, material, equipment, and design services that are typically required for the completion of the Work are included in this design/build proposal. All Work shall comply with the applicable federal, state and local requirements.

    B. All sections in the Outline Specifications carry a one (1) year Standard Construction Warranty and Guarantee against labor and material defects including Work performed by subcontractors. All equipment warranties greater than one (1) year will be passed to the Owner at project completion.

01002 INSURANCE AND BONDS

Design/Builder's Liability Insurance:

    A. Design/Builder shall purchase and maintain in a company or companies authorized to do business in the state in which the Work is located such insurance as will protect the Design/Builder from claims set forth below which may arise out of or result from operations under the Contract by the Design/Builder or a subcontractor of the Design Builder, or by anyone directly or indirectly employed by any of them, including:

1. Claims under workers' or workmen's compensation, disability benefit and other similar employee benefit laws which are applicable to the Work to be performed;
2. Claims for damages because of bodily injury, occupational sickness or disease, or death of the Design/Builder's employees under any applicable employer's liability law;
3. Claims for damages because of bodily injury, sickness or disease, or death of persons other than the Design/Builder's employees;
4. Claims for damages covered by usual personal injury liability coverage which are sustained by a person as a result of an offense directly or indirectly related to employment of such person by the Design/Builder;
5. Claims for damages, other than to the Work at the site, because of injury to or destruction of tangible property, and
6. Claims for damages for bodily injury of death of a person or property damage arising out of ownership, maintenance or use of a motor vehicle.

B. The insurance required by the above subparagraph shall be written for not less than limits of liability specified in the insurance certificates submitted with the bid of _____.

C. The Design/Builder's liability insurance shall include contractual liability insurance applicable to the Design/Builder's obligations under AIA A191 Part 2, Paragraph 11.7.

D. Certificates of Insurance shall be delivered to the Owner prior to commencement of design and construction. These Certificates, as well as insurance policies required by this Paragraph, shall contain a provision that coverage will not be canceled or allowed to expire until at least thirty day's prior written notice has been given to the Owner.

E. Builder's Risk Insurance can be provided by the Design/Builder, but is not included in the bid.

Design/Builder's Errors and Omissions Insurance:

A. Design/Builder shall carry Architects and Engineers Professional Liability insurance with the following limits (example only):
1. $2,000,000 per Claim
2. $2,000,000 Aggregate
3. $100,000 S.I.R.

Performance & Payment Bonds:

    A. Design/Builder shall provide a Payment and Performance Bond for the overall construction project value.

    B. Design/Builder's Surety will assume no responsibility for any design work performed in connection with this project.

01003 ALLOWANCES

    A. Allowances refer to items of scope or cost which have not been sufficiently defined to date. The stipulated Allowance amount has been included in the base proposal price. Actual billings against these items will be supported by supplier and subcontractor invoices. Actual costs of less than the original Allowance will result in a reduction of base contract price. Actual costs greater than the original Allowance will be billed at cost plus a 15% General Contractor's Fee and result in an increase to the base contract price. Allowance items if anticipated are clearly noted in the Construction Budget Summary.

01004 DESIGN AND SUPERVISION

    A. This proposal includes all required architectural, structural, plumbing, mechanical and electrical engineering design with stamped drawings and corresponding specifications for the garage structure. The cost associated with peer review by the State of _____ is also included.

    B. Supervision:

        1. Design/Builder will assign a Project Manager to this job that will be responsible for all project activities from design through construction including coordination with the Owner, Regulatory Agencies, other Prime Contractors, etc.

        2. Design/Builder will assign, on site, a full-time superintendent solely for this project.

01050 FIELD ENGINEERING

    A. Field engineering services required for proper completion of the Work including but not limited to:

        1. Extend base lines and elevations from initial site survey provided by owner.

        2. Locate and protect control points before starting work on the site.

        3. Layout of all window and door frames.

01310 PROJECT SCHEDULE

    A. Design/Builder will provide an overall design and construction schedule. The schedule will be updated monthly.

01500 TEMPORARY FACILITIES AND CONTROLS

A. Temporary facilities and controls needed for the Work including but not limited to:
1. Telephone service for the Design/Builder office trailer.
2. Portable sanitary facilities located on the site for Design/Builder personnel only.
3. Field offices/sheds for Design/Builder construction and office personnel.
4. Temporary electric power and lighting connection to an existing supply within 25' of the site. Metered electricity usage is at Design/Builder's expense.
5. Temporary construction water connection to an existing supply within 25' of the site. Metered water usage is at Design/Builder's expense.

B. Temporary barricades:
1. Elevated deck edge fall protection and deck opening protection.
2. Safety barricades around major excavations in accordance with OSHA guidelines including warning tape and lighted flashers if required.
3. Temporary barricades, traffic barriers, safety lighting etc. if required for partial occupancy are not included in this proposal. The scope of services can be added at a future time when it is defined.

C. Temporary chain link fencing, 6'-0" high including construction safety signs and warnings for the parking garage site is included. Removal at project completion.

01700 CONTRACT CLOSEOUT

A. To provide an orderly and efficient transfer of the completed Work, upon substantial completion of all work:
1. The project will be inspected with representatives of the Owner and Design/Builder for the purpose of itemizing a final punch list.
2. The project will be turned over broom clean and ready for use.
3. Closeout submittal to include but not be limited to:
   a. Project record documents i.e. "as built" drawings, specifications, shop drawings, etc.
   b. Operation and maintenance manuals as available.
   c. Warranties and bonds.
   d. Keying and keying schedule.
   e. Spare parts and material extra stock.
   f. Release of liens.
   g. List of subcontractors, service organizations and principal vendors.

01710 CLEANING
   A. Throughout the construction period, Design/Builder will maintain the building and site in a standard of cleanliness consistent with safe and efficient construction operations.
      1. Design/Builder will provide dumpsters for the use of all trades under its contract on this project.
      2. All storm drains will be protected from debris during construction.
   B. Final cleaning of the structure.
      1. Remove all trash associated with the installation work.
      2. Clean and wash all glass inside and out.
      3. Clean and all wrappings on door and window frames.
      4. Clean all floors around work area of debris like screws, etc.

DIVISION 02 – SITE WORK

02110 SITE PREPARATION
   A. The door and window openings site will be cleared and frames will be anchored to the existing structure by the Design/Builder.

DIVISION 03 – WINDOWS and FRAMES

03100 WINDOW FRAMES
   A. Provide frames for all cast-in-place frames within the structure.
      1. Structure walls.
      2. All frames will have some type of locking mechanism for operating windows.

03200 CONCRETE REINFORCEMENT
   A. Shop fabricated non-epoxy coated reinforcing bars including all required accessories for all cast-in-place concrete frames, into the walls.
   B. Welded wire fabric (not epoxy coated):
      1. 6×6 - $W1.4 \times W1.4$ for grade level pads for stairs and utility rooms.
      2. 6×6 - $W2.1 \times W2.1$ for slabs at maintenance areas.
   C. Bolsters, chairs, spacers and other devices for spacing, supporting and fastening frames reinforcement in place.

03300 CAST-IN-PLACE FRAMES
   A. Reinforced concrete work includes pile cap foundations, raised slabs for the stair pads and utility room floor, foundation walls and miscellaneous concrete work.
      1. Standard gray, ready mix concrete for all cast-in-place frame requirements.
      2. 4,000 psi concrete or greater will be used for all slabs, foundations, and walls.

3. Form finish for all exposed concrete with fins removed, snap tie holes filled and honeycomb repaired.

4. All work in accordance with ACI Standards and Procedures.

B. Cast-in-place concrete forms for frames and closure strips at cross joints of precast double tees.

03400 WINDOW GLAZING

A. Any glass in the exterior windows shall be laminated and be bullet resistant for the front lobby area meeting the requirements of UL 752.

B. Window glazing shall also meet the specifications for blast protection as outlined in ASTME E330-97e1, the Uniform Building Code (UBC), and any other applicable codes and standards.

03500 INTRUSION DETECTION

A. Intrusion detection design and installation will be provided by others.

B. Provide holes and string to make connections for the wires for the intrusion detection system in the frame during installation of the frame.

DIVISION 04 – DOORS

04200 DOOR FRAMES

A. Wood door frames will be installed meeting the following criteria:
1. Hollow Walls:
   a. The space will be reinforced to minimize the threat from spreading the frame.
2. Anchoring the frame:
   a. The frame will be anchored
   b. Screws 3 inches or greater in length shall be used to anchor the frame to the wall.

B. Metal door frames shall meet the following criteria:
1. _____

DIVISION 05 – HINGES

05500 HINGES

A. All hinges shall meet the following minimum criteria
1. All hinge pins shall be on the inside of the door and not visible or accessible from the exterior of the door unless:

B. The hinges are spot welded

C. Fast riveted

D. Non-removable hinge pin.

E. Safety stud

F. Hinges shall be fastened to the wall and door using machine screws.

05600 LOCKING HARDWARE
   A. Locking devices shall meet the requirements set forth in the locking and hardware bid specifications.

DIVISION 06 – WOOD AND PLASTICS

06100 ROUGH CARPENTRY
   A. Wood, nails, bolts, screws, framing anchors and other rough hardware and other items needed to complete the Work requirements for form-work, wood blocking, framing, cants, etc., required to properly install all doors, frames, finish hardware, roofing, glass and glazing.

DIVISION 07 – THERMAL AND MOISTURE CONTROL

07200 BUILDING INSULATION
   A. Blanket insulation at exterior walls.
   B. Board insulation below topping at office areas.

07270 FIRESTOPPING
   A. Fire rated doors and frames shall be used in all fire-rated partitions and areas.
   B. Fire rated sealants at all penetrations of fire-rated partitions, floors, and ceilings.

07920 CAULKING AND SEALANTS
   A. Caulk and sealant joints to provide a positive barrier against passage of moisture and air.
      1. Control joints between precast double tees.
      2. Precast deck pour strips at interface of precast double tees and cross joints.
      3. Precast tee/precast spandrel interface.
      4. Sealant around all columns penetrating parking decks.
      5. Caulking of all door frames.
      6. Standard color for all caulks and sealants.
      7. Joint filler to be 1/2" thick premold.
      8. Caulking will be two part urethane by.

DIVISION 08 – DOORS, WINDOWS AND GLASS

08110 STANDARD STEEL DOORS AND FRAMES
   A. 18 gauge hollow metal door and hollow metal frame, fire ratings as required by code.

08200 FLASH WOOD DOORS
   A. Five-ply solid core flush wood doors.

08710 FINISH HARDWARE

    A. Butts, hinges, locksets, latchsets, dead bolts, closures, push plates, door pulls, exit devices, door stops and tamper-proof screws, as required, for all doors stated in Sections 08110 and 08200.

    B. Hardware finish shall be US32D - Dull Stainless

    C. Interior hardware to be commercial, medium duty. Exterior hardware to be commercial heavy duty.

DIVISION 09 - FINISHES

09250 GYPSUM BOARD

    A. Gypsum board assemblies, including fire-rated and non-rated partitions, ceilings, and bulkheads.

09900 PAINTING

    A. All doors, frames and window frames will be painted with a standard color finish coat to match the color scheme of the building design.

       1. All doors and frames will be painted to match the building color scheme.

CHAPTER 12

Defense-in-Depth

Defense-in-depth is a term coined by the government to mean an all encompassing, multi-layered approach to security. Like an onion as you peel away one layer of protection there is another layer of protection underneath. The layered approach security is similar in that as you move through one layer there is another directly behind the layer you just removed. Even with Defense-in-Depth as a strategy for implementing security perfectly, 100%, security cannot be achieved. The reason for the layered or Defense-in-Depth approach is simple, all systems can be compromised especially by those who are determined and possess the training, equipment, etc., and have much to gain by entering the facility. The other way systems are compromised is by the people who work at the facility. People will do things un-intentionally or intentionally that will undermine the security in place. Most security compromises are done unintentionally by those who are not educated as to the consequences of their actions will cause a security compromise. Other security compromises are intentional and in most cases are caused by not following policies or procedures, while other compromises are for personal gain or revenge. Not following policies or procedures are a big problem and the only way to ensure that there is compliance awareness training and consequences for not complying are necessary. An unintentional compromise of security for example, occurs when someone is "being helpful" and holds an access controlled door open for a fellow employee known or unknown and allowing that person to enter the facility, building, secure area, etc. People also block open doors so they can exit and enter again without a badge or key. An example of an intentional compromise of security would by the copying or emailing of proprietary information for the purpose of selling it to a competitor for personal gain or to get a job at a competitor. By doing these things the security systems are compromised. So people are an important part of the security system.

Defense-in–depth is overall and encompassing approach to security using a number of layers for implementing security at a facility, building, etc. The concept of "Defense-in-Depth" includes the following security components:

1. People

2. Physical security

3. Electronic systems (technology)

4. Procedures

PEOPLE AND DEFENSE-IN-DEPTH

The people part of the layered approach consists of training the personnel assigned to a location, facility, etc. and letting them know their role in security and that they are an important part of the overall security program. It is important to spend the time "selling security" through security awareness training and other means to convey the message that people are an integral part of the security program. People as previously stated are also the weakest link in the security program since they can easily compromise electronic systems by holding doors open or propping the doors open. Sometimes people do things that are unintentional but still compromise security. This could be as simple as loaning an access card to a fellow employee because they forgot their card at their desk. The problem is the person lending the access card may have access to locations the person the card is given to may not for security reasons. This simple act can put the facility at risk. Even doors that are alarmed are propped open. To minimize the effect from people, security awareness and training sessions are conducted as is disciplinary action for non-compliance.

Establishing policies that address security are important to the success of the facility's security plan. Not only must the policies be developed they must also be communicated to the people at the facility so they know what is expected. The purpose of the policies is to help shore up the weakest link in security which is the people. So people are an important part in the success of the Defense-in-Depth or any approach to security. Without their cooperation all the best security plans and technology will fail. Policies and procedures need to be communicated to the organization.

There are other things that can be done but since this book is about the architectural features of security we will move on to the other components of Defense-in-Depth which are the physical security features.

Physical Security

The design of the physical security components of Defense-in-Depth is the basis of the book. An important part of planning for physical security is to determine which one or combinations of the following is the objective:

1. Deter

2. Detect

3. Delay

4. Response

All physical components address one or more of the four elements listed above. For example, some physical security features such as the use of three or four rolls of concertina wire and two fences with a clear zone in between with armed guards watching the fence line for prison is a deterrent to the inmates from attempting an escape through the fence. Another physical security such as a fence intrusion detection system will detect anyone attempting to climb, cut or otherwise compromise the fence.

A delaying tactic would be to add the concertina wire on a fence over eight feet high with a clear zone and another fence with rows of concertina wire on a fence over eight feet high. Each fence and concertina wire adds another layer for an intruder to tackle thereby slowing him or her down.

Response is used in conjunction with intrusion detection and delaying. The response can be from on-site security personnel or local law enforcement by automatic alarm.

Physical security is an important part of facility planning process and should be a part of the design process. It is better and more cost effective to design-in and add security into the initial facility design and construction rather than add it later as a retrofit. Retrofitting is costly because labor will cost more to add card readers, electronic door locks, instruction detection, and CCTV cameras, due to the need to run cables in areas that are hard to get to after the construction is completed. These spaces include door frames that are cast in concrete, window frames cast in concrete, etc. It is more difficult to run the cables for the intrusion device or electric lock in a door when the surrounding wall is concrete. This adds to the cost because it will take longer to "fish" the cable for the lock and the card reader for an access control door due to the concrete. Physical security like any building or site improvements takes planning to ensure that the proper systems are put in place to address the threats and vulnerabilities of the facility location or proposed location of the facility. As we have seen so far, physical security has many facets. Below is a list of the physical security elements that are important to providing Defense-in-Depth security to a facility:

1. Perimeter fence

2. Protective barriers

3. Protective lighting

4. Access control

5. Intrusion detection

6. CCTV

7. Locks and keys

8. Windows and doors

9. Blast and bullet resistant protection

10. Fire protection

11. Protected zones

IMPLEMENTING THE PHYSICAL SECURITY

To implement the Defense-in-Depth strategy, especially the physical security components, you must do the following:

1. First, perform an assessment to identify the threats.

2. Second, perform a vulnerability analysis so it can be determined what threats are the most likely to occur.

3. Third, you need to develop a plan for mitigating the most serious threats by implementing the proper countermeasures to minimize the risk. Chapter 2 details the threat and vulnerability assessments and how to categorize the risk.

4. Last, develop the physical security countermeasures designed to address and minimize the threat.

The Defense-in-Depth strategy not only addresses the threats from intruders but also from those who have the authority to enter the site and are set on doing harm, damage or theft to the facility and the personnel. Physical security counter measures include the items listed above which are the elements that make up physical security.

The natural barriers are the first line of defense. Natural barriers include the following as previously stated in Chapter 4:

• Lakes

• Rivers

• Rugged terrain

THE PERIMETER FENCE AND NATURAL BARRIERS

The design of the physical security systems should incorporate the natural barriers if there are any on the site. The facility layout can be influenced by the natural barriers on the site that the facility will be constructed. For example, the most important part of the facility, i.e. where secret, special proprietary equipment will be located should be placed where the physical barriers will serve as another layer of security and be the first line of protection such as a sheer cliff in the rear of the property that goes down to the ocean. The cliff will make it very hard for an intruder attempting to use the cliff to enter the facility grounds undetected. To enhance the protection provided by the natural barrier, the cliff, microwave detection can be used or a perimeter fence detection system or both can be used. The addition of the intrusion detection system will provide another layer and an early warning system that an intruder is attempting to gain entry.

The perimeter fence has a role in the physical security of the facility but not to stop someone from entering the location. Remember a chain link fence will not stop someone, in other words the fence is not a good delaying tactic but can be used to detect the intruder by using a fence detection system. In most cases the chain link fence will not even slow down an intruder and cannot be considered as a delaying tactic. There are perimeter fences like the 8-foot wrought iron fence with outward pointing spade like pickets that are harder to compromise and will slow down an intruder and when used with detection may provide a good method for delaying and detection. Few fences other than those used to surround prisons or military installations will be an affective deterrent to an intruder. Most jurisdictions do not permit the use of razor or concertina wire on fences for commercial properties. Chapter 3 has more details about fence types and vulnerabilities.

Back to our example, the area just near the cliff's edge would be a wrought iron fence with sensors, most likely microwave, just before the fence line and sensors on the fence itself to detect any intruders that are attempting to climb or cut through the fence. The tripping of an alarm sensor will alert security which will also necessitate a response to the incident to determine the reason for the alarm.

Natural barriers can be used to enhance security and should be a part of the initial design process to make sure the barriers are used to their fullest. Some natural barriers can be used as a deterrent to intruders especially for the not-so-determined ones. The cliff in our example may deter an intruder since the concentration of security will be on the other three sides of the facility which more likely increase the chances of detection. When using natural barriers to enhance security, consideration must be given to maintaining the clear zone around the perimeter fence line. There is a zone of 5 feet on either side where there are no obstructions for an intruder to hide to evade detection.

PROTECTIVE LIGHTING

The lighting in the rear of the facility would be bright enough to be able to see an intruder's face and not just an image. The lighting for the exterior of the facility should also include motion–senor-operated glare lighting that illuminates out from the facility and will shine directly into the eyes of an intruder but will not cast the security officers inside the perimeter fence in the light. This will give the security officers the advantage of seeing the intruders and the intruders not being able to see the security officers because of the glare lighting. Normal exterior lighting should be bright and not cast shadows. The security lighting should cover the entire area and not provide areas that are dark and provide cover for an intruder to move about without detection. There are various types of lighting used for security. Choose the lighting that will meet the needs of the facility. In our example the lighting should be connected to emergency back up power so, if there is a loss power from a storm, electrical failure or the deliberate cutting of power to the facility, the lights will still provide the proper illumination for the facility. Chapter 5 outlines the requirements for protective lighting.

ACCESS CONTROL

Access control adds another layer and way to keep unauthorized people from entering the facility. The access control system allows those who have authorized access to an area to enter by unlocking the door when a card, biometric, or PIN is presented to the reader. The reader will read the information on the card that is presented to the reader usually swiped or inserted for magnetic strip type cards. Then the information is checked with information stored in the access control system's data base to see if the card has a valid access to the area. If there is a valid access the door is unlocked permitting the person to enter. If there is not a valid access the door will not unlock and a report is generated. For those that have authorized access there is a method to track the access. Doors with access control have door switches and will alarm if the door is held open too long. The "open too long" time is decided in the access control system data base. For entry the time is usually set to allow a person with a valid entry card enough time to enter through the door. The time will vary and most access control systems have set times for the valid entry times.

Doors that are operated by an access control system usually have CCTV surveillance to make sure that the person presenting the access control card to the door's reader is in fact the person who is presenting the card. This is accomplishing by matching the picture on the card from the access control data base and the CCTV image of the person presenting the card. If there is not a match an alarm is sent to the console for appropriate action and if there is a match the door is unlocked.

Access has advantages to the mechanical locks and keys because there is no need to keep a record of who has keys. The access control data base will keep the records and will also control who has access to what areas of the facility. Another advantage is the access control system will keep record of who entered which and at what time.

Sometimes dual technologies are used to grant access to an area or door. This follows the tenant in security of access being granted on one or more of the following tenants of access control:

1. Something you have like an access card, fob, etc.

2. Something you know such as a PIN for a keypad

3. Something you are like biometrics

Sometimes access control is granted using dual technologies to unlock the door. This provides more layers. The two technologies can include an access card and biometrics like hand geometry or a retina scan. The access card swipe is used to pull up a template for the second technology to be compared against. The use of dual access control technologies provides at least two layers before entry is permitted so if one fails or is compromised the person will not be granted access without the second one like the retina scan and a card swipe before entry is granted. This will minimize the possibility that an employee who has access will have their card stolen and an intruder will use the card to gain entry to a sensitive area because the biometric retina scan cannot be compromised.

INTRUSION DETECTION

Intrusion detection systems play an important role in alerting the facility that an intruder has gained entry. The intrusion detection system is the electronic part of Defense-in-Depth. The systems help increase the chances that an intruder will be detected and stopped before any damage is done or anything is lost. Think of the intrusion detection system like radar as an early warning device to let the security officers or others know that an intruder has gained or is attempting to gain entry to the facility. We have discussed perimeter intrusion detection earlier in the chapter. Now we will move from perimeter intrusion detection to the facility intrusion detection. Facility intrusion includes some the following devices:

- Window and door contact switches

- Glass break sensors

- Vibration sensors

- Microwave

- Photoelectric beams

- Infrared motion sensors

- Ultrasonic

- Pressure mats

There are more devices than those named above and Chapter 7 has more devices and information about how the devices work. It is advisable that several different devices be used to protect an area. The reason is simple if one fails, or is compromised, than another device will detect the presence of an intruder or the attempt to gain entry to the facility. In most cases the devices are used as dual technologies for example window contact switches used in conjunction with motion sensors. If the intruder cuts the glass rather breaking it the window contacts or glass sensor will not detect the intrusion but the motion sensor will. The same can be said for door contact switches and motion sensors it the door switch is compromised then the motion sensor will detect the intrusion.

Layers of intrusion detection systems (dual technologies) will help in making penetrating the facility harder. The harder you make the target the more likely except for the determined few, most intruders will think twice about attempting to gain entry for fear of being detected. After all that is the purpose of Defense-in-Depth, to make the target harder and not so easy to compromise.

CCTV

The use of CCTV will assist by providing surveillance of the perimeter. The CCTV cameras should be set to record with motion. The cameras would go into "alarm" and begin recording. The CCTV system should be connected to the security console or monitoring station. The CCTV system will record on a hard drive using a DVR (digital video recorder). The camera would record when there is a change in the field of vision is detected like an intruder moving toward the facility. Since the cameras will be used outdoors for nighttime recording as well as daytime recording, it is advisable to use a camera lens that is capable of recording in low light. These types of cameras usually will record in color when there is sufficient light and in black and white in low light. Chapter 9 provides more insight into CCTV systems.

Well-designed CCTV systems will provide an extra set of "eyes" to help ensure that intruders are detected that may otherwise slip past a layer of security such as a perimeter fence or outdoor intrusion detection device like microwave sensors.

LOCKS AND KEYS

To help secure the facility, tight control should be maintained for locks and keys. The best types of locks to enhance security are ones where the keys cannot be duplicated. Most major lock manufacturers have a security lock that has keys that cannot be duplicated by any locksmith, since special blanks are used and a special machine is used to cut the keys.

Key control is an important and often overlooked part of security. A good key control program will help when someone leaves the company since an accounting of the keys can be done and the lock cores can be changed easily and new keys issued to the right people so there is minimal if any disruption. The key control program should account for all those persons that are issued keys. The best way to track who has keys and what the keys will unlock is to use some kind of automated system. More can found about locks and keys in Chapter 10.

Some systems for key control, especially in a temporary environment will require a lock box. The old systems had a sign-in-and out sheet to account for keys. The newer lock boxes can be opened and keys removed using a driver's license or an access control card from someone who has authorization to remove the key. The driver's license or card access will activate the electronics and release the key and the cards will stay in the box's slot under the key storage space until the keys are returned. This is a good to way to make sure the keys are returned. With the old sign-in-and-out sheets it was difficult to account for the keys.

WINDOWS AND DOORS

The windows and doors of a facility are weak points in the perimeter of the outer walls. Windows can be easy entry points for an intruder if they are not properly protected. All exterior windows should have contact switches if the windows are operable if not the windows should have a unbreakable window pane of Plexiglass or Lexan instead of glass to prevent easy breakage or cutting of the window to gain entry.

Exterior doors should be protected using contact switches. For example balanced magnetic switches will send an alert if contact is broken and the switches are not as easily compromised as mechanical contact switches. In keeping with the layered approach that is Defense-in-Depth, you would also add infrared motion sensors so if the door switches are compromised the motion sensors will detect the intruder. Other combinations of sensors will work as well. For example, the door switches used in conjunction with ultrasonic sensors, or a photoelectric beam.

Exterior doors should be sturdy so that they cannot be easily compromised. Doors that are used for exit only should not have exterior hardware like door handles to prevent them from being compromised by removing the hardware. All exterior doors should have the hinge pins on the exterior and if this is not possible then the hinges should be pinned, spot welded, or riveted to prevent easy removal. Store front doors used for lobbies and storefronts for aesthetic purposes should have balanced magnetic switches and glass break sensors and motion sensors inside the area of the doors. This will help to detect an intruder that has compromised the glass doors. If electronic access control is used for entry then make sure the REX is set to shunt the alarm only, so a forced exit alarm is not received. Do not set the REX to unlock the door as this will allow someone on the outside to trip the REX and gain entry. Windows and doors and explained in greater detail in Chapter 11.

BLAST AND BULLET RESISTANT PROTECTION

Blast protection has now become an important part of Defense-in-Depth since the recent incidents involving bombs that have destroyed facilities or severely damaged them. To help minimize the damage to surrounding buildings from the effects of a bomb-doors and windows have been developed that provide blast protection.

Windows use a special laminated glass that keeps the window from producing glass shards when a blast occurs. Glass shards cause damage to the window and permit the effects of the blast to be transmitted to the building. The shards of glass become flying missiles and the open window allows debris to enter the building causing damage. Windows that are blast resistant will not shatter during the explosion and will remain intact even though the window is broken and looks like an automobile windshield after an accident.

Windows are also made to be bullet resistant. See Chapter 11 for more details. The windows that are bullet resistant can with stand shots from handguns to high-powered rifles. To make a window, bullet-resistant laminate is used to hold the window together to prevent the bullet from penetrating the window. Lexan and Plexiglass are also used to make a window bullet resistant.

Doors are also made to be bullet and blast resistant. Chapter 11 has more information about doors that are bullet and blast resistant. Adding blast and bullet resistant doors to the facility will help enhance security.

FIRE PROTECTION

Fire protection is an element of Defense-in-Depth because the facility must be protected from damage or destruction by fire. Chapter 17 addresses fire protection in detail. To protect a facility from damage due to fire there are several things that can be done:

1. Design the facility using fire-resistive construction features

2. Include in the design automatic fire detection and suppression systems

3. Develop and implement good fire prevention procedures

By using fire-resistive materials in the construction the risk of a fire totally destroying the facility will be minimized. There still may water and smoke damage but the overall structural damage will be minimal.

In order to protect sensitive documents and equipment that could be damaged by smoke and water, the fire suppression systems should be designed with this in mind. Water fire sprinklers are usually used to protect the facility from complete destruction since these systems are designed to protect the structural features of the building while gaseous fire suppression systems like carbon dioxide and FM 200 systems do not use water to suppress a fire. Dry chemical systems are also available. The gaseous systems especially carbon dioxide are inherently dangerous to life since the system displaces all the oxygen to suppress the fire. The gaseous systems have one major drawback. They are not suited for deep seated fires and do not have any cooling characteristics and any hot surface in contact with combustible materials may cause re-ignition after the gas has dissipated. This is where good fire prevention procedures come into play by limiting the amount of combustibles that are stored in an area protected by a gaseous system.

Fire-resistant safes can be used for storing important papers that may be damaged by fire sprinklers. There are also new sprinkler systems that will shut off when the fire is suppressed and not continue to flow water causing more damage. More about these systems can be found in Chapter 16.

Fire extinguishers are required to be installed by the fire and building codes. Personnel working in the facility should be taught how to use a fire extinguisher to fight small fires to keep them from becoming large and activating the fixed suppression systems. In some facilities and high-rise buildings hose cabinets are required by the fire and building codes. The hose in the cabinet is 1 1/2 inch hose with a plastic adjustable nozzle. The hose like a fire extinguisher is considered a first aid fire fighting appliance. A properly trained person can keep a small fire from becoming a large one and extinguish the fire safely. Facility personnel should be trained in the use of small hose steams as well.

Finally every facility should have an evacuation plan and hold practice evacuation drills at least semi-annually so all the personnel and visitors in the facility will know what to do in the event of an emergency. To detect fires in the early stages smoke detectors are used. The detectors also will activate an alarm so the occupants can safely evacuate.

PROTECTED ZONES

Protected zones are a method for protecting the most sensitive areas of a facility. There can be broken down in the following zones:

• Clear zone

• Controlled zone

• Restricted zone

The clear zone is the 5 feet on both sides of the perimeter fence. The purpose of the clear zone is to have both sides of the perimeter fence visible from in side and outside of the perimeter to detect any intruder that may be attempting to enter the facility. The clear zone traverses the outside public area, outside the perimeter with the controlled zone inside the perimeter. Usually this area has control points such as gates, doors, etc. to control access.

The controlled zone is the area just inside the perimeter. This is where access to the facility is controlled. This can be done with security officers and a gate or an access control system. Visitors enter the facility through the controlled zone. This is the lobby where entry to the facility is secured by a locked, card access controlled door. The lobby is usually staffed by a receptionist or a security officer whose duties are as follows:

- Meet and greet visitors
- Make sure visitors complete the visitor log
- Issues a visitor badge

The lobby is the first point of contact for visitors and must be secured. When planning the lobby layout make sure to include a portal that can be secured. The portal can consist of a swinging door that is locked and controlled by an access card, or a revolving door that is controlled by a card access system. The revolving door is known as "Mantrap" since only one person can enter at time. This will prevent someone with or without a valid access card from entering with someone with a valid access card. The system is designed to stop if two people are detected in the revolving door at the same time. The door will then go into reverse and back out both people to the non-controlled area. This is based on the one card one entry and helps eliminate "tailgating" and "piggybacking" at entry doors that access card controlled.

The restricted zone is an area that contains the most sensitive/or important information or equipment in the facility. The restricted zone is set up to only permit those with a need-to-know access. Not everyone in the facility has access to the restricted zone. Visitors will not have access to the restricted zone and if there is a need they will be escorted at all times.

CHAPTER 13

Secure Areas in a Building

The secure room is one of the secure areas and is designed to be shielded from electromagnetic interference, attack, and information leakage. The purpose of the room is obvious which is to prevent or to make it extremely difficult for listening in on conversations by competitors, governments, etc. for information that is important or secret that could be useful to other than the current holder. This is also known as competitive intelligence in the private sector or spying in the government sector.

Competitive intelligence is a growing concern, especially in today's global market place. Getting and edge on the competition can mean the difference between success and failure for a company. There are legal ways to get competitive intelligence on another company and there are entire books written on the subject. For our discussion the point is that it does occur and not all companies around the world obtain the information on a competitor. Some will use the techniques that government intelligence agencies use, like electronic surveillance. This is why some companies in highly competitive industries are concerned and will use measures to help protect their most valuable secrets. One of the measures used is to design and construct secure rooms where business can conduct meetings without the information being "leaked" to the outside through electromagnetic waves and vibrations through exterior windows. Also, the secure rooms that are used for sensitive research can have access controlled to make sure that unauthorized company employees or others do not have access. Everything that is taken into the room and carried out of the room is closely inspected, including the employees themselves.

Think of the secure room as a room within a room. It is a vault not unlike a bank vault except the room does not hold money but does contain valuable information, equipment, secure meeting room, etc. The room is used to prevent communications during important meetings from being "leaked out". All conversations during meetings produces electromagnetic waves and these waves can be captured with the proper equipment. The electromagnetic waves will cause the windows, if there are any in the meeting room, to vibrate. It is this vibration which is the electromagnetic waves that are captured by "listening" devices. To be effective the secure room should be located and built without any special attention being drawn to the project. In other words the design and construction of a secure room should be anonymous.

There are also what is known as secure areas. These areas are usually found in warehouses and are used to store high value cargo or products. High value cargo includes, DVD players, plasma screen TVs, computers, etc. The area is a fenced area with the fence that is special mesh material that cannot be cut with wire or bolt cutters that extends from the floor to the ceiling. The entrance to the fenced in or caged area is what is known as a "man door" and the door is controlled by an access control card. The caged area has alarms and CCTV monitoring so any attempt to try and enter the secure area will be detected.

This chapter will discuss the design and construction of the secure room and the secure area.

DESIGN AND CONSTRUCTION OF THE SECURE ROOM

The secure room design and construction is different than the rest of the facility since the room's purpose is to more secure than the rest of the facility. The secure room is considered a physical security countermeasure that is designed to thwart intruders and those that are intent on stealing sensitive information or designs of special equipment.

The following are the design considerations for the secure room:

1. Keep the project low key and don't draw attention to it. Make sure that are not any signs stating that sensitive information or equipment is located in the facility or exactly where the information or equipment is located within the facility.

2. The number of exterior doors to the secure room should be minimized. There should be only one or two exterior doors to the area. The number of doors will depend on the square footage, whether there are fire sprinklers in the room and building, etc. Make sure that there is compliance with the local fire and building codes relating to life safety.

3. The doors to the room should be solid, fire resistive, in plain sight of the security staff and never be permitted to be blocked open. The solid wood door should by at least 1 3/4 inches thick. The wood door should be covered with metal cladding completely around the entire door, front and back.

4. To limit access and to know who has entered the room, there should be dual technology card access system to the room. The dual technology

would include a card swipe and a biometric device such as a retina scan. The door should also be a "mantrap" design to allow only one person per card to enter.

5. To know how long someone was in the secure room, there should be a card reader for exiting as well.

6. The room should not have excessive exterior windows. Any windows should have locks on them.

7. The doors and the room should be monitored by CCTV.

8. The walls should extend to the full height, that is to the bottom of the roof deck or plate of the floor above. The ceiling and walls should be constructed of rated material. The interior walls that are constructed of drywall should have wire mesh inserted between the layers of drywall. This will help prevent someone from simply going through the wall to avoid tackling a secure door and frame.

9. The room, doors, and any windows should by monitored by an intrusion detection system.

10. Keys and combinations for window, door, file, and other locks shall be maintained by appropriate authorities to ensure there is no breach. When someone leaves, all the locks need to be changed as well as combinations to prevent compromises.

11. Alarms to alert when any piece of equipment is disconnected from the system

12. All ducts, pipes, and vents that pass through the security room and are 96 square inches or larger must be protected by bars or grills or an instruction detection system must be installed. If bars are chosen then the bars must be 1/2 inches in diameter and welded in place 6 inches on center. If grills are used they must be 9–gauge expanded steel.

13. If the room is a vault then the following criteria as outlined by the Federal Government's Manual on "Physical Security Standards for Sensitive Compartmented Information Facilities" by the Director of Central Intelligence Directive (DCID) must be met. The manual sets the standard for all government SCIFs (Standards for Sensitive Compartmented Information Facilities).
    a. Vault Construction Criteria
        1. Reinforced Concrete Construction: Walls, floor, and ceiling will be a minimum thickness of eight inches of reinforced concrete. The concrete mixture will have a comprehensive strength rating of at least 2,500 psi. Reinforcing will be accomplished with steel reinforcing

rods, a minimum of 5/8 inches in diameter, positioned centralized in the concrete pour and spaced horizontally and vertically six inches on center; rods will be tied or welded at the intersections. The reinforcing is to be anchored into the ceiling and floor to a minimum depth of one-half the thickness of the adjoining member.

GSA-approved modular vaults meeting Federal Specification FF-V-2737, may be used in lieu of a 4.1.1 above.

2. Steel-lined construction: Where unique structural circumstances do not permit construction of a concrete vault, construction will be of steel alloy-type of 1/4" thick, having characteristics of high yield and tensile strength. The metal plates are to be continuously welded to load-bearing steel members of a thickness equal to that of the plates. If the load-bearing steel members are being placed in a continuous floor and ceiling of reinforced concrete, they must be firmly affixed to a depth of one-half the thickness of the floor and ceiling.

3. If the floor and/or ceiling construction is less than six inches of reinforced concrete, a steel liner is to be constructed the same as the walls to form the floor and ceiling of the vault. Seams where the steel plates meet horizontally and vertically are to be continuously welded together.

4. All vaults shall be equipped with a GSA-approved Class 5 or Class 8 vault door. Within the US, a Class 6 vault door is acceptable. Normally within the United States a vault will have only one door that serves as both entrance and exit from the SCIF in order to reduce costs.

b. SCIF Criteria for Permanent Dry Wall Construction

Walls, floor and ceiling will be permanently constructed and attached to each other. To provide visual evidence of attempted entry, all construction, to include above the false ceiling and below a raised floor, must be done in such a manner as to provide visual evidence of unauthorized Penetration.

c. SCIF Construction Criteria for Steel Plate

Walls, ceiling and floors are to be reinforced on the inside with steel plate not less than 1/8" thick. The plates at all vertical joints are to be affixed to vertical steel members of a thickness not less than that of the plates. The vertical plates will be spot welded to the vertical members by applying a one-inch long weld every 12 inches; meeting of the plates in the horizontal plane will be continuously welded. Floor and ceiling reinforcements must be securely affixed to the walls with steel angles welded or bolted in place.

    d. SCIF Construction Criteria for Expanded Metal

Walls are to be reinforced, slab-to-slab, with 9-gauge expanded metal. The expanded metal will be spot welded every 6 inches to vertical and horizontal metal supports of 16-gauge or greater thickness that has been solidly and permanently attached to the true floor and true ceiling.

    e. General

The use of materials having thickness or diameters larger than those specified above is permissible. The terms "anchored to and/or embedded into the floor and ceiling" may apply to the affixing of supporting members and reinforcing to true slab or the most solid surfaces; however, sub-floors and false ceiling are not to be used for this purpose.

14. Protect cables, wires, etc. from the inadvertent or intentional removal. Protecting cables from damage also needs to be considered. There are cable intrusion detection devices to alert a response if the cable is moved or cut. With the use of fiber becoming the norm this feature is built into the cable.

15. Design an emergency backup electrical system to augment the normal electrical system. The system should be designed to keep the critical sensitive equipment, ventilation, lights, etc. operating even with the loss of power, accidental or otherwise.

Also as a part of the design and planning process, emergencies need to be considered such as fires. As previously stated, check with the local fire and building codes to ensure compliance. The design will need to be approved by the local authorities and a permit obtained prior to beginning any work. The room should be protected by an automatic fire suppression system. Smoke detectors will also be required by the fire code so the occupants can be alerted to evacuate as soon as fire is detected. More about smoke detectors is in Chapter 17. Locations for storing fire extinguishers so they can be easily found during a fire emergency should also be included in the design. The local fire code official will look on the plans for the room for the exits, fire extinguishers, fire doors, suppression system, emergency lighting, etc. before approving the drawings. The personnel should be trained to properly use fire extinguishers in the event of a fire. Fire extinguishers are an effective tool in trained hands to keep a fire from becoming large and causing severe damage to the room and facility. Fire extinguishers must be placed within 75 feet travel distance for ordinary hazard facilities, and every 50 feet travel distance for high hazard facilities or areas with in the facility, according to the fire codes. For more information on fire codes see Chapter 17.

The room design should include proper ventilation climate control for the comfort of those working in the room as well as any special equipment that needs to be maintained at a specific temperature. For computer equipment the temperature of the room must be kept at between 50 and 80 degrees Fahrenheit with a humidity of between 20 to 80 percent. The constant temperature applies to after hours, holidays and even when the room is not occupied.

The room should not have a large amount of storage. There should be enough storage for what is necessary for the functioning and operations that take place in of the room. Excessive storage will only cause a compromise of security because access will not be limited only to those that have a need to know.

When sensitive equipment is in the room it is important to design the systems so that critical sensitive equipment is kept separate from general non-sensitive equipment. This will help minimize the possibility that the general equipment will cause collateral damage to the sensitive equipment during a failure. Also, it will limit the amount of traffic in the secure room to work on equipment and minimize the possibility of working on the wrong equipment.

As was previously discussed earlier in the chapter, to design sound protection into the secure room consideration needs to be given to shielding. Vaults provide good shielding especially if they are designed to do so. The vault is a metal room inserted into a concrete block room. The shield will help protect conversations in the room from anyone outside being able to "listen" in by preventing the electromagnetic waves from leaving the room. The shield will also prevent the capturing of "leakage" (information) from computers by shielding the electromagnetic waves that are produced by the computers.

Finally in the design of the secure room there must be a backup power supply to operate emergency lights, IDS and access control to the room. The back up power supply must be tamper resistant by having some kind of IDS to ensure that it will operate when needed. The back up or emergency power system must be protected from tampering and IDS should be installed in the area where the back up system is stored. Also, alarms should be added that will detect any attempt at removing any of the components of the emergency back up power system.

Design and Construction of the Secured (Caged) Area

Secured or caged areas are useful and help store sensitive or high value equipment. In a warehouse setting the caged area is also known as the high value storage area. These high value storage areas are used to store everything of high value from computers, other electronics, to TV sets, etc. The area chosen for the high value or caged area is usually in the center of the warehouse so there are not windows and doors that lead to the exterior to secure.

The design of the high value storage area would consist of the following:

1. An area that is coordinated off from the rest of the warehouse. The area should be located preferably in the center of the warehouse or building not near any exterior door, windows and skylights. This will help in securing the area since the possibility of entry directly into the area from the exterior can be eliminated.

The area will also have locked containers within the high value storage area of smaller articles to prevent pilfering. The containers shall be shipping containers.

2. A ceiling to floor fence with a fence across the top so there is a box made of special mesh chain link fence will make up the perimeter boundaries of the high value storage area. The reason for chain link fencing is so the area is visible from outside the fence which will provide good surveillance of the area by security personnel. The sides of the fencing would by secured to the fence across the top of the box. The sides of the fence would be secured into the floor to prevent the lifting of the fence to enter the secure area.

3. Intrusion detection systems installed in the area would include more than one type of system. For example, infrared motion detection can be used in conjunction with the perimeter fence motion sensors, or fence motion sensors and photoelectric motion sensors, etc. The IDS system will sound an audible alarm as well as a visible alarm with strobe lights.

   An IDS system will be installed for all of the shipping containers that are within the high value storage area to detect movement of the containers that are in transit. Containers that are permanently stored at the location can have IDS installed to detect when there is an attempt to attack the integrity of the container.

4. CCTV that is set to record on motion and when an entry is made through the gate ("man door") into the secure area. A camera will be used to capture the person swiping the card for entry, and as the person moves through the door and into the secure area.

   The IDS systems will be integrated with the CCTV system so video will be recorded of any event that activates the IDS system. This will take coordination between the CCTV installation and the IDS. The CCTV will be set to record on motion only when the secure area has not been access through a proper access card and biometrics read.

5. Access control will be granted by a card swipe and a biometric device. The door lock will be an electric strike and will be opened using the access control system. The biometric device could be a hand geometry reader. The door to the secure area would be two doors one outer and one inner. The inner door would need to shut and latched before the inner door' card reader and biometric device will work. Also there should be pressure mat between the doors that will detect if there is more than one person outside the inner door. If there is more than one person then the card reader and biometric device would not work and an alarm will sound. Another method would be the use of a turnstile that allows one entry per card. The turnstile will eliminate the

need for two doors but still accomplish the desired result of eliminating the opportunity to tailgate into the secure area.

There will probably be a need for a fork lift door or gate so pallet loads of high value cargo and/or product can be shipped. The fork lift door would also be controlled by a card and biometric reader. When the fork lift door is opened, security will need to be present to make sure that the area remains secure. All the items or pallet-loads of the high value cargo and/or products need to be scanned just like any one item being removed would be.

6. To further protect the high value cargo and products, a system of bar coding can be used and security tagging. The security tag will be read by a reader that is in the door frame of the entry and emergency exit doors. Any cargo that is to be removed during normal operations will have the bar code read by a bar code reader prior to removing the security tag and moving the cargo out of the secure area. Once the bar code is read and the tag is removed the reader at the doors would be shunted so an alarm would not be sent. On the other hand, if the cargo or products are removed without authorization then the reader will detect when any cargo is removed from the secure area and an alarm will sound. The bar code would also serve the purpose of tracking the movement of the cargo like tracking bar code numbers are now used to track packages sent via package carriers.

7. There should be at least one emergency exit from the secure area. The emergency exit is a gate that has panic hardware in the inside for exiting. The door will be alarmed and will send an audible and visual alarm if the door is used. A camera will record the activity at the door when the panic hardware is activated.

EMERGENCY POWER

Planning for emergencies should be part of the design process. Just like the secure room, emergency power back up for the secure area needs to part of the design. Since the secure area will be storing high value cargo it makes sense to have an emergency power system to back up the normal power supply. The access control system, electronic locks, CCTV cameras, and the IDS. The emergency back up power supply should not be overlooked because it will create a large vulnerability to the high value storage area in the event of a loss of power. The secure storage area, since it is important, should have its own back up emergency power supply form the rest of the warehouse. If the emergency power supply is not separate from the rest of the warehouse then the emergency power supply should be protected from tampering. This can be accomplished by providing a locked room with limited access using access control to house the back up power system. The room should have an IDS system using dual technology of infrared motion and door contact switches. CCTV should also be included in the monitoring of the room. An automatic fire detection and suppression system should also be installed and will most likely be required by the fire and building codes.

Emergency back up power will be provided for the secure room as well using the same principles as for the secure area emergency back up power.

The normal power supply should also be protected to prevent tampering for both the secure room, and the secure area as well as the rest of the facility or warehouse. The power supply room will have locked power boxes and the boxes that provide power to the secure room and secure area will have tamper switches installed. The electrical room will have limited access by using a card reader. CCTV will be installed at the entrance door to the electrical room and inside the electrical room as well. The cameras will be set to record on motion at all times. This way all activity in the electrical room and at the entrance to the electrical room will be recorded.

DESIGN CONSIDERATIONS FOR SECURE ROOMS AND SECURE AREAS

What follows is an abbreviated sample of design specifications to guide you so you can write your own design specifications for your project.

PART 1 GENERAL

1.1 RELATED DOCUMENTS

1.2 GENERAL REQUIREMENTS

1.3 SUBMITTALS

1.4 QUALITY ASSURANCE

1.5 DELIVERY, STORAGE AND HANDLING

1.6 WARRANTY

PART 2 PRODUCTS
This part outlines the type of secure room or secure area will be built including the materials of construction the dimensions, diameter, etc. This section also outlines finishes, etc.

PART 3 EXECUTION

3.1 EXAMINATION

3.2 INSTALLATION

3.3 FIELD QUALITY CONTROL
The related documents section outlines what other sections or documents are related to this document or are included in other sections of the document in the

sections that follow and any related sections. The general requirements section outlines what is required for the project.

- Drawings and how many copies

- Fence material for the secure area

- The vault for the secure room

- Hardware (locks) and door schedule

- Copies of approved hardware, and door material schedule for the subcontractors (windows and door installer)

- Installation instructions

- Other

The section on quality assurance addresses such things as:

- The length of time the installer has been in business

- Contractor's license number

- Attend a pre-installation meeting

- Ensure door and window material meets the standards set forth in the submittals.

Sample design specifications for window and door design/build installation are presented below:

DESIGN/BUILD – OUTLINE SPECIFICATIONS FOR THE SECURE ROOM OR SECURE AREA

The Qualifications section provides specific clarification of scope issues not necessarily identified in the Outline Specifications.

If a specific material or brand name product has been referenced, it is only to show the quality of material being used. In the final specification and during construction of this project, "or equal" products may be installed.

DIVISION 01 – GENERAL REQUIREMENTS

01001 GENERAL

All facilities, labor, material, equipment, and design services that are typically required for the completion of the Work are included in this design/build proposal. All Work shall comply with the applicable federal, state and local requirements.

All sections in the Outline Specifications carry a one (1) year Standard Construction Warranty and Guarantee against labor and material defects including Work performed by subcontractors. All equipment warranties greater than one (1) year will be passed to the Owner at project completion.

01002 INSURANCE AND BONDS

Design/Builder's Liability Insurance:

Design/Builder shall purchase and maintain in a company or companies authorized to do business in the state in which the Work is located such insurance as will protect the Design/Builder from claims set forth below which may arise out of or result from operations under the Contract by the Design/Builder or a subcontractor of the Design Builder, or by anyone directly or indirectly employed by any of them, including:

Claims under workers' or workmen's compensation, disability benefit and other similar employee benefit laws which are applicable to the Work to be performed;

Claims for damages because of bodily injury, occupational sickness or disease, or death of the Design/Builder's employees under any applicable employer's liability law;

Claims for damages because of bodily injury, sickness or disease, or death of persons other than the Design/Builder's employees;

Claims for damages covered by usual personal injury liability coverage which are sustained by a person as a result of an offense directly or indirectly related to employment of such person by the Design/Builder;

Claims for damages, other than to the Work at the site, because of injury to or destruction of tangible property, and

Claims for damages for bodily injury of death of a person or property damage arising out of ownership, maintenance or use of a motor vehicle.

The insurance required by the above subparagraph shall be written for not less than limits of liability specified in the insurance certificates submitted with the bid of _____.

The Design/Builder's liability insurance shall include contractual liability insurance applicable to the Design/Builder's obligations under AIA A191 Part 2, Paragraph 11.7.

Certificates of Insurance shall be delivered to the Owner prior to commencement of design and construction. These Certificates, as well as insurance policies required by this Paragraph, shall contain a provision that coverage will not be canceled or allowed to expire until at least thirty day's prior written notice has been given to the Owner.

Builder's Risk Insurance can be provided by the Design/Builder, but is not included in the bid.

Design/Builder's Errors and Omissions Insurance:

Design/Builder shall carry Architects and Engineers Professional Liability insurance with the following limits (example only):

$2,000,000 per Claim

$2,000,000 Aggregate

$100,000 S.I.R.

Performance & Payment Bonds:

Design/Builder shall provide a Payment and Performance Bond for the overall construction project value.

Design/Builder's Surety will assume no responsibility for any design work performed in connection with this project.

01003 ALLOWANCES

Allowances refer to items of scope or cost which have not been sufficiently defined to date. The stipulated Allowance amount has been included in the base proposal price. Actual billings against these items will be supported by supplier and subcontractor invoices. Actual costs of less than the original Allowance will result in a reduction of base contract price. Actual costs greater than the original Allowance will be billed at cost plus a 15% General Contractor's Fee and result in an increase to the base contract price. Allowance items if anticipated are clearly noted in the Construction Budget Summary.

01004 DESIGN AND SUPERVISION

This proposal includes all required architectural, structural, plumbing, mechanical and electrical engineering design with stamped drawings and corresponding specifications for the garage structure. The cost associated with peer review by the State of _____ is also included.

Supervision:

Design/Builder will assign a Project Manager to this job that will be responsible for all project activities from design through construction including coordination with the Owner, Regulatory Agencies, other Prime Contractors, etc.

Design/Builder will assign, on site, a full-time superintendent solely for this project.

01050 FIELD ENGINEERING

Field engineering services required for proper completion of the Work including but not limited to:

Extend base lines and elevations from initial site survey provided by owner.

Locate and protect control points before starting work on the site.

Layout of all window and door frames.

01310 PROJECT SCHEDULE

Design/Builder will provide an overall design and construction schedule. The schedule will be updated monthly.

01500 TEMPORARY FACILITIES AND CONTROLS

Temporary facilities and controls needed for the Work including but not limited to:

Telephone service for the Design/Builder office.

Portable sanitary facilities located on the site for Design/Builder personnel only.

Temporary electric power and lighting connection to an existing supply within 25' of the site. Metered electricity usage is at Design/Builder's expense.

Temporary construction water connection to an existing supply within 25' of the site. Metered water usage is at Design/Builder's expense.

Temporary barricades:

Elevated deck edge fall protection and deck opening protection.

Safety barricades around work area within the facility and/or major excavations in accordance with OSHA guidelines including warning tape and lighted flashers if required.

Temporary barricades, traffic barriers, safety lighting etc. if required for partial occupancy are not included in this proposal. The scope of services can be added at a future time when it is defined.

Temporary chain link fencing, 6'-0" high including construction safety signs and warnings for the parking garage site is included. Removal at project completion.

01700 CONTRACT CLOSEOUT

To provide an orderly and efficient transfer of the completed Work, upon substantial completion of all work:

The project will be inspected with representatives of the Owner and Design/Builder for the purpose of itemizing a final punch list.

The project will be turned over broom clean and ready for use.

Closeout submittal to include but not be limited to:

Project record documents i.e. "as built" drawings, specifications, shop drawings, etc.

Operation and maintenance manuals as available.

Warranties and bonds.

Keying and keying schedule.

Spare parts and material extra stock.

Release of liens.

List of subcontractors, service organizations and principal vendors.

01710 CLEANING

Throughout the construction period, Design/Builder will maintain the building and site in a standard of cleanliness consistent with safe and efficient construction operations.

Design/Builder will provide dumpsters for the use of all trades under its contract on this project.

All storm drains will be protected from debris during construction.

Final cleaning of the structure.

Remove all trash associated with the installation work.

Clean and wash all glass inside and out.

Clean and all wrappings on door and window frames.

Clean all floors around work area of debris like screws, etc.

Security Design 14

The design of the security is a part of the facility, building, or project planning process. It is far better to design security into the project rather than do a retrofit later on. Security should be designed from the ground up when planning the design/build project of a new facility or the expansion of an existing one.

In this chapter we will design security for a fictitious company using the concepts and information contained in the book. The company chosen for this example is completely fictitious and is not based on any real company in location, or facility. The facility will be small but it will be of critical importance to the company and will be considered a high security facility because of the type of work that will be performed. Even though some of the security design is probably more than is necessary for most facilities the requirements set forth for this project are for a high security facility doing research for the development of vaccines for biological hazards and warfare.

Following is a narrative about the company and the proposed facility that is being designed to be built on the proposed site address in the narrative. Since security is an important part of the facility, the design and specifications of security are being designed into the overall facility design. This is a unique opportunity to develop a security system that meets the facility needs of being a high security facility.

XYZ PHARMACEUTICAL COMPANY

The company is called XYZ Pharmaceutical Company and the new facility will be a research and office building. The research to be performed is to develop vaccines for biological hazards and weapons so the facility is a high security facility. The location for the new facility has been chosen and will be at 13746 Jones Road, Maplewood, CA 95226. The facility will be three stories, the first two floors will be offices and the third floor will be research labs. The square footage of the building is 300,000 square feet, approximately 100,000 square feet per floor. The proposed location of the building is a small city, old industrial and agricultural, based economy in the Central Valley of California bordering a large city. The city has its own small police department and has agreements with the neighboring large city and the county sheriff's department for mutual aid. The industrial area of Maplewood is on the border of the larger city and which is known for its crimes of drug sales, prostitution, vehicle thefts, burglary, and crimes against persons including robbery. To make the facility as safe as possible, the security measures that are put in place will be important.

The type of research to be performed at the facility is critical to the company and Homeland Security and is highly sensitive in nature. The research projects that will be undertaken at the facility will aid in the Homeland Security effort.

Security Design for the XYZ Pharmaceutical Company

The following are the steps that will need to be taken to plan for and design security into the facility design of the new XYZ Pharmaceuticals Company's (from this point known as the "Company") office and research center in Maplewood, CA.

1. Contact local law enforcement agencies and request crime statistics for the following:

    a. Maplewood, CA PD
    b. Neighboring Big City PD
    c. County Sheriff's Office

2. Notify CAP Index and send to them the address and order a report of the CRIMECAST® statistics, maps, charts, etc. for the proposed location. The cost of the report for 1–5 sites is $165.00 per report.

3. Perform a Threat and Risk Assessment based on the statistics and the CAP Index (see Chapter 2 for more details).

4. Develop a plan for security for the proposed site.

5. Prepare the security design based on the assessment

The CAP Index and local crime statistics indicate that there are issues with the following types of crimes (see Table 14-1 for a sample CRIMECAST(r) Report):

1. Crimes against persons
    a. Assaults
    b. Robbery
    c. Rape
    d. Homicide

TABLE 14-1   Spreadsheet

XYZ Corporation			03/01/03
			National Current CAP Index = 294

CAP Index

Crime · Loss · Risk Prevention Solutions

CRIMECAST®Site Report
CAP Index, Inc.
800-227-7475
www.capindex.com

View Map | Sort by CAP Ind | Print | Help

Site ID	XYZ001		
Site Name	Main Office		
Address	999 City Ave.		
	Philadelphia, PA 19999		

Current Scores (2003)	National Scores	State Scores	County Scores
CAP Index	294	470	1412
Homicide	510	541	854
Rape	331	491	1231
Robbery	277	460	1537
Aggravated Assault	231	320	1418
Crimes Against Persons	247	360	1376
Burglary	96	213	448
Larceny	126	167	494
Motor Vehicle Theft	170	248	518
Crimes Against Property	125	183	490

Past Scores (1990)	National Scores	State Scores	County Scores
CAP Index	290	404	1424
Homicide	482	478	851
Rape	285	400	1113
Robbery	292	413	1636
Aggravated Assault	303	363	1678
Crimes Against Persons	298	377	1576
Burglary	143	273	619
Larceny	175	209	640
Motor Vehicle Theft	188	261	567
Crimes Against Property	170	224	626

Projected Scores (2008)	National Scores	State Scores	County Scores
CAP Index	273	466	1299
Homicide	476	527	787
Rape	317	491	1167
Robbery	257	458	1415
Aggravated Assault	191	285	1209
Crimes Against Persons	213	333	1203
Burglary	83	197	400
Larceny	111	154	451
Motor Vehicle Theft	150	230	466
Crimes Against Property	110	169	445

2. Crimes against property
   a. Theft
   b. Vandalism
   c. Burglary

The spread sheet in Table 14-1 and the map in Figure 14-1 are samples of what the report would look like. For our purposes here let's just say that the

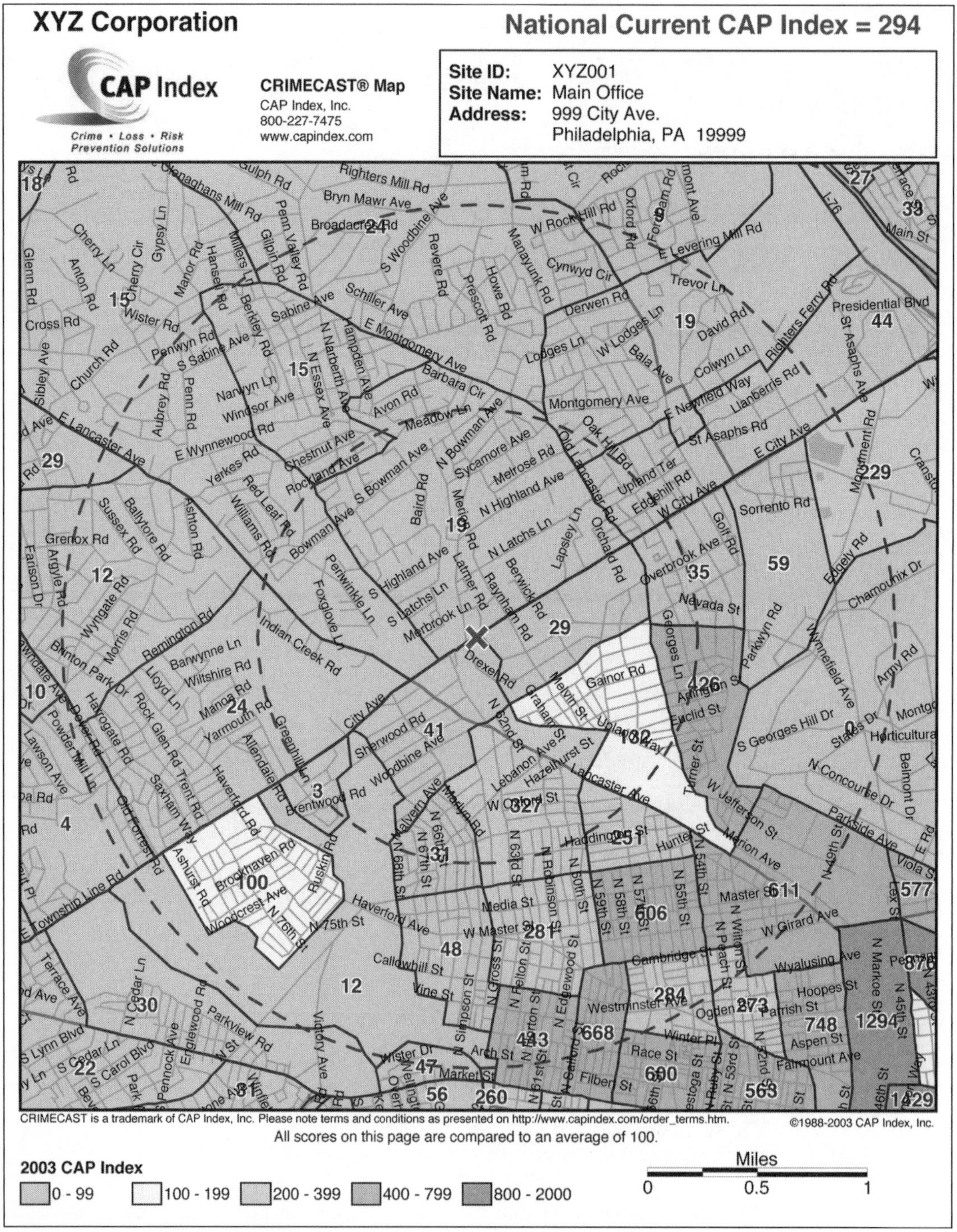

XYZ Corporation

National Current CAP Index = 294

CAP Index

Crime • Loss • Risk
Prevention Solutions

CRIMECAST® Map
CAP Index, Inc.
800-227-7475
www.capindex.com

Site ID:	XYZ001
Site Name:	Main Office
Address:	999 City Ave.
	Philadelphia, PA 19999

CRIMECAST is a trademark of CAP Index, Inc. Please note terms and conditions as presented on http://www.capindex.com/order_terms.htm.　　©1988-2003 CAP Index, Inc.

All scores on this page are compared to an average of 100.

2003 CAP Index

	0 - 99		100 - 199		200 - 399		400 - 799		800 - 2000

Miles

0　　　0.5　　　1

FIGURE 14-1 Crimecast® map

statistics in Table 14-1and Figure 14-1 are for our fictitious location in Maplewood, CA not the XYZ Company in Philadelphia, PA. With this in mind let's plan the security for the proposed office and research facility starting with the perimeter security.

PERIMETER SECURITY

The perimeter of the facility will be bordered on one side by the street and on two sides by heavily wooded areas and the fourth by a fast flowing river with steep banks. So the natural barrier of the river with its steep banks will be included in the security plan of the facility. Even though there is a river with steep banks in the rear of the facility, the rear of the facility will be fenced as well. This is keeping with the defense-in-depth concept of security which will be used to design the security of this critically important facility.

Based on the information obtained in the CAP Index CRIMECAST® Report and the threat assessment crimes against persons and property has a high risk and must be addressed in the security design of the facility. Also, since the facility is performing work that is sensitive, the security will be designed to be high to protect the integrity of the work being performed.

The perimeter will have the following security measures.

1. The entire perimeter will be fenced using an 8-foot high black wrought iron fence with a second inner fence 30 feet from the outer fence of 8 foot black wrought iron fence. The area between the fences will be clear of all vegetation that will block the view of the fence and perimeter. The two fences will be used on three sides of the facility, the rear and the two sides. The fences will have outward facing spikes pointing at a 45 degree angle with tips. The fence will have detection installed on the fence. See the IDS section in this chapter for more details.

2. The gates for the employees' entrance and the entrance for deliveries will have electrically operated gates. The gates will be operated by using an access control card.

   For the employees entrance gate to the parking lot there will be a card reader and a camera hidden in the reader so the person swiping the access card will have their face captured and it will be compared to the database for a match. All employee's vehicles will have a bar code that will read as the employee presents the access card. The bar code will be a match to the employee's ID badge before the gate will open. For car pools the ID badge of the driver and passengers will match the bar code on the car pool decal. If there is not a match, the gate will not open and the security console will receive an alarm and will respond. There will be a second camera to record the license plate of the vehicle as it enters the facility.

For deliveries there will be a security officer who will look at the driver's license of the delivery vehicle driver and scan it into a database for future reference, Also, the driver will be asked to show the company ID card of the delivery company. All the information is recorded as well as the information on the manifest and the vehicle number and license plate number. The vehicle is inspected inside and out for any bombs, etc. A check is made to verify that a delivery is expected then gate is opened to allow the truck to enter. All the checks of the vehicle and the delivery driver are captured by CCTV.

3. There will be CCTV cameras all along the perimeter that are monitored 24 hours a day. The cameras are set to record on motion after hours except for those remote locations in the back of the facility.

4. The entire fence is monitored by a fence intrusion detection system. The fence IDS will be integrated with the CCTV system so any trip of the detection system will be recorded and will alert security for a response. There will also be perimeter IDS in the form of motion sensors. The motion sensors will be microwave sensors.

5. Perimeter lighting will consist of all four types of lighting listed below and based on the illumination requirements set forth in Table 14-2 below.
   a. Continuous lighting
   b. Standby lighting
   c. Movable lighting
   d. Emergency lighting

TABLE 14-2   Illumination requirements

LOCATION	FOOT-CANDLES ON HORIZONTAL PLANE AT GROUND LEVEL
Perimeter of outer area	0.15
Perimeter of restricted area	0.4
Vehicular entrances	1.0
Pedestrian entrances	2.0
Sensitive inner areas	0.15
Sensitive inner structure	1.0
Entrances	0.1
Open yards	0.2
Decks on open piers	1.0

CONTINUOUS LIGHTING

Glare lighting will be used as a part of the continuous lighting system and is designed to provide lighting that projects a glare to the outside of the facility. The glare lighting will assist the security officers by allowing them to see what is on the outside of the perimeter fence but any intruder will be blinded by the light and not able to see the security officers. When designing the glare protection lighting make sure that the lights do not point to any roadway since you don't want to blind drivers and cause an accident.

The other type of continuous lighting will be street lights for lighting parking lots, pedestrian walkways, perimeter fence, and entrances. The street light is a light on a pole that illuminates below the light. The light also extends out to the sides. These lights will provide a minimum of 2.0 foot-candles of illumination.

STANDBY LIGHTING

Standby lighting will also be used and will be set to be illuminated by motion sensors. The lighting will provide glare to the outside of the facility to blind anyone approaching the perimeter fence in the rear and the sides that border the wooded area.

MOVABLE LIGHTING

Movable lighting will be used in the rear of the facility and operated by security personnel when there is an alarm from an IDS, either fence or perimeter. The lights will be illuminated and will be manually moved by the security officer on duty at the console. The lights will be glare protection type lights to assist in response to security incidents that occur along the perimeter.

EMERGENCY LIGHTING

All the security lighting will be connected to a backup emergency power supply that will automatically become the power supply in the event of loss of the normal power supply.

The emergency power supply shall consist of a battery back up and an emergency standby generator. UPS systems do not work well for security lighting and should not be used.

Lighting for the perimeter fence line will be quartz lamps. The rest of the perimeter lighting will be halogen lamps. The halogen lamps produce a bright white light. Halogen lights will be used to illuminate the parking lot.

Lighting of entrances used for pedestrians to go to and from the site should be controlled lighting. The lighting should provide enough illumination for the recognition of people and examination of ID badges, etc. This requires a minimum of 2.0 foot-candles of illumination.

Vehicle entrances on the other hand, should have lighting that produces enough illumination so a complete inspection of passenger cars, trucks and freight cars (rail), including the contents, can be done safely.

Security officer gatehouses usually have a lower intensity of illumination inside the gatehouse so officers can see approaching vehicles and pedestrians. If the illumination intensity inside the gatehouse is too high then the officer will not be able to see out as easily but they would easy to see from the outside.

A part of the perimeter security is the security of the employee entrances and the building lobby for visitor entrance. All employee entrance doors into the building, of which there will be three, will have controlled access. The access control system will be a card reader system using proximity card readers and will be used in conjunction with the dual technology of a biometric reader. The employee will swipe the proximity card on the door reader and then place their hand in the hand geometry reader. The employee entrance doors will be revolving doors so that only one card and biometric read will allow only one entry. When two people enter the door at the same time either exiting or entering the door will back them both out and not allow any entry. All of the doors that have access control will have contact switches on the doors to monitor the door position.

All other exterior doors that are for emergency exiting only will have a blank face on the exterior which means there will not be any hardware since the door will not be used for re-entry. All of the doors will be alarmed, will be self closing, and will alarm if propped or held open.

CCTV will be used to monitor the employee entrance doors as well as the emergency exit doors. The cameras will be monitored by the security officers at the security console and will record when motion is detected at the emergency exit doors and upon the activation of the card reader for the employee entrance doors.

INTERIOR SECURITY

The lobby will have a receptionist sitting behind a Lexan® window. The door to the office will be controlled by the use of an access card. The door is not an employee entrance door since only on method of verification is used for the access control which is the card swipe. There will no biometric reader on the door. The door will also be monitored by CCTV on the outside of the door in the lobby and inside the office as well. The CCTV like all of the doors will record on motion and activation of the door card reader.

The lobby will have CCTV cameras monitoring the entire lobby area. One camera will monitor the reception desk and the other cameras will monitor the rest of the lobby. All of the CCYV cameras in the lobby will be monitored by the security officers on the security console monitors.

All visitors will sign at reception and be issued a visitor's badge. The visitor's badge will not be an active badge and therefore will not allow access through doors. The visitor will need to be accompanied by a company employee at all times while in the facility.

The reception desk will have a duress button to be used by the receptionist during an emergency. The duress button will alert the security officers at the security console and the lobby CCTV cameras will also come on the security officer's screen when the duress button is activated. The security officers will respond to the lobby to address the situation.

Elevators to the second floor of the office and the third floor research area will be operated by card access only 24/7 and the elevator lobby doors will require not only a card swipe but also a biometric read to enter.

The doors to the secure areas will not only card in but also employees will be required to use their access card to exit the secure areas as well. The secure areas are all the research areas on the third floor and the office areas that work, prepare, and maintain the company's strategic planning and the IT server room and help desk. These secure office area doors will have card biometric readers for access and a card access for exiting. The doors to secure areas will be either a revolving door or a man trap, which will be two doors so piggybacking and tailgating will be eliminated. The doors will be a one card one person enters access system. Exiting the secure areas will be the same, one card one person exits. All other access doors will have REXs on them for exiting except for after hours exiting so the intrusion detection system can be re-armed. The Rexs will be set to shunt the forced exit door alarms only and not to unlock the door for exiting. The doors will have door switches which will monitor the position of the door.

Access to the IS server room will be done by a card reader and a biometric hand geometry reader. The door to the IS server room will consist of a revolving door that will only allow one person to enter per card swipe and hand geometry read. To exit the IS server room there will be a card reader and hand geometry reader to activate the revolving door. Access to the Information Data Systems rooms will be done by using a card reader and hand geometry readers.

CCTV

CCTV will be located throughout the interior to monitor doors to secure areas for the purpose of monitoring traffic through the doors. The CCTV system will be integrated into the access control system for management and monitoring. The CCTV in sensitive areas will be designed to record on motion after hours even though the operation of the research area will be 24/7. Security will monitor all CCTV cameras and will have the capability to operate the pan tilt zoom (PTZ) cameras from the security console. All CCTV cameras will record on a digital video recorder (DVR). The DVR has replaced the VHS recorder tape systems.

There will be CCTV cameras in the IS server room and all the Information Data System rooms. This will help identify any potential issues that may happen in these critical rooms.

FIRE PROTECTION

The entire facility will be protected by an automatic fire suppression system using fire sprinklers. All applicable fire and building codes for the design and installation of the sprinkler system will be adhered to. Smoke detectors will be placed throughout the facility in accordance with the applicable fire and building codes. The smoke detectors when activated will initiate an alarm so the occupants can safely evacuate the facility. The fire alarms will be monitored by the security console and, to meet the fire codes, the fire alarm system will have its own monitoring panel located in the lobby of the building.

The building will have an emergency back up generator for illuminating all the emergency lights including providing power to the security console and the IT room in the event of a power failure. There will be a separate generator for the perimeter lighting and intrusion detection.

Portable fire extinguishers will be located every 75 feet travel distance in the office areas and every 50 feet in the research areas on the third floor. The placement on fire extinguishers is the fire code and is 75 feet travel distance for ordinary hazards (office locations) and 50 feet travel distance for high hazard (research areas).

INTRUSION DETECTION

All intrusion detection alarms will be monitored by the security console. The intrusion detection system will be integrated into the access control system. This will combine the CCTV, alarm monitoring, and access control into one system making it easier for the security officers to monitor and manage. By integrating the systems and managing it through one system the security officers will only need to monitor one system even though the fire codes require a separate annunciation panel for the fire systems. The fire systems can be monitored through the access control system, however there still needs to be a separate panel for the fire alarm system.

Exterior intrusion detection will consist of photo electric for the perimeter just outside of the fence and the 30 foot space between the fences and a fence detection system for the fence. See Figure 14-2 for a picture of a fence detection system from the Army Field Manual 3-19.30 for Physical.

Sensors (buried line sensors) will also be placed in the ground in the flower beds near the windows to detect anyone approaching the windows.

Intrusion detection for doors on the first floor will consist of door contact

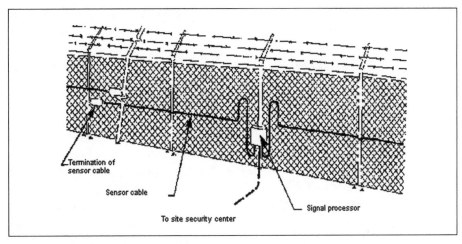

FIGURE 14-2   Fence detection system

switches that are balanced magnetic switches for doors whether they have access control on them or not. See Figure 14-3 for pictures of balanced magnetic switches from the Army Field Manual 3-19.30 for Physical Security. The doors that have card readers and biometric will shunt the alarm when the door is accessed with a valid card and biometric read. The balanced magnetic switches will alarm if the door is forced and the card reader and biometric reader are bypassed.

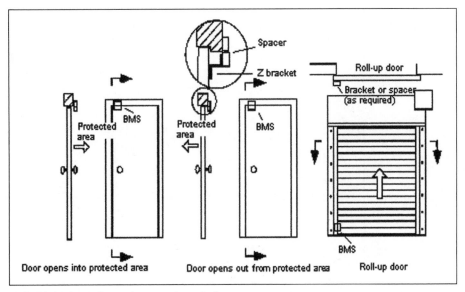

FIGURE 14-3   Balanced magnetic switches

Any doors that held open too long will alarm as well. The time limit for entry will be set at 15 seconds before the alarm is sent indicating that the door has been open too long.

Window intrusion detection will consist of balanced magnetic contact switches for operating windows. For fixed or non–opening windows there will not be any contact switches. All the windows on the first floor will be laminate and dual technology glass breaks will be deployed on the first floor.

Passive ultrasonic sensors and infrared motion sensors will be deployed in the office area that will be activated after hours. See Figure 14-4 for the pattern of a typical passive ultrasonic detector. Passive ultrasonic detection ranges can be found in Table 14-3 from the Army Field Manual 3-19.30 for Physical Security. The disarming of the intrusion detection system will occur when a valid access card is swiped at the entrance door to the office on the second floor and through one of the three employee entrances on the first floor. The system will be re-armed when the employee swipes the access to exit the facility.

The intrusion detection system will divided into zones known as detection zones. The detection zones should be long and straight so the number of detection devices can be kept to a minimum. The detection zones are based on the existing terrain, contour, and the activities in the perimeter. The detection zones will be included as a part of the software installation of the system. All entry

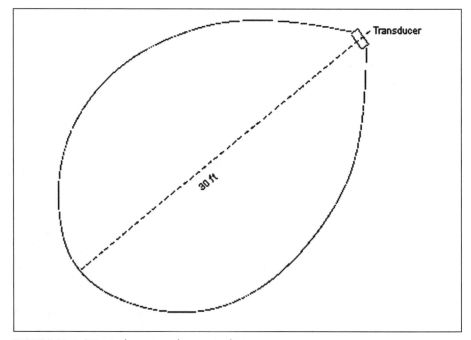

FIGURE 14-4   Typical passive ultrasonic detector

TABLE 14-3 Pattern of a typical passive ultrasonic detector

Penetration	Distance (in Feet)
Cut 1/4-inch-thick expanded metal with bolt cutters	55
Cut 5/8-inch reinforcing bar with bolt cutters	45
Use acetylene cutting torch	39
Cut wood with circular saw	30
Cut 5/8-inch reinforcing bar with hacksaw	19
Drill through brick	15
Drill through 1/8-inch steel plate	6
Cut 1/8-inch steel plate with hacksaw	4
Drill through cinderblock	3

points will be configured as separate independent detection zones. This will allow for the deactivation of the sensors without affecting the whole or a large portion of the detection zone during normal working hours as long as the security officers are manning the entry points.

The length of each detection zone is to be no more than 300 feet. The 300 foot cutoff allows the security officer to more effectively monitor the CCTV system and to do alarm assessment. The design of the zones is important and needs to be done before the information is added to the access system for monitoring.

All the alarms for the IDS sensors will be integrated through the access control system and a map of the area for exterior alarms will show where and what type of alarm has been tripped and the information will be displayed on the monitor by blinking on the screen of the console as well as activating the CCTV camera in the area.

To adequately protect the integrity of the IDS system all sensor related enclosures that contain circuitry and associated wiring will have tamper switches installed. The tamper switches will alarm at the security console and the security officers will respond immediately to address the situation. The wall or screens containing grid-wire sensors are susceptible to being removed or re-positioned and will be equipped with tamper switches to prevent them from being moved or repositioned.

ALARM ANNUNCIATION

Alarm annunciation is an important part of the IDS system. Without monitoring the system is useless. Monitoring will include a response to the alarm both in the system at the monitor and a physical response as well. Our example of the fictitious company's new facility that we are designing the security for includes alarms and, as a part of the design, the alarm annunciation needs to be considered. The design specifications sample at the end of the chapter depict the design of the entire system including IDS, access control, door contacts, etc.

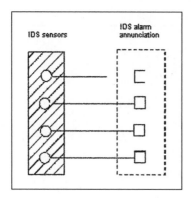

FIGURE 14-5   Block diagram of the point-to-point system

There are two methods for alarm annunciation:

1. Point–to–Point

2. Multiplexed

Point–to–Point is for small installations and each alarm point with a separate transmission line to the security console for each alarm point. See Figure 14-5 from the FM 19-30.3 of a block diagram of the point-to-point system.

The multiplexed system on the other hand is for larger systems. The digital multiplexed system allows multiple systems to be sent to the security console using one data communication link. See Figure 14-6 from FM 19-30.3 of a block diagram of the multiplexed system.

The alarm-annunciation is monitored by the access control system's main server. In Figure 14-7 from FM 19-30.3 is a block diagram of a typical alarm annunciation configuration system. The central computer in the diagram would be the access control system's main server and magnetic tape is the hard disk and floppy disks are CDs used today. The diagram still provides a good layout of the system's configuration. All of the "local processors" are desk top computers and are the "clients" of the main server.

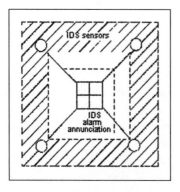

FIGURE 14-6   Block diagram of the multiplexed system

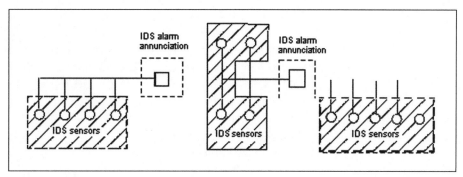

FIGURE 14-7   Block diagram of a typical alarm annunciation configuration system

With today's systems all of the alarms, CCTV, and access control are monitored by one system which is the access control system's main server. The CCTV system will be monitored through the access control system's main computer but will still have its own DVR (Digital Video Recorders). To help pinpoint an alarm the system will have floor plans for each floor of the facility loaded into the data base and when an alarm is received it will bring up the floor plan and the alarm type and location will be shown according to its location on the floor plan.

The fire alarm system must have its own annunciation panel separate from the security system to meet the fire codes. The fire alarms can also be monitored by the security system through the security console.

SAMPLE DESIGN SPECIFICATIONS

The design specifications for the project would look like those below. Also included below are the "Instructions to Bidders". The document contains information to the project bidders. The more detail you provide in specification the easier it will be for companies to bid the job. The documents submitted for bid will provide you with the information necessary to make a decision on what contractor will get the job of doing the installation of the security systems. What follows is an abbreviated sample of design specifications to guide you so you can write your own design specifications for your project.

SECTION 17000 – ELECTRONIC SECURITY SYSTEM (Access Control and IDS)

PART 1 – GENERAL

1.1 RELATED DOCUMENTS

    A. All drawings and the General Provisions of the Contract including the General and Supplementary Conditions and Division 1 Specification Sections, apply to this Section.

1.2 PROJECT SCOPE:

A. The system being developed under this design is a electronic intrusion detection, egress control system that incorporates the technologies shown below. For the purpose of clarification, the following parties will be referenced in this document in the following manner:

1. The XYZ Corporation   The Client
   13746 Jones Road
   Maplewood, CA. 94588
   209-224-7955 Tel
   209-224-7964 Fax
   www.xyz.com

2. The ABCD Consultants Inc.   The Consultants
   4847 Fresno Street
   Stockton, California, 95338
   209-832-8534 Tel
   209-832-1219 Fax
   www.abcdconsult.com

3. The XYZ Corporation   The Facility(s)
   Maplewood, California

B. In all new facilities, the system is being installed for the purpose of controlling traffic in the Client's facility. It is a requirement of the system that all technologies be integrated into one system to allow for instantaneous alert and response to any alarm condition that may be activated in the secured area. The system will be controlled through one central processor located in the facility. Archived information is to be sent via the "NET" to the remote server located in the Client's offices in Maplewood, California. The system must be compatible from the standpoint of the ability to read existing access control cards and to provide the same report formats to allow for standardization of a global network.

C. It is also a requirement of the system to monitor all building management services as they relate to the facility. The operations manager shall have the ability to both monitor and control building management equipment through the access control screen located at the systems management console (SMC).

D. This Section calls for the contractor of choice to provide all labor, materials, equipment, and service necessary for the completion of the integrated electronic security system and subsystem(s), as indicated on the drawings and as described herein. The internal "NET" shall be supplied by the Owner however it is the responsibility of the contractor to verify that communication pathways are open and compatible with all components within the global system. The Owner reserves the right to supply other components if they are needed for this project. The system technologies called for within this Scope of Work are:

1. Access Control cards, readers, and field panels;
2. Closed Circuit Television camera and monitors;
3. Intrusion Detection Devices;
4. Duress Reporting Devices;
5. Video digital recording devices; and
6. Components required for installation

E. The Contractor shall provide all labor, materials, equipment, software, and programming required to provide the Client with an integrated security system that is compatible with existing components in other offices operated by the Client.

F. Contractor shall ensure the system meets the operational and functional needs of the Client as specified herein, and as indicated on the drawings. The drawings are diagrammatic only. Equipment and labor not specifically referred to herein, or on the plans, that are required to meet the functional and operational intent, shall be provided without additional cost to the Client.

G. Contractor shall be responsible for coordinating with other trades and contractors to provide a system that is totally integrated and operational as required for this project.

H. The Contractor shall be responsible for providing with their Submittal, a one year spare parts list with single component (itemized) and quantity pricing. Should any particular component be in redesign stage that would possibly cause it to be a non-production item within the 1 year period, this component shall be identified as such and the substitute or new component be identified on this spare parts list.

1.3 RELATED SECTIONS

A. The contractor shall review the following sections of the total project to ensure compliance with:

1. Division 2 Site Work
2. Division 7 Fire stopping
3. Division 8 Doors and Door Hardware
4. Division 16 Electrical

   All specification divisions are identified by The Construction Specification Institute
   Master Format

1.4 SUBMITTALS

A. Contractor shall submit bid data containing original catalog cut sheets that provide complete technical data as required by the Owner to allow evaluation of the material and equipment proposed. The information should include component dimensions, wiring and block diagrams, wire/cable sizes, conduit sizes, performance data, ratings, operational characteristics, control sequences, and other descriptive data to describe the items proposed.

B. The Contractor's submittal shall include a complete list of equipment, materials, and installation instructions. All prices shall be itemized in single component prices as well as quantity pricing with any discounts so indicated. Alternative proposals are acceptable under this specification and shall comply with all standard requirements for the bid package submittal.

C. The Contractor receiving the award shall submit within two weeks (14 days) of the award date a complete set of shop drawings. These drawings shall contain complete wiring and schematic diagrams, software descriptions, calculations, and any other details required to demonstrate that the system has been properly coordinated and installed to function as described within the specifications.

D. The Contractor shall upon the completion of the project, provide to the Client or their designated representative, a complete and accurate set of As-Built drawings. The submittal shall be in AutoCAD V2000 and supplied on a disk along with five copies of system(s) manuals and drawings. The submittal shall be completed and delivered to the Client and/or their designated representative at least two weeks prior to final acceptance testing. Punch item corrections will require a re-submittal if the list is substantial.

1.5 QUALITY ASSURANCE

A. Manufacturer's Qualifications:

The Contractor shall only represent a Company that specializes in the business of having provided Electronic Integrated Security Systems for a period of at least five (5) years. The supporting documentation supplied by the Contractor shall demonstrate the Manufacturer's as well as the Contractor's experience by including:

1. Installations for at least five (5) facilities of equal size and comparable technical requirements utilizing the equipment submitted.
2. For each facility, the information should include:
   a. Name and address of facility;
   b. Date of the Installation and System Acceptance;

      c. A point of contact for either the Owner or the Owner's designated representative;

      d. The name of the project or construction manager, if applicable; and

      e. The name of the Architect of Record, if applicable.

    3. A description of the technical aspects of the system describing how the system functions in comparison to the System described within this specification.

  B. References and Regulatory Requirements.

    1. All workmanship and materials supplied under this Section shall comply with the requirements of the following agencies and authorities:

      a. International Electrical Engineers (IEE)

      b. European Committee for Electro technical Standardization (CENELEC)

      c. International Electro technical Commission (IEC)

      d. National Fire Protection Association (NFPA) US Standard

      e. National Electric Manufacturers Association (NEMA) US Standard

      f. Life Safety Code (NFPA 101) (1999) US Standard

      g. National Burglar and Fire Alarm Association (NBFAA) – Standards of Application – US Standard

      h. Closed Circuit Television Manufacturers Association (CCTMA) – US Standard

      i. Underwriters Laboratories (UL) – European Equivalent

1.6 REQUIREMENTS OF THE DESIGN

  A. THE SYSTEM – The design for this system consists of several components. The intent is to allow full monitoring of all security and security related activities, including building management services (HVAC, Fire, Power, etc.) at the systems management console (SMC). The monitored functions shall consist of but not be limited to:

    1. All access control devices for access and egress to and from the facility;

    2. Intrusion detection equipment as it relates to fire doors, duress buttons, and other similar devices;

    3. Delayed Egress Locking Devices;

    4. Closed circuit surveillance cameras with a processor integrated into the overall system to provide reactive design functions and a digital recording device; and

    6. Any additional components required for a complete installation but not identified within this specification.

B. THE INSTALLATION – The Contractor shall provide, install, terminate, and submit for final acceptance testing the electronic system required for this design. All work will be inspected during the installation process and final acceptance testing will be conducted prior to the system being accepted by the Client. The contractor shall advise the Client at each point of substantial completion to allow periodic inspections. Final acceptance testing shall be conducted when contractor advises the system is ready. Punch list corrections shall be completed within two weeks after list development. The testing process is on all items prior to acceptance of the system by the Client. The Client reserves the right to require complete system testing a second time if the punch list is of considerable size.

1. CENTRALIZED MONITORING – This design of this system is such that monitoring will be required in two locations. The primary monitoring of CCTV and all alarms will be at the systems monitoring console (SMC) located in the main console room. A second monitoring station at the Security Command Center (SCC) may be required for each site. This workstation will be monitored by security officers and shall mirror the information being sent to the SMC... This station will be a workstation with all security and security related functions reporting to this location as well as the SCM. The system shall archive all access control, intrusion detection alarms, BMS functions, and CCTV video storage information at the main system server located in Livermore, California. The information shall be sent via the owner provided "NET" on a pre-programmed basis established by the Client and programmed by the Contractor.

2. The system shall provide for automatic display of alarm point locations at the SMC and SCC. The components of the integrated system shall include but not be limited to:

A. The Front-end processor for each site complete with software license;
B. One workstation, complete with software license;
C. One (1) Net-controller unit;
D. Power supply with battery backup;
E. Software to accommodate 32 card readers;
F. Software to accommodate up to 4 biometric readers (hand-geometry);
G. Field panels as required to monitor all points identified within this specification and on the drawings;
H. Building management systems (BMS) monitoring and control capability for up to 100 points;
I. Four (4) card reader units with locking and egress devices;

J. One (1) Hand Geometry reader unit;

K. Door position switches for each access control door leaf and other egress points within the facility;

L. Duress reporting devices (3) to be located at a later date;

M. Four (4) emergency break glass release units;

N. One (1) intercom master with 1 external slave unit;

O. Twelve (12) dual technology volumetric protection devices with adjustable lens units;

F. Training, manuals, service, and maintenance as specified; and,

G. Any additional components required, but not specifically mentioned within this or other sections.

E. CLOSED CIRCUIT SURVEILLANCE - The Contractor shall provide, install, terminate, program, and submit for final acceptance testing, a processor based Closed Circuit Television Surveillance system (CCTV). This system shall be integrated through the matrix switcher and the access control front end central processor to provide video coverage of each alarm point and/or surveillance locations identified for this project. Monitoring shall be required at the SMC and SCC with video storage both on site and at the Livermore, CA server. The system shall be reactive in design with all programming being done in accordance with this specification and the accompanying drawings. Each location shall be supplied with a 32 channel digital recorder that will serve as the video signal processor and shall be installed in such a manner as to allow it to integrate with other system components. The CCTV system shall consist of the following components:

1. Cameras - Fixed & Autodome

2. Monitors for SMC and SCC;

3. Video Matrix processor capable of handling up to 32 cameras with 8 outputs;

4. Digital Video Recording Unit;

5. Housings as required;

6. Power supplies as specified;

7. Training, manuals, service, and maintenance as specified; and,

8. Any additional components required, but not specifically mentioned within this or other sections.

F. INTRUSION DETECTION: The Contractor shall provide, install, terminate, and submit for final acceptance testing, door position switches as indicated on the drawings accompanying this specification. Each door position switch shall be interfaced into the system in order that either intrusion or egress alarms through secured doors are reported to both the SMC and SCC. The IDS also shall interface with the camera controller unit to activate the camera system for the purposes of alerting the personnel in the monitoring areas and also to activate the recording functions of the system. This system shall be integrated through the Contractor provided cabling for the purpose of activating the video and security response techniques required for both interior as well as limited exterior areas. The system shall consist of the following components:

1. Door Position Switches; and
2. Any additional components required, but not specifically mentioned within this or other sections.
3. Fence sensors
4. Passive ultrasonic
5. Photo-electric beam
6. Dual technology glass breaks
7. Balanced magnetic switches

G. DURESS REPORTING – The contractor shall provide, install, terminate, program, and submit for final acceptance testing, duress buttons at the locations indicated on the drawings accompanying this specification. The duress system shall, when activated, report to the SMC as well as the SCC. Additionally, the cameras selected by the Client and programmed by the Contractor shall be activated for the purpose of viewing the controlled area and recording all events that take place during the alarm. The components required for this portion of the system shall consist of:

1. Duress buttons – desk mounted
2. Any additional components required, but not specifically mentioned within this or other sections.

H. STRIKE PLATES – All access control doors and all egress points from within the controlled space to the outside of the facility shall have strike plates installed to protect against direct attacks against the lock bolt of the door.

I. DELAYED EGRESS LOCKING UNITS – Certain of the facilities covered under this specification may require the use of delayed egress locking devices. The contractor shall provide, install, terminate, service and submit for final acceptance testing, delayed egress locking devices at the locations indicated on the drawings accompanying this specification. The locking system shall be integrated with the fire alarm system to ensure compliance with all codes relative to the use of this device. Signage and other required components such as power supplies, etc., will the responsibility of the contractor to provide, install, terminate, service and maintain. The locking system, when activated, shall report to the SMC as well as the SCC. Additionally, the cameras selected by the Client and programmed by the Contractor shall be activated for the purpose of viewing the areas of egress and recording any events that take place during the alarm. The components required for this portion of the system shall consist of:

1. Delayed Egress Locking Units – mortise locking units;
2. Key cylinders;
3. Strike plates to fit each individual application;
4. Power supplies and transformers; and
5. Any additional components required, but not specifically mentioned within this or other sections.

1.7 WARRANTY

A. Warrant material and workmanship for a period of one year from the date of system final acceptance.

B. Warranty shall include the repair, replacement, and upgrade of defective security components and/or materials including the correction of defective work when given notice by the Client during the warranty period.

C. Warranty response time shall be within 8 hours upon receipt of request from Client or their designated representative during normal working hours. Weekend response shall be extended to a period not to exceed 12 hours.

1.8 RECORD DOCUMENTS

A. The Contractor shall provide project record drawings identifying the system architecture and rack/component distribution.

B. The "document package" shall include three sets of system manuals for the overall system concept as well as individual components within the system. Manuals shall consist of:

1. Operations manual – provide all information for operation of the system, including but not limited to, trouble shooting information, as well as software operational information;

2. Installation manual – provide drawings describing all circuits, power distribution, equipment placement, and cable routing, in an As–Built drawings (C size) format. This manual shall also include reference to any conduit routing;

3. Maintenance/Service Manual – Provide all trouble shooting information, data that is applicable to on-site software manipulation, programming information, and service/maintenance records.

C. The "drawing package" shall include three (3) sets of As-built drawings. These drawings shall be supplied to the Client or the Client's designated representative for final acceptance testing, punch list development, and system acceptance. The drawings shall be corrected as required for final system acceptance. The As–Built drawings shall not be considered complete until accepted by the Client.

1.9 OPERATION TRAINING AND MAINTENANCE DATA

A. Included with the shop drawing submittal should be a syllabus outlining the training program that will be provided to the Client or their designated representative with reference to the operation of this system. This syllabus should include a minimum of 16 hours training with demonstrations of the features and functions of the primary system and integrated subsystems.

B. The training classes should be conducted with competent supervisors or factory trained technicians and shall be conducted on site. The Client shall designate which individuals from their organization shall receive the training.

1.10. OPERATION AND MAINTENANCE DATA MANUAL

1. Assemble a set of three (3) manuals in hard bound covers, presenting for the Client's guidance, full details for care and maintenance of visible surfaces, and of equipment included in the work.

2. Include manufacturer's literature relating to components and other equipment, catalog cut sheets, parts list, wiring diagrams, instruction sheets, and other pertinent information which will be useful to the Client in overall system operation and maintenance.

3. Include a list of installers and service representatives with company names and addresses, names of individuals to contact, and telephone numbers.

4. Prepare operating instructions, complete and explicit, including, but not limited to, instructions for start–up, operating, and stopping.

1.11 MAINTENANCE SERVICE

A. The contractor shall test and service system on a quarterly basis during the warranty period. Each quarterly inspection shall "cover" up to 30% of the installed components.

B. After each quarterly maintenance inspection the Contractor shall provide written notification to the Client of the system's condition before and after service, exact components that were tested and serviced, and overall status of the system. All notices shall be sent to Mr. Mike Arata, XYZ Corporation, 5667 Gibraltar Drive, Maplewood, California, 94588.

PART 2 - PRODUCTS

2.1 INTEGRATED ELECTRONIC SECURITY SYSTEM (IESS):

A. Refer to individual Integrated Electronic Security System Specification section for selected equipment and operational requirements.

2.1.1 DELAYED EGRESS LOCKING DEVICES:

A. Required Performance Features:

    1. The contractor shall provide, install, terminate, and submit for final acceptance testing, a delayed egress locking device that provides the following features:

        a. A request to exit switch shall be built into the device to detect attempts to use the door for unauthorized egress;

        b. Each unit shall be supplied with a lamp that indicates the disposition of the locking device. The lamp shall be protected by a masked bezel design that provide wide angle viewing along with the capability of providing three signals to indicate the armed status of the unit. The three signals shall be as follows:

            1. A continuously lighted lamp indicates the device has just been armed and as soon as the rearm timer expires the unit will be fully armed;

            2. A slow flashing light shall indicate the device being armed with no re-arm timing activation; and,

            3. A flashing indicator shall indicate the unit is in an alarm condition.

        c. The application of less than 15 pounds of pressure to the push pad shall cause an internal switch to start an irreversible alarm cycle;

        d. Activation of the internal switch shall cause an internal horn to sound at a minimum volume of 85 db at 6ft. The internal horn shall be supplied with the ability to select activation or non-activation during a fire alarm condition;

        e. The unit supplied shall also be capable of controlling nuisance alarms by being equipped with firmware that will provide a non-activation time of at least two seconds should the push pad be pushed by mistake;

        f. If the push pad is held for two seconds or more, the unit will revert to normal operating conditions, thereby activating the timing sequence as well as the internal sounding device causing the unit to release as designed for delayed egress requirements;

        g. Each unit supplied shall have a set of relay contacts rated at 1 ampere, 24 VDC, for external alarm indication and remote monitoring. The contacts should be designed to close when the device goes into the irreversible alarm condition. The internal relay contacts shall also be capable of driving a horn, lamp, or other indicative devices in accordance with the design;

        h. The contractor shall provide, install and terminate with each delayed egress device, a surface mounted door position switch to provide added monitoring capabilities to the secured door. The delayed egress locking device supplied shall have the ability to interface with this door position switch to allow activation of the alarm system should the door not close when the system is armed, the door is forced open when the system is armed, or to monitor anti-pass back activities through the shortening of re-arming times;

i. The unit shall be capable of being re-armed from the security console (SMC or SCC);

j. Each unit supplied shall be integrated into the fire alarm system to allow immediate disabling of the timing sequence and unlocking of the device in the event of a fire evacuation need. The unit shall be interfaced with the building's fire alarm system that should provide a set of normally closed contacts which open on alarm;

k. Each unit supplied shall be capable of accepting console "override" by being supplied with a external inhibit input device to allow interfacing capability with card readers, wall mounted key switches, and/or remote security console controls. The override feature shall be controlled by a normally closed switch that in an open position disarms the unit;

l. The firmware supplied with the unit shall have the ability to accommodate an adjustable re-arm time of from 2 to 28 seconds based on two second intervals or an infinite re-arm setting based on the status of the external door position switch. This adjustable time shall be changeable at the unit;

m. Each unit shall be capable of being adjusted to meet the requirements of the local AHJ (authority having jurisdiction, i.e., Fire Marshal) by providing up to 15 or 30 seconds of time delay as standard with adjustable capabilities of from 0 to 60 seconds based on 2 second increments. The contractor shall, for any delay adjusted longer than 15 seconds, receive and provide to the Client a letter of acceptance from the local AHJ confirming acceptance of the extended time delay;

n. The delayed egress devices shall also be supplied with an internal auxiliary locking device that is designed to engage when the unit is armed. This locking device shall be capable of withstanding forceful blows as well as pressures of more than 75 pounds on the push pad;

o. Each unit shall be supplied with a key switch designed to allow manual arming, disarming, and resetting of the unit. The contractor is responsible for verifying the need for the keyed unit with the Client prior to the units being supplied. If the key is not required, the unit shall be supplied with a blank cylinder; and,

p. The units supplied shall have been tested and accepted in accordance to ANSI A156.3, 1984, Grade 1, and shall meet all requirements for NFPA 101, Special Locking Arrangements.

2. The acceptable manufacturers for the delayed egress locking devices are as follows:

a. Von Duprin

b. Security Door Controls

c. Locknetics

END OF SECTION

INSTRUCTIONS TO BIDDERS

A. Definitions

1. Bid Documents

Bid documents include the bid advertisement/invitation, instructions to bidders, sample documents, the bid form, contract documents and any addenda issued prior to the bid opening date.

2. Addenda

Any narrative or graphic material issued by either the Client, or the Clients designated representative which would modify or change the bid documents by the addition, deletion, correction, or clarification of individual items contained in the bid documents, instructions, or specifications.

3. Bid

All qualified bidders shall submit a complete and properly executed bid statement to the Client or their designated representative. Proposals will include an offer to supply, install, terminate, and check out a complete and operational system as specified. All work will be performed in accordance with any specifications, drawings, and data included in the bid documents. The bid statement has to be signed by a person in position of authority for the bidder. Lump sum pricing is acceptable for the bid statement, however, itemized pricing must be supplied in the bid package as support materials.

4. Base Bid

A properly executed statement outlining the cost for hardware, work and services which the bidder proposes to perform, and which may be adjusted accordingly, at the option of the Client, by an alternate bids included with the base bid package.

5. Alternates

Additional amounts that could be added (Add-Alternates) or deducted (Deduct Alternates) from the base bid for components, installation techniques, systems, or interfaces pertaining to the system design, which the Client does not wish included in the primary system. All prices submitted for alternates must be signed as required for the base bid, and will be subject to the same terms and conditions as the base bid.

6. Unit Pricing

All bids must be itemized showing unit prices for materials and labor in order for the bid submittal to be considered complete.

7. Definition of the term qualified bidder

A prime business entity that was invited to bid on this project, and submitted a bid for work described in the documents and specifications of this bid package.

8. Definition of the term qualified sub-contractor

A corporate entity submitting pricing information for equipment and services related to a portion of this project. The pricing is submitted to the bidder for inclusion in the total package.

9. Definition of the term prime contractor

The corporate entity proposing to be totally responsible for the services called for in the bid package submitted to the Client. The party accepts total responsibility for all sub-contractor performance related to the provision of equipment, installation, service, warranty, and any other conditions or requirements related to this project.

B. Bidder Representation

1. Each bidder, by the action of submitting a bid package, is classified as a prime contractor and represents that:

   a Contract documents, specifications, and supporting documents have been read and are fully understood by the bidder and all sub-bidders involved with the bid package.

   b The bidder is fully responsible for the procurement, coordination, installation, and start-up of a complete and operational system and its related components, including all necessary accessories and peripheral equipment, whether or not specifically indicated by the contract documents.

   c The bidder will make every effort to ensure that the various components of the project are purchased and installed in a coordinated, efficient manner.

   d As limited by information contained in this proposal, the bidder fully understands the conditions under which the work is to be performed. Full disclosure of information will be made to bidders invited to enter into final negotiations. The bidders final offering represents a full understanding of all issues, including but not restricted to:

      1. Transportation

2. Disposal
3. Handling and storage of materials or equipment
4. Availability of labor, water, power and roads
5. The uncertainties of the weather in this region
6. Coordination of construction efforts
7. Conditions of the surface and subsurface around the project
8. Shipping restrictions of certain suppliers and equipment manufacturers.

2. Submission of a proposal warrants that the bidder fully understands and agrees to coordinate with all other contractors (trades) on the project, and that this effort will include, but not be limited to:

a. Scheduling of construction activities in the sequence required to obtain the best results when part of the work is depending upon the installation of other components.

b. Coordinate installation of different components, where availability of space is limited, to assure maximum accessibility for required maintenance, service, and repair.

c. Make adequate provisions to accommodate any items, components, or systems, scheduled for later installation.

d. Where and when necessary, prepare memorandum for distribution to each party involved outlining special procedures required for coordination. This memorandum may include but not be limited to items such as required notices, reports, and attendance at meetings.

3. The bidder guarantees coordination of schedules and timing of required administrative procedures with other construction activities to avoid conflicts, and ensure orderly progress of the work. Such administrative activities should include but not be limited to:

a. Schedule preparations
b. Installation and removal of temporary facilities
c. Delivery and processing of submittals
d. Progress (construction) meetings
e. Project close out activities

C. Documents

1. Bid documents may be obtained in accordance with the provisions of this specification.

2. All bidders are responsible for preparing and submitting a complete set of bid documents.

3. The Client, in duplicating the bid documents and making available the same, does so only for the purpose of obtaining bids for the

work, and does not confer a license for, or grant any other use of the documents by any party either involved in the bid process, acting as a sub-bidder, or only having come into contact with the documents, unless so authorized by the Client.

4. All bidders and sub-bidders must immediately advise the Client, or the Clients designated representative, of any inconsistency or error discovered while examining the bid documents or of the site and local conditions.

5. All requests for clarification or interpretation will be submitted in accordance with the procedures outlined in the bid advertisement.

6. All interpretations, changes, additions, or deletions to the documents of this project will be made by addendum issued by the Client, and/or the Clients designated representative.

7. Substitution requests for system equipment, components, or installation procedures must be submitted with the bid package and documented.

8. All addenda to this project will be mailed, FAXED, or delivered via overnight services to all parties known to the Client as having received a copy of the bid documents for this project.

D. Bidding Process

The following instructions apply to the bid process:

1. Bid Submittal Format

    a. All bids will be typed and submitted complete.

    b. Telephone or oral bids not acceptable.

    c. Blank pages, sections or other spaces must be marked accordingly.

    d. All pricing submitted for the bid must be itemized.

    e. Each copy of the bid will include the legal name of the bidder and a statement indicating whether the bidder is the sole proprietor, a partnership, corporation, or other legal entity. Each copy will be signed by the person or persons legally authorized to bind the bidder to the contract. All bids by corporations will further give the state of incorporation and have the corporate seal affixed. A bid submitted by an agent shall have a current power of attorney attached certifying the agents authority to sign the bid documents, and subsequently bind the bidder to the project.

2. Submission Procedures

    a. Each submission will be typed and will include copies of the bid, the bid security, and other documents as required, in a sealed envelope addressed in accordance with the bidder instructions. The envelope will be identified with the following information:

    a. Clients representatives address as specified in the bid instructions.

b. The title of the project.

c. The Bidders name and address.

d. The Bidders license number if applicable.

e. All bids must be delivered by the time and date, and in accordance with the manner specified in the bidder instructions.

f. The bidder is fully responsible for timely delivery of the bids. Bids received after the time and date designated within the bidder instructions will be rejected.

3. Separate Contracts

The Client reserves the right to enter into separate contracts for this work. The bidder will properly coordinate to the best of their ability with all other contractors to schedule and connect the work required under the scope of this project.

4. Bid Modification or Withdrawal

a. The bid may not be modified, withdrawn, or canceled after the stipulated closing time for bid submittal.

b. Bids withdrawn before the stipulated closing time may be resubmitted prior to the designated closing time and will be considered if they are fully in compliance with submittal requirements, and the security is in an amount sufficient to meet the requirements of the bid security section.

E. Consideration of Bids

a. Rejection

The Client reserves the right to reject any and all bids when such action is in the Client's best interest.

b. Unacceptable Bids

All bids based on the following will be unacceptable for this project:

1. Any bid not based on the specifications included in this design and bid package.

2. Bids not signed by any person(s) having legal authority to bind the bidder to the submitted bid package.

3. Bids containing quotations qualified by memoranda.

4. Alternates, substitutions, additions, or deletions, submitted by the Bidder, and which are found by the Client, or the Client's designated representative, not to be in compliance with the intended design of this specification.

c. Acceptance of Bids

1. The Client reserves the right to waive any informality or irregularity in the bid when such action is found to be in the Clients best interest.

2. It is the intent of the Client to award the contract to the bidder showing the best combination of factors including; compliance

with the bid format and submission requirements, compliance with technical specifications, bidders stability, strength and reputation, and that the bid is found to be reasonable in cost and schedule. Bids will not necessarily be awarded on the basis of any one factor, such as cost.

3. The Client reserves the right to request a best and final proposal from any or all bidders should it be deemed necessary.

d. Unit Pricing

1. Unit prices (for individual hardware or software applications) will be considered in the process of awarding this contract.

2. Quantities specified in this design are approximate. Should additional hardware be required, prices will be modified at the same rate as the itemized price originally quoted.

INSTRUCTIONS TO BIDDERS

A. Definitions

1. Bid Documents

Bid documents include the bid advertisement/invitation, instructions to bidders, sample documents, the bid form, contract documents and any addenda issued prior to the bid opening date.

2. Addenda

Any narrative or graphic material issued by either the Client, or the Clients designated representative which would modify or change the bid documents by the addition, deletion, correction, or clarification of individual items contained in the bid documents, instructions, or specifications.

3. Bid

All qualified bidders shall submit a complete and properly executed bid statement to the Client or their designated representative. Proposals will include an offer to supply, install, terminate, and check out a complete and operational system as specified. All work will be performed in accordance with any specifications, drawings, and data included in the bid documents. The bid statement has to be signed by a person in position of authority for the bidder. Lump sum pricing is acceptable for the bid statement, however, itemized pricing must be supplied in the bid package as support materials.

4. Base Bid

A properly executed statement outlining the cost for hardware, work and services which the bidder proposes to perform, and which may be adjusted accordingly, at the option of the Client, by an alternate bids included with the base bid package.

5. Alternates

Additional amounts that could be added (Add–Alternates) or deducted

(Deduct Alternates) from the base bid for components, installation techniques, systems, or interfaces pertaining to the system design, which the Client does not wish included in the primary system. All prices submitted for alternates must be signed as required for the base bid, and will be subject to the same terms and conditions as the base bid.

6. Unit Pricing

All bids must be itemized showing unit prices for materials and labor in order for the bid submittal to be considered complete.

7. Definition of the term qualified bidder

A prime business entity that was invited to bid on this project, and submitted a bid for work described in the documents and specifications of this bid package.

8. Definition of the term qualified sub-contractor

A corporate entity submitting pricing information for equipment and services related to a portion of this project. The pricing is submitted to the bidder for inclusion in the total package.

9. Definition of the term prime contractor

The corporate entity proposing to be totally responsible for the services called for in the bid package submitted to the Client. The party accepts total responsibility for all sub-contractor performance related to the provision of equipment, installation, service, warranty, and any other conditions or requirements related to this project.

B. Bidder Representation

1. Each bidder, by the action of submitting a bid package, is classified as a prime contractor and represents that:

   a Contract documents, specifications, and supporting documents have been read and are fully understood by the bidder and all sub-bidders involved with the bid package.

   b The bidder is fully responsible for the procurement, coordination, installation, and start-up of a complete and operational system and its related components, including all necessary accessories and peripheral equipment, whether or not specifically indicated by the contract documents.

   c The bidder will make every effort to ensure that the various components of the project are purchased and installed in a coordinated, efficient manner.

   d As limited by information contained in this proposal, the bidder fully understands the conditions under which the work is to be performed. Full disclosure of information will be made to bidders invited to enter into final negotiations. The bidders final offering represents a full understanding of all issues, including but not restricted to:

1. Transportation
2. Disposal
3. Handling and storage of materials or equipment
4. Availability of labor, water, power and roads
5. The uncertainties of the weather in this region
6. Coordination of construction efforts
7. Conditions of the surface and subsurface around the project
8. Shipping restrictions of certain suppliers and equipment manufacturers.

2. Submission of a proposal warrants that the bidder fully understands and agrees to coordinate with all other contractors (trades) on the project, and that this effort will include, but not be limited to:
   a. Scheduling of construction activities in the sequence required to obtain the best results when part of the work is depending upon the installation of other components.
   b. Coordinate installation of different components, where availability of space is limited, to assure maximum accessibility for required maintenance, service, and repair.
   c. Make adequate provisions to accommodate any items, components, or systems, scheduled for later installation.
   d. Where and when necessary, prepare memorandum for distribution to each party involved outlining special procedures required for coordination. This memorandum may include but not be limited to items such as required notices, reports, and attendance at meetings.

3. The bidder guarantees coordination of schedules and timing of required administrative procedures with other construction activities to avoid conflicts, and ensure orderly progress of the work. Such administrative activities should include but not be limited to:
   a. Schedule preparations
   b. Installation and removal of temporary facilities
   c. Delivery and processing of submittals
   d. Progress (construction) meetings
   e. Project close out activities

C. Documents
   1. Bid documents may be obtained in accordance with the provisions of this specification.
   2. All bidders are responsible for preparing and submitting a complete set of bid documents.
   3. The Client, in duplicating the bid documents and making available the same, does so only for the purpose of obtaining bids for the

work, and does not confer a license for, or grant any other use of the documents by any party either involved in the bid process, acting as a sub-bidder, or only having come into contact with the documents, unless so authorized by the Client.

4. All bidders and sub-bidders must immediately advise the Client, or the Clients designated representative, of any inconsistency or error discovered while examining the bid documents or of the site and local conditions.

5. All requests for clarification or interpretation will be submitted in accordance with the procedures outlined in the bid advertisement.

6. All interpretations, changes, additions, or deletions to the documents of this project will be made by addendum issued by the Client, and/or the Clients designated representative.

7. Substitution requests for system equipment, components, or installation procedures must be submitted with the bid package and documented.

8. All addenda to this project will be mailed, FAXED, or delivered via overnight services to all parties known to the Client as having received a copy of the bid documents for this project.

D. Bidding Process

The following instructions apply to the bid process:

1. Bid Submittal Format
   a. All bids will be typed and submitted complete.
   b. Telephone or oral bids not acceptable.
   c. Blank pages, sections or other spaces must be marked accordingly.
   d. All pricing submitted for the bid must be itemized.
   e. Each copy of the bid will include the legal name of the bidder and a statement indicating whether the bidder is the sole proprietor, a partnership, corporation, or other legal entity. Each copy will be signed by the person or persons legally authorized to bind the bidder to the contract. All bids by corporations will further give the state of incorporation and have the corporate seal affixed. A bid submitted by an agent shall have a current power of attorney attached certifying the agents authority to sign the bid documents, and subsequently bind the bidder to the project.

2. Submission Procedures
   a. Each submission will be typed and will include copies of the bid, the bid security, and other documents as required, in a sealed envelope addressed in accordance with the bidder instructions. The envelope will be identified with the following information:
   b. Clients representatives address as specified in the bid instruction

    c. The title of the project.

    d. The Bidders name and address.

    e. The Bidders license number if applicable.

    f. All bids must be delivered by the time and date, and in accordance with the manner specified in the bidder instructions.

    g. The bidder is fully responsible for timely delivery of the bids. Bids received after the time and date designated within the bidder instructions will be rejected.

3. Separate Contracts

The Client reserves the right to enter into separate contracts for this work. The bidder will properly coordinate to the best of their ability with all other contractors to schedule and connect the work required under the scope of this project.

4. Bid Modification or Withdrawal

    a. The bid may not be modified, withdrawn, or canceled after the stipulated closing time for bid submittal.

    b. Bids withdrawn before the stipulated closing time may be resubmitted prior to the designated closing time and will be considered if they are fully in compliance with submittal requirements, and the security is in an amount sufficient to meet the requirements of the bid security section.

E. Consideration of Bids

  a. Rejection

The Client reserves the right to reject any and all bids when such action is in the Client's best interest.

  b. Unacceptable Bids

All bids based on the following will be unacceptable for this project:

    1. Any bid not based on the specifications included in this design and bid package.

    2. Bids not signed by any person(s) having legal authority to bind the bidder to the submitted bid package.

    3. Bids containing quotations qualified by memoranda.

    4. Alternates, substitutions, additions, or deletions, submitted by the Bidder, and which are found by the Client, or the Client's designated representative, not to be in compliance with the intended design of this specification.

  c. Acceptance of Bids

    1. The Client reserves the right to waive any informality or irregularity in the bid when such action is found to be in the Clients best interest.

    2. It is the intent of the Client to award the contract to the bidder

showing the best combination of factors including; compliance with the bid format and submission requirements, compliance with technical specifications, bidders stability, strength and reputation, and that the bid is found to be reasonable in cost and schedule. Bids will not necessarily be awarded on the basis of any one factor, such as cost.

   3. The Client reserves the right to request a best and final proposal from any or all bidders should it be deemed necessary.

  d. Unit Pricing

   1. Unit prices (for individual hardware or software applications) will be considered in the process of awarding this contract.

   2. Quantities specified in this design are approximate. Should additional hardware be required, prices will be modified at the same rate as the itemized price originally quoted.

IV. AGREEMENT/SUBMITTAL FORMS

  A. Introduction

The following forms will be required, as described by the specification:

  a. Bond Forms, Proof of Bond Capability with submittal

  b. Insurance Forms, Proof of coverage with submittal

  c. Surety Consent Forms, None required with initial submittal

  d. Licensing Certificate of Compliance. Required with submittal

  f. Bid Summary Form. Required with submittal

  B. Bond Forms

Required from selected vendor prior to final award of contract:

  a. Performance Bond

A performance bond shall be supplied for the full value of the work to be performed as called for within the specifications and drawings.

  b. Payment Bond

A payment bond shall be supplied for the full value of all work to be performed by sub-contractors and suppliers or for other financial obligations required under this project.

  C. Insurance Forms

Certificates of Insurance

Certificates of Insurance will be in the amount of $1,000,000 liability for each occurrence, combined liability, each occurrence and property damage, listing the ABCD Corporation as an additional insured.

  D. Surety Consent Statements

  a. Consent of Surety Company to elimination of further retainer at 50% contract completion.

  b. Consent of Surety Company to Final Payment.

  c. Licensing Certificate of Compliance

Before work is performed at the site, file or record the construction contract with proper governmental or regulatory officials if such filing is required. Submit a statement of compliance signed by the issuing agency stating that filing has been accomplished.

V. UNIT PRICES
A. Introduction

This section specifies administrative and procedural requirements for unit pricing.

All pricing must be quoted in US Dollars. However, the Client reserves the right to pay the amounts due in local currency.

Unit prices are amounts proposed by bidders and should be indicated as the price per unit of materials or services. Unit prices are also required for change orders that will be added to or deducted from the Contract Sum, in the event the estimated quantities of work required by the Contract Documents are increased or decreased.

Unit prices include necessary material, overhead, profit, and applicable taxes. Any costs or taxes unique to work in the European Economic Community must be included.

B. Schedule

The unit price schedule should include all items comprising the specified systems.

The Client reserves the right to reject the Contractors measurement of work-in-place that involves the use of established unit prices, and to have this work measured by an independent surveyor acceptable to the Contractor at the Clients expenses.

Protection of Utilities (Electric, Phone, Water)

The protection of the site utilities is important since the infrastructure is critical to operating any facility and the physical security of the site should take into account the planning and design to protect the infrastructure. The utilities are critical to keeping the site operating without them nothing will work. For example, without electricity the computers, lights, equipment, etc. would not operate. Since water is essential to life then a site without water would not last long. The heating ventilation and air conditioning and system (HVAC) is important for providing the air for people to breathe. The fiber or T1 line for the computers is important to keep data flowing so there are not any interruptions. Phones, and fax machines are a communication tool that needs communications links to keep working.

The protection of the utilities is important to maintaining the integrity of the site. There are ways to protect this critical infrastructure. Designing security for fiber, T1 lines, phone lines, electricity, HVAC, etc. is best done in the design phase of the facility. Retrofitting protection of these critical infrastructure components is sometimes the only option but not the desired one.

There are various methods used for protecting the utilities on a site. The following is a list of these methods:

1. Securing the T1 and fiber lines

2. Securing the manhole covers

3. Securing the electric utility vaults

4. Securing the electrical switchgear rooms

5. Securing the telephony room

6. Securing the emergency back up power system

7. Securing the water lines or wells on, the site

PROTECTING FIBER DATA LINES AND T1 LINES

Today computers are used extensively in all businesses, without them most businesses would grind to a halt. If you think I am kidding or exaggerating think of the last time that that computers were down, how much work got done? We rely on computers to do our jobs and when they are not available we can't do our jobs, or school work, etc. even with the advent of wireless connections. Most companies do not rely entirely on wireless and still use T1 and fiber for data lines. So protecting the fiber or T1Circuit is important.

The T1 line or fiber comes to the facility via the street through a network of underground utility tunnels filled with conduit. There is not much that can be done to with the conduit that is in the utility's manhole and tunnel, but when the conduit comes onto the facility's property there are things that can be done to help protect the fiber.

The following are some ways to help protect the fiber infrastructure when it leaves the street and comes onto the facility:

1. Protect the cable by placing it conduit. This will help when the cable is buried in a trench across the grass and flower beds from the street to the building. The conduit may protect the cable from being damaged if it is grabbed by a backhoe doing work in the area.

2. Lock the manhole covers on the property down by screwing them down with a special bolt. Welding is another option, however it will be difficult to get into the manhole for any work.

3. Install manhole intrusion detection system. The system is designed to send an alert when someone attempts to remove the manhole cover without having approved access. When maintenance is to be done on any utilities residing under the manhole cover, the IDS is shutdown.

4. Install a fiber optic monitoring system. There are several types of monitoring systems:

   a. Vibration sensor monitoring—The vibration sensing system does just that it monitors the fiber optic cable for any movement which is measured by the vibration of the cable.

   b. Real time monitoring systems—Real time monitoring is when the fiber cable is monitored in the here and now. In other words there is no delay whatever is occurring is actually happening now and is not recorded or captured in a log file.

   c. Phase modulation of the signal—The phase modulation of the signal monitors the cable for tapping which is one of the threats to the fiber optic cable.

Fiber can also be monitored by using one of the fiber optics that is not being used and use it to detect motion in the fiber. There is no way to set up zones so all the alarm will do is tell the cable has been moved. This could be because a rat as big as a cat is standing on the fiber but it will give you an alarm.

A T1 line can be fiber or copper and uses two wire pair, one for transmitting, the other one for receiving. T1 lines are used mostly by businesses because of their fast speed of 1.54 Mbps (Mega bits per second). The T1 line is vulnerable to a single point of failure. There is no redundancy built into the system. A T1 is a leased line and runs between two points of contact as a part of the Wide Area Network (WAN). If any part of the circuit is interrupted, the connection is lost. So a remote office will not have contact with the main office and the remote office will not have a network connection.

The T1 will be in conduit as it comes in from the street to protect it from inadvertent damage caused by a back hoe or some other machinery working in the grass and flower beds leading up to the facility

The protection of the circuits on the site is important. The T1 circuit is to be placed in a room with other circuits and switches. The room is to be monitored by balanced magnetic switches on the door for intrusion detection. The door will have card access and biometric readers for entry and only those that need access will be given access. Limited access is important to prevent intentional and unintentional damage to equipment in the room. The intrusion detection system for the room will be monitored continuously. The alarm will be shunted by a valid card and biometric access. To exit the room there will be a card access reader and a biometric reader and upon a valid read of both the alarm will be shunted to allow exiting.

Redundancy may need to be considered for the T1 line. The decision will based on, among other factors, the critical nature of what will be done at the facility when it is completed for a new one and for a facility that is already built, the critical nature of the work that is being done. The number of outages of any of the T1 lines also needs to be part of the decision process for redundant T1 lines. With the advent of and more widespread use of fiber cable maybe the back up line can be the T1 and the primary line can be the fiber. Another backup to the T1 line is the Frame Relay circuit. Frame relay operates on packet switching so, if any segment of the network cloud has a problem or failure, the packet is switched to another part of the operation.

There are sensors that can be placed in the conduit of a copper T1 line to detect any movement of the line that may indicate that the line is being tapped into. The tapping into the line is the purpose of capturing information.

Protecting the T1 and the fiber cables from intentional or unintentional damage is a part of the physical security program and it is a largely overlooked aspect. Protection of the T1 and fiber cable also includes the protection of the circuits. The circuits that are or will be on site can be protected as previously discussed earlier in the chapter.

SECURING THE MANHOLE COVERS

As previously mentioned above manhole covers on site can be secured by locking them with a locking bolt and installing intrusion detection. The issue here is that only the manhole covers on site can be secured but the manhole covers off site that belong to the phone company, power company, water company and the like cannot be secured by using a locking bolt since the manhole covers belong to the utility company and they need to have access to them regularly. Even if you could get the utility company to allow you to install locking bolts on the manhole covers near the facility how far out do you go? What is far enough to ensure the security of the fiber, T1, power lines, water, and/or telephone lines? The key thing to remember here is that you can design a certain amount of utility security into the facility's site plan but there is a significant part of the system

FIGURE 15-1 Manhole cover lock made by STABILOC®

FIGURE 15-1A In the locked position from inside the manhole.

of delivering utilities to a site that you will not have any authority or control to secure. Since the terrorist events of recent years the utility companies are securing more of their infrastructure than they have in the past. For example, more attention is being given to securing substations and switching yards. Manhole covers are also being secured as well but overall the problem of securing manhole covers today has not been sufficiently addressed. We still have a long way to go since the only protection in most cases is the 150 pound weight of the manhole cover which is not adequate security and is easily overcome making the manhole cover vulnerable.

See Figure 15.1 for a picture of a manhole cover lock made by STABILOC® and the manufacturer recommends two locks be installed in each manhole. The manhole cover needs to be retrofitted for the lock.

In Figure 15.1A, The STABILOC® shows the lock in the locked position from inside the manhole. The STABILOC® also comes with an option for adding an intrusion detection sensor and also has the option to come with a high security bolt that has a tungsten carbide insert which will deter any attempt to drill through the bolt head to gain entry. There are over 500,000 geometric patterns than can be used to make the bolt heads of the lock and all information related to the bolt heads is kept confidential by the manufacturer which helps to maintain the integrity of the locking system.

Figure 15.2 shows another type of manhole cover lock made by McGard, Inc. called the Intimidator™. The manufacturer recommends that each manhole be fitted with two locks per manhole cover. The bolt is specially grooved so it can only be turned using a special wrench known as a "key wrench". There are no two blots grooved the same in any geographical region so the wrench from one locking system will work in a neighboring locking system. The bolt is counter sunk so it can not be removed with gripping tools. The bolts are made of alloy steel to prevent being removed using various tools. To further protect the integrity of the locking system the key wrenches are tightly controlled by the manufacturer and are available only to authorized end-users that are registered in the

FIGURE 15.2 Manhole cover lock made by McGard, Inc. called the Intimidator™

system. The wrenches have serial numbers on them so they can be inventoried and controlled thereby minimizing the risk of an authorized access to a manhole for occurring. No special modifications need to be done to place the locks on the manhole covers.

Another type of manhole lock is a pan-type lock. The pan-type locks do not require any retrofitting for the lock to be installed. The pans are corrosive resistant and durable. The locks come in standard sizes or can be made to order to fit any manhole cover. The pan-type lock blocks any access to the manhole even if the cover is removed since the pan covers the entire opening. The pan is slightly recessed into the manhole and a padlock is used to secure the pan in place.

Another pan-type manhole device is made by Barton Southern Company. The device is called the LockDown-LockDry™. The lock covers the opening to the manhole so entry cannot be made even if the manhole cover is removed. Another feature of the pan-type manhole covers is that can be made to be water tight. This may be important since a large amount of water in a utility manhole and the underground tunnels that carry the utility services may lead to a failure of the equipment or lines that provide the services. Figure 15.3 shows a picture

FIGURE 15-3 Lock in place for the topside

FIGURE 15-3A The device from the bottom side in the locked position

of the lock in place for the topside and Figure 15.3A show the device from the bottom side in the locked position.

The LockDown-LockDry™ device is locked in place on the topside using a padlock. There is a guard that goes over the padlock to prevent tampering. There are locks that have intrusion detection as a part of the locking device. The locks can be ordered separately and are not part of the standard locking package. The padlock guard can be seen in Figure 15-3 which is the small device in the center of the picture. Part of the lock is visible the left of the small device. Notice that the lock hasp is covered and protected by the device. The lock cover adds another element of security. Manhole intrusion sensor technology is now option that was not readily available several years ago. The sensors used is new technology but the use of existing technology in a new way.

When selecting a manhole intrusion detection system design the following features should be considered:

• The type and sensitivity of the sensor

• The method of communication of the sensor

• The range of the sensor communication system

• The power requirements to operate the sensor

Choosing the right sensor is important for the following reasons:

1. Is the sensor designed to work in the environment it will be placed in?

2. Placement of the sensor is important for proper function.

3. Contact sensors need to be aligned with the sensors on the manhole cover and the frames for them to function properly.

4. Infrared sensors do not need to be aligned to function properly.

5. The sensor must send an alarm as soon as the manhole cover is removed or moved in any way.

6. Each system communicates differently using differently technologies and communication strategies. For example some sensors send a continuous signal to a monitoring station and if the signal is interrupted then an alarm is sent. While other sensors send an alarm only when the manhole cover is disturbed.

7. Some systems are hardwired and others are wireless. Each of these present their own set of logistical problems. Wireless systems have limits on the distance that their communications are effective. Also with the wireless systems there are issues with power supplies. In some cases fire optics may not fill the bill. So the decision has to include an analysis of the situation to choose the right sensor for the job and conditions.

8. Power supplies for the sensors is important and some manholes do not have a readily available power source so batteries are used. The use of batteries adds the additional problem of keeping them charged and ready for use.

9. Fiber optic does not require a power source so it may be an option.

The selection of a manhole to use in the design or retrofit will depend on doing an assessment.

The types of sensors being used for manhole cover intrusion detection are as follows.

1. Mechanical switches

2. Magnetic switches

3. Infrared motion

4. Fiber optic

The mechanical switches are similar in design to those that are used for windows and doors. The systems operation is simple; the two parts need to be in contact with one another to close the circuit. One has a plunger and the other keeps the plunger depressed If one them is moved and contact is broken the plunger is released and the circuit is open an alarm is sent. To disarm the intrusion detection of the STABILOC® system which has a microchip in the system, the maintenance crew uses handheld device readers and scans the chip in the sensor. The information from the chip is sent back to the central monitoring station that is part of the system's SCADA, which stands for Supervisory Control And Data Acquisition used by utilities to centrally monitor their system to deactivate the alarm.

The magnetic switch intrusion detection systems operate like those used for doors and windows. The magnetic sits up a magnetic field between the manhole lid and the sensor. When the field is broken an alarm is triggered. Deactivation for maintenance purposes can be done in a similar way as the mechanical sensor since there is also a microchip in the magnetic sensor or by notifying the central monitoring station to deactivate the sensor using a code to verify the identity of the person making the request to deactivate the alarm.

Infrared motion sensors are used to detect movement of the manhole cover. A wireless sensor is installed on the frame of the manhole and used to shoot a beam across the cover if the beam is broken an alarm is sent. Another infrared sensor systems uses off the shelf technology and there a sensor at the bottom of the manhole frame that shoots a bema up to the cover if the cover is removed and alarm is triggered. The alarm is then sent using SCADA to the central monitoring station.

Fiber optic sensors are designed to measure a loss in signal strength the fiber optic cable. The cable is looped through the manhole and frame in a predetermined pattern. The detector is programmed to see a certain pulses of light in a predetermined pattern so if the light is disrupted because of movement of the cable, removing or moving the manhole cover, then an alarm is triggered.

There are several types of fiber optic sensors on the market today:

1. The LightLoc™ system is different than the one described above because it is a not a contact system. The system is made of sensors that are placed around 1/2 inch for the bottom of the manhole cover with the monitoring station being remote from the manhole. The sensor contains a fiber optic loop with a magnet to hold the fiber optic sensor in place. When the magnetic field is broken the cable is pushed by a spring form its resting place and this causes a change in the attenuation of the continuous fiber optic signal causing an alarm.

2. LightGuard (patent pending) makes a sensor that consists of a LightGuard control system that has fiber extending from it and a detector mounted on a non-metallic flat surface that is within 500 feet of the manhole cover for the hardwired system and 400 feet for the wireless version. The fiber loop is placed underneath the manhole frame. Then the cable is spliced and reconnected using two half moon-shaped connectors. The two moon-shaped connectors are then mounted, one on the manhole cover and the other mounted on the frame adjacent to the one on the manhole cover making the fiber cable continuous when the manhole cover is closed. The system when activated sends a randomly pulsed signal through the fiber loop. Opening the cover with sensor activated will cause the connection between the fibers to be broken triggering an alarm. The alarm is sent to the central monitoring station by using a control panel, SCADA, or by some other means.

PROTECTING THE ELECTRIC UTILITY VAULTS

The electrical vault is a critical infrastructure that needs to be secured so there is not any interruption in the normal power for any extended period of time. Some sites have more then one feed from the power company. This redundancy of two vaults builds in some protection since there are two vaults that will have the transformer and associated equipment. If the vaults are located on opposite sides of the facility, it is harder to have damage to both at the same time. The electric utility vault needs to be protected from the following vulnerabilities:

1. Fire

2. Vandalism

3. Sabotage

To protect an electric utility vault from fire there must be an automatic detection and suppression system installed. The electric utility vaults usually have switchgear and a transformer in the vault and a large amount of heat is produced during normal operations so the vault will need to be ventilated with grating and ventilation fans.

The type of fire suppression system that works best on live electrical equipment fires is Carbon Dioxide. The CO_2 system is a gaseous system. Since the CO_2 displaces the oxygen, it is immediately dangerous to life and health. The system will need to be disarmed when anyone is the vault. Also since CO_2 is a gas it will dissipate quickly and in order to get the proper concentration of gas to suppress the fire the vault needs to sealed during a fire. The detection system will need to shut down the ventilation fans. Most of the detection systems for gaseous systems are dual technology. The first detector will shut down the fans and the second detector will activate the system to discharge.

Vandalism is not a major issue for electric utility vaults. However, the grating cover and any other openings to the vault need to be locked at all times to keep unauthorized persons from entering the vault. The electrical vault is extremely dangerous when the transformer and switchgear are hot and operating. Intrusion detection will need to be installed on the entrance gates or grates to alarm when someone is attempting to enter the vault. The IDS will be balanced magnetic contact switches.

The vault should have an adequate drainage system including a pump to pump out large amounts of rainwater to prevent damage. The pump should be designed to automatically come on when the water reaches a certain level in the vault.

Finally, sabotage is a vulnerability that needs to be addressed especially for facilities that are sensitive. The threat of sabotage is still a possibility for other facilities however the possibility is remote.

The purpose of the sabotage is to disrupt or stop the operations at the facility. To help minimize the effect of a power outage, all critical operations will be on the emergency back up power system and the emergency generator. A UPS (Uninterruptible Power Supply) system will help eliminate the disruption to sensitive equipment and processes. With the UPS system the power is uninterrupted by using batteries as a backup.

Sabotage to electrical vaults with transformers and associated equipment can be done in a number of ways. Such as some the following:

1. Fire/Turning off the fire detection and suppression in the vault

2. Damaging the transmission line to the vault

3. Damaging and/or shutting down the ventilation system in the vault

We discussed the threat from fire previously. Installing an automatic fire detection and suppression system will help with a fire but tamper switches and alarms need to be installed to help alert security that the fire detection or suppression system was shut down. By shutting down the fire detection and suppression system a fire will be more damaging than normal because it will not be detected and contained early enough.

The power lines coming into the vault need to be protected as well. The power lines are to be placed underground to protect them from the weather and other elements but to also secure them from being tampered with. Even though tampering with live high voltage electric lines is dangerous there are people who will take the chance to sabotage or cause vandalism. Overhead lines are targets for damage by taking down the power poles that hold the lines.

To protect the vault against sabotage use an IDS system as previously mentioned. Also CCTV can be added to monitor the vault area. The CCTV can be set to motion sensors and to alarm if there is any movement in the vault. The security console will get an alarm and the cameras displaying the vault area will come up the security console monitor. The security officers will able to assess the situation by manually rotating the cameras. A response to the area above the vault by the security officers will also be part of the plan. There will be an audible and visual alarm above the vault that will be activated with the IDS system to signal that there has been a possible breach in security. The light will be a strobe light flashing red and a horn sounding an audible warning. Other alarms such as overheating of the electrical switchgear, shut down, also known as the tripping of the breaker, and water levels during storms or other run-off, will also be monitored by the security console and the cameras can be used to help assess the situation during an overheating or shut down alarm without having to send someone into the vault. This will help provide an element of safety since going into the vault during normal operations should be avoided if possible.

SECURING THE ELECTRICAL SWITCHGEAR ROOM

The electrical switchgear room needs to be secured for safety and security reasons. The switchgear room has high voltage equipment in the room and associated cabling. The room also has all the main breakers for the switchgear and some of the large equipment used at the facility. The room is usually protected by an automatic fire suppression system. In most cases the fire suppression system is water, but for some switchgear rooms have two fire suppression systems. One system is CO_2 and the other is a water sprinkler system that is used to protect the building if the CO_2 system fails to suppress the fire. CO_2 is a health and life hazard and, when the room is occupied for maintenance or to take readings, the CO_2 system is usually disarmed.

Access control will be used to control access to the room for safety and security. To enter the room the person entering will swipe an access card on the reader and for added security a biometric reader. The action of using the card and biometric readers will disarm the CO_2 system. To exit the person will swipe their access card and the door will open shunting the alarm. To exit during an emergency evacuation the panic bar will be pushed for immediate exit. Any time the panic bar is used an alarm will be sent to the security console. CCTV will be used to monitor the inside of the room and a camera will be positioned at the entry door to record who enters and leaves.

SECURING THE TELEPHONE ROOM/OR CLOSET

The telecommunications equipment needs to be secured and protected from tampering. The greatest vulnerability to the telecommunications equipment not being secured is for someone to enter the room or closet and place a wire tap on the phone lines of the executives. Most telephony phone switches have all the wiring labeled by phone extension number or name. This makes it easy to trace the lines but it also makes it easy for someone to place a wire tap on the executive's phone. It is advisable to use a numbering system to identify what line belongs to whom and not leave the paper with the numbering scheme in or around the phone switch panel.

The door to the closet or room will have access control so entry to the room can be controlled and the room will be locked at all times. By using electronic locks and the access control system for the door the door will be monitored. The telephone company representative will have an access card that will be kept at the reception desk and upon presenting and surrendering a valid driver's license the access card for the telephony closet will be given to the company representative. The driver's license is given back to the telephone company person when the access badge is returned. The access control badge will only open the telephony rooms/or closets and no other locations. Most telephony rooms are left unlocked or have locks and keys and the control system is nonexistent so there is not any security for the telephony equipment.

CCTV will be used for recording who enters the telephony room/or closet. There should be two cameras used, one outside the room/closet and one in the room/closet. Figure 15.4 is an excerpt for the State of Virginia Housing Authority outlining the design requirements for Electrical and Telecommunications Closets and Computer Rooms.

TOPIC 8. ELECTRICAL AND TELECOMMUNICATIONS CLOSETS AND COMPUTER ROOMS

1. GENERAL PROVISIONS FOR NEW BUILDINGS

   a. Provide at least two means of egress from switchgear rooms, transformer vaults, generator rooms, and rooms over 1800 mm (6 feet) wide containing equipment rated over 1200 amperes. Provide egress to the exterior on grade or into a corridor. Egress by means of a ladder in an areaway is prohibited.

   b. Provide paddle operated door hardware on all doors leading from switchgear rooms, transformer vaults and generator rooms with door swing in the direction of exit travel.

   c. Provide standard hardware on doors of electrical and telecommunications closets. Doors must swing out.

   d. Stack all electrical and telecommunications closets vertically, except for electrical closets in VA Hospital Building System (VAHBS) as indicated in paragraph 3d.

   e. Refer to the HVAC Design Manual for necessary mechanical ventilation or mechanical cooling system to maintain indoor temperatures as required for proper operation of the equipment for all electrical and telecommunications closets, elevator machine rooms, emergency generator rooms, fire alarm equipment rooms and computer rooms.

2. SWITCHGEAR ROOMS AND TRANSFORMER VAULTS IN NEW BUILDINGS

   a. Locate switchgear rooms and transformer vaults as close as practical to the utility service entrance side of the building. Locate these areas on or above grade, but not in pipe basements.

   b. For switchgear rooms and the vaults, provide one wall with double swing doors to the exterior, on grade with access to a service road. Establish the required size of switchgear rooms and transformer vaults after the electrical loads and equipment layouts have been determined. For high and low voltage switchgear, allow a minimum clearance of 4200 mm (4 ft.) on both ends and rear, and 1800 mm (6 ft.) in front, from any wall, column or other equipment.

3. ELECTRICAL CLOSETS IN NEW AND MAJOR ALTERATIONS TO EXISTING BUILDINGS

   a. Except for the VA Hospital Building System (VAHBS) concept, provide one centrally located electrical closet for each wing length of 45 000 mm (150 ft.) or less. When the wing length exceeds 45 000 mm (150 ft.), provide a minimum of two electrical closets. Where feasible, centrally locate electrical closets in the area to be served. The minimum size of electrical closets containing step down transformers should be 2400 mm (8 ft.) by 3000 mm (10 ft.). Size closets that do not contain transformers per the number of panels installed with space allotted for a future normal panel and a future emergency panel. Walk in closets should be a minimum 2100 mm (7 ft.) wide.

   b. Where only one or two panels are to be installed in an area, shallow closets may be permitted. The depth of the closet should be 600 mm (2 ft.) minimum. The length should be 1800 mm (6 ft.) with double doors that swing 180 degrees out into the corridor.

   c. Position closet locations such that structural beams do not have to be core drilled and that the conduit feeder risers are routed vertically through the stacked closets.

   d. For the VAHBS concept, to reduce voltage drops, do not design electrical closets to serve large areas greater than 45 000 mm (150 ft.) from the service bays. Design electrical closets to be served horizontally from the service bay on the same floor.

FIGURE 15-4 Design requirements for Electrical and Telecommunications Closets and Computer Rooms.

(continued on next page)

4. TELECOMMUNICATIONS CLOSETS IN NEW BUILDINGS

   a. Design the quantity and locations of telecommunications (combined computer, TV, radio, fire alarm, nurse call and telephone communications) closets the same as electrical closets above and follow the guidelines identified in Electrical Design Manual for Hospitals PG-18-10, Chapter 8, Telephone/Data Systems, Paragraph 8.15, Telecommunications Closets. Contact CSO Telecommunications Consultants Division (194D) at 301.734.0350 for technical assistance for these rooms.

   b. For the VAHBS concept, locate the telecommunications closets in the equipment bay.

5. MAIN TELEPHONE EQUIPMENT ROOMS FOR ELECTRONIC PRIVATE AUTOMATIC BRANCH EXCHANGE (EPABX) - See Electrical Design Manual for Hospitals PG-18-10, Chapter 8, Telephone/Data Systems, Paragraph 8.11, Telephone Equipment Room, Paragraph 8.12, Physical Security, Paragraph 8.13, Basement Installations and Paragraph 8.14, Telephone Console Room for minimum room size and physical requirements for these areas. Contact Telecommunications Consultants Division (194D) at 301.734.0350 for technical assistance for these rooms.

6. MAIN COMPUTER ROOM - Locate with one wall adjacent to mainframe telephone equipment rooms. See PG-18-3, Topic 10 Computer Systems, for additional requirements. Coordinate the final size of room with VA Medical Center.

7. SPECIAL PROVISIONS FOR THE ABOVE ROOMS - Do not locate any of the described areas above directly below laboratories, kitchens, dishwashing areas, toilets, showers, or other areas where water service is provided. No roof drains, pipes containing liquids or gases, or air conditioning ducts not serving these rooms should pass through these rooms except for approved supervised automatic sprinkler systems serving these rooms.

8. EMERGENCY GENERATOR ROOMS - Locate emergency generators in a separate building, on grade and near the normal power switchgear room. Locate an emergency generator in an Energy Center or Boiler Plant where space is available. Size the emergency generator building to fit the equipment required with maintained clearances of 1500 mm (5 ft.) between two generators and 1200 mm (4 ft.) between a generator and a wall or large piece of equipment. Refer to the Architecture Design Manual for Hospitals for recommended ceiling heights.

9. FIRE ALARM EQUIPMENT ROOMS - Preferably, locate fire alarm equipment at the Engineering Control Center (ECC). If an ECC is not included, locate the fire alarm equipment in a room adjacent to the hospital telephone switchboard room. The size of the room should be 7.5 m2 (80 sq. ft.) minimum.

10. ALTERATIONS TO EXISTING BUILDINGS - Follow the recommended space requirements as described herein for new buildings.

FIGURE 15-4   Design requirements for Electrical and Telecommunications Closets and Computer Rooms. *(continued)*

SECURING THE EMERGENCY BACKUP POWER SYSTEM

The emergency back up power UPS and generator will be discussed in more detail in Chapter 17. The emergency back up power system whether it is a UPS system or generator or both is usually in a separate room especially a generator. The UPS battery systems are sometimes placed in a cabinet. However the emergency back up power supply is stored, it needs to be secured.

To secure the cabinets that house the UPS batteries the door must be locked and alarmed. This way if an unauthorized person attempts to enter the cabinet an alarm will be sent. The keys to the cabinet which is inside the room where the cabinet is located can be kept in a box that uses card access for retrieving the keys. The access card cannot be removed until the key is replaced. To exit the room a card access badge is needed so this will help ensure that there is some key control. Also the type of key used is the kind that cannot be duplicated. The kind of key that cannot be duplicated is a special blank with no grooves.

SECURING THE WATER LINES AND WELLS ON SITE

All the water lines and wells on the site need to be secured. The section on manhole cover intrusion detection systems and manhole cover locks earlier in the Chapter will help provide some guidance.

The following are some ways to help secure water lines and wells on site:

1. Secure the manhole covers by locking

2. Using a pan-type, watertight, locking device for the manhole

3. Installing intrusion detection

4. Installing cameras below the manhole covers and outside the manhole near the cover.

As can be seen from the information presented there are things that can be done to improve the security of the site's infrastructure:

1. Locking devices for manhole covers. The limitation is that you cannot secure manhole covers that are offsite and belong to the utility companies.

2. Intrusion detection for manhole covers offers some choices and the technology used for some of the systems is no different than the technology for any intrusion detection system. For example, infrared motion sensors.

3. Securing switchgear and telephony rooms is no different than security any other room

4. CCTV to monitor the doors and manhole covers

5. Fiber optic cable detection systems are available but cannot be separated into zones. The system provides one alarm anytime there is cable movement.

Before selecting an intrusion detection or access control system to help secure the site's infrastructure you need assess your needs and then choose the system that best meets the needs. One solution is to add redundancy to the utility services so there are back up systems and the failure of one will not cause an outage. This will help minimize or eliminate a single point of failure.

CHAPTER 16

Blast Protection

There are various options to help protect a site or building from the effects of a blast caused by an explosion, whether intentional or accidental. Accidental explosions may be a more remote possibility if there are no hazardous chemicals present or any materials that are explosive or extremely reactive. Then the possibility of an intentional explosion needs to be considered.

The definition of an explosion in non-scientific terms is the very rapid release of energy with an audible sound of a blast. The energy from the explosion is released in part by thermal radiation and by an air blast and ground shock waves. The air blast is what accounts for most of the damage caused by an explosion. What happens is that during the release of the energy the air becomes displaced pushing out in all directions from the center of detonation, and then rushes back in causing the shock waves and the air blast. The air blast is the over pressurization of the surrounding air to several orders of magnitude higher than the ambient pressure. The air pressure will increase until it reaches a peak and then will fall rapidly. There is another phenomenon associated with an explosion and it is called the air blast drag loading. The air blast drag loading produces the high velocity winds caused by the explosion. The high velocity wind will spread debris over a large area causing damage to other buildings and people.

Now, protecting buildings from exterior explosions has been getting more attention. Studies and research have been conducted on what will be needed to protect a building, its components, and occupants from the effects of an explosion on buildings. The purpose of the research is to develop ways to harden the soft targets of civilian buildings and structures. The military has been hardening its structures, buildings, etc. from bomb blasts for years and some of that technology is finding its way to the civilian design and construction industry to help minimize the effects of an explosion on a building. For example, designing windows that will not produce large glass shards that become airborne and cause extensive damage to people and surrounding buildings. Blast-resistant doors have also been developed and are being used to help protect buildings against exterior explosions. The design of the blast-resistant doors will minimize damage because the force of the explosion will not be communicated into the building.

To design blast protection into the design of the structure, a threat and vulnerability assessment needs to be done to determine the asset value of the target. According to FEMA (Federal Emergency Management Agency) there are several things to consider when developing blast protection design for a building.

FEMA lists the following process to help make the assessment:

1. Define and understand the building's function, office building, health care facility, etc.

2. Identify the critical infrastructure elements of the building.
   a. Critical components/assets
   b. Critical telecommunications systems and utilities
   c. Life safety systems and safe areas
   d. Security systems

Each of the components listed in the assessment process developed by FEMA help identify the critical elements of the process. By identifying the elements necessary for planning, the assessment is more focused on the critical infrastructure to be protected.

Identifying and understanding what the function of the building is or will be is important in determining if the building is or will be a high-risk one. High-risk buildings include hospitals, government buildings, schools, etc.

The critical components and assets of the building include things like the personnel who are always a first consideration. The next critical component is the infrastructure which includes the following:

• The support columns

• The walls – interior and exterior

• The emergency exits

• Any openings – windows, doors, ventilation shafts and the like

Is critical, sensitive information stored in the building? Are there backups for the information? A good business disaster and continuity plan will help minimize the risk in this area.

The critical telephony and computer fiber optic and T1 lines and associated switchgear need to be identified by type and location. The location of the rooms where the equipment is housed needs to be identified. The equipment should not be placed on an exterior facing wall or near any other structural components that could cause more damage than initial blast does. This damage could include partial collapse of the structural components onto the telephony and computer equipment or water damage from broken water pipes and sewer lines.

The electrical and water utilities need to be identified, including their locations. These systems are critical to the operation of the building and need to be protected. The backup power system needs to be located so that it can be protected and will be available when needed. Losing both the normal and backup power in an emergency can become a major issue and needs to be prevented by protecting and maintaining the backup power system so it is available when needed.

The crucial life safety systems and safe areas of a building need to be identified. The life safety systems include the following:

- Fire alarms and evacuation instructions

- Smoke detectors

- Fire sprinklers

- Illuminated exit signs

- Emergency lighting

- Smoke free evacuation stairs for high rise buildings

- Smoke dampers to shut down the HVAC so smoke won't be pumped throughout the building

- Safe area to evacuate to during an emergency. These safe areas are used in high rise buildings since evacuating the entire building may not be possible. The safe areas need to be protected from fire, smoke, and be blast protected.

Security systems include such things as:

- Access control (Badges, card readers, biometrics, etc.)

- Intrusion detection systems (door alarms, windows, motion sensors, etc.)

- CCTV(Closed Circuit Television)

- Security officers or some type of response to security incidents

- Network security

- Protecting utilities

ASSESSMENT FOR BLAST PROTECTION

As stated earlier, the first step in the assessment process for designing blast protection for a building or structure is to define the use. This will help in determining the risk factor of being a bombing target. Targets for bombing are usually buildings defined as soft targets that are easy to get close to and experience the most damage. The following questions from FEMA will help in defining the building's main purpose or function:

1. What are the building's primary services or outputs?

2. What are the critical activities that take place at the building?

3. What goes on in the building? Are there many visitors and who are they?

4. What external sources are required for the building's success?

The answers to the questions above outline what the building does or will do. This is important in defining the risk. For example, buildings with large numbers of people that have a direct effect on the economy are at greater risk than an empty storage building. Health care, schools, government buildings are also considered to be a high risk.

After the building's main function has been identified, the next step is to identify the key infrastructure of the building. The reason for identifying the key infrastructure is because that is where blast protection design will applied.

The most important part of any building is the people and the correlation to the damage of the infrastructure and the number of people that can be killed in a bomb blast needs to be evaluated. Damage to the infrastructure that results in partial or total collapse of the building needs to be protected so the loss of the infrastructure will not result in a catastrophic loss.

What goes on or will go on in a building is an important part of the assessment. A health care facility that has a large number of ambulatory patients is a high risk since the occupants cannot evacuate to a designated safe area without assistance.

Are there a sufficient number of exits to launch a full scale evacuation of the entire building? What if one exit is destroyed or otherwise impassible? If there are only two exits, will the remaining one be adequate? This is an important question that needs to be addressed because if the number of evacuation routes will not be adequate to handle the number of people if one exit is lost, then the decision to provide some means of blast protection needs to be considered.

FEMA has developed a rating matrix that is used to categorize the asset value of each critical building component. People rate the highest on the scale. The scale is from very low to very high and a numerical value from 1-10. Table 16-1 shows the matrix rating system in a table format. One table can be used to rate all of the assets until completed. Each asset is given a rating based on the table

TABLE 16-1 FEMA Rating Scale

ASSET	VERY LOW 1	LOW 2-3	MEDIUM LOW 4	MEDIUM 5-6	MEDIUM HIGH 7	HIGH 8-9	VERY HIGH 10

and then that rating would be included in showing an overall rating for all of the building's assets. Those assets with ratings that are considered unacceptable in the "high to very high" range would be part of the risk mitigation plan.

After the assets are rated, a threat and hazard assessment (vulnerability assessment) is done. This is similar to any threat and vulnerability assessment. FEMA recommends that the threat and vulnerability be obtained from local law enforcement, emergency management, FBI, or Homeland Security. The vulnerability and threat assessment risk will be rated from high to low or the FEMA table used above can be used to rate the vulnerabilities and threats. The point is not what rating system is used but to quantify the risk so it is meaningful and the risks can be prioritized. By prioritizing the risks, a plan can be developed to mitigate the highest risks which would include blast protection for new and existing buildings especially those buildings that are high risk or a high value asset.

The vulnerabilities were outlined by completing the information for Table 16-1. All assets were identified and then prioritized by importance. Now the threats need to be identified. A threat is what could happen to the vulnerability to have an incident.

The information on how to perform a risk analysis is in Chapter 2. There is also a rating system form low to high that can be used or the same rating system and table presented earlier, developed by FEMA, can be used to rate the risk.

The vulnerability assessment can be done using a form that covers all the elements to be reviewed. It is part of doing the physical security assessment. There are a number of forms available or you can make your own form. The form in Figure 2-2 in Chapter 2 can be used by adding the sections that address the blast vulnerabilities of the facility. The sections that are different from the standard vulnerability form are the following items except for the security systems and security master plan:

1. Information about the site

2. Security systems

3. Security master plan

4. Architectural

5. Structural systems

6. Utility systems

7. Fire alarm systems

8. Building envelope

9. Mechanical systems (HVAC)

10. Telephony and computer equipment

11. Electrical systems

12. Equipment operations and maintenance

13. Plumbing and gas systems

When doing an assessment it is a good idea to document the vulnerabilities with digital photographs. The digital photos can be incorporated into the report to illustrate the vulnerability. Photos help in the identification of the vulnerability and it will make it easier to evaluate rather than trying to describe the vulnerability with words alone.

Physical Security Survey

The physical security survey is a part of the vulnerability assessment. The weaknesses in the physical security will also be vulnerability for a building's asset. For example, if the perimeter security is nonexistent or the perimeter is uncontrollable because of the location of the building, then it would be easy for someone with bad intent to gain access to the building and probably would do it undetected. This makes the target or building a soft target. Remember that hardening the target from a security perspective is also important to control who enters the building or site and, if it is easy, burglary will be an issue as will other types of crimes.

The information obtained by the physical security survey will give you a pretty good idea of what the vulnerabilities are to the building or site. Then a plan can be established to close the gaps in security. The physical security survey goes hand and hand with asset assessment for determining the vulnerability of a building to the assessment for blast protection.

The security survey is then used to develop a security master plan which can be viewed as a security budget plan for the site. The security master plan will address the deficiencies that were noted in the surveys. The plan helps prioritize the issues that need to be addressed from high to low. The low-risk items probably will not get done due to budget constraints but the high-risk items will be addressed in the plan and should be given immediate attention. There are trade-offs that do occur in budgeting so the security plan should provide more than one option for mitigating the risk. This way, management has some choices and can clearly see what each option will provide and cost so an informed decision can by made for security expenditures.

Blast-Hardening

In recent years there has been a great of research and studies into blast-hardening of new and existing structures and the main focus has been on making windows safer so that large shards of glass are not produced that become flying missiles causing severe damage. The research in the civilian area has expanded to address blast protection beyond the windows to the structure. These research studies have been conducted by university engineering departments and the government, particularly the Armed Forces. The military has been studying blast protection for at least 15 years or more. Now, some of their findings are available for civilian use in commercial buildings since these buildings are the likely targets for terrorist attacks, domestic or foreign. The building's critical support structure members need to be identified, and a plan for protecting them from the effects of a blast needs to be developed. Studies that address the effects of explosions on the structural members of a building have and are being done to help minimize the threat and risk from the effects of a blast. The measures include the following as outlined in the U.S. Army Technical Manual TM 5-853. For obvious security reasons there is not any detail in the manual:

- Physical space planning that deliberately uses architectural location and organization of spaces

- Other nonstructural features to minimize the effects of an explosion on people and property

These measures are known as blast-hardening. Blast-hardening encompasses all the measures used to reduce the effects of a blast. Remember, the purpose of blast-hardening is to minimize the effects of a blast and not to stop the damage completely. The techniques for blast-hardening can be applied to the building design just like any design feature. Designers incorporate designs for seismic, wind, and fire protection into buildings and the blast-hardening features can also be designed into the building.

The site selection of the building has an impact on the blast-hardening design because, if the access to the building can be tightly controlled, there is less of a risk for delivering and planting explosives in or near the building.

Locations to avoid for a building would be as follows:

- Congested urban areas
- Too close to the street
- Where there is a large, uncontrolled right-of-way

The congested urban area site for a building adds to the problems of being too close to the street and having an uncontrolled right-of-way. Perimeter security is limited because of the large, uncontrolled right-of-way not under control of the building's owner making the building a soft target. Since the urban area is congested, the building may be close to the street with not much room for large building setbacks. Being near to the street makes it easier to deliver a vehicle bomb because the bomb can be close to the building to effect the maximum amount of damage. Part of the assessment for a new building or an existing building that is not a high-value target is to determine what the surrounding buildings' functions are and make a determination of whether they are considered a high-value target. This is important because the proximity of the surrounding buildings to the new building or an existing one is important for designing blast protection. The new or existing building near a high-value target will be a target as well due to the proximity of the buildings in a congested urban area.

Another issue of congested urban areas is that the buildings are close to parking lots and narrow alleys where a bomb could be detonated. A bomb intended for one building will cause damage to surrounding buildings as well. Sometimes this may not be an option because of the cost of land. Also the owners of commercial buildings may not be able to control the areas around their buildings so it comes down to designing in or retrofitting the blast protection to minimize damage from an explosion. Also in urban areas, an explosion may be caused by phenomena other than bombs, for example, a gas line rupture.

The uncontrolled right-of-way makes it easy for someone to get near the building to plant an explosive device either in a vehicle or in a briefcase, back pack, etc. With a right-of-way that can be controlled, perimeter security can be set up to make it harder for someone to enter the zone near the building undetected and plant an explosive device.

There are some design options that will help in minimizing damage from explosions. The following are some of these design options:

1. Hardening of the mail and receiving areas if the facility is prone to receiving a large volume of unsolicited mail or packages. The large amount of unsolicited mail or freight receiving can make it easy to deliver a bomb to the site unnoticed. If the mail or shipping and receiving area cannot be hardened, then designate a remote area of the site for the processing. Another option would be to take the mail and shipping and receiving function off-site.

2. Limit or control the amount of hazardous materials on-site since these materials can contribute to the fire caused by an explosion or be the source of an explosion. The hazardous materials and fire suppression systems, especially fire pumps, need to be stored away from any evacuation route so that they will not be damaged if there is an explosion of the materials.

3. When designing the structure, locate vulnerable functions far from the uncontrolled public areas to minimize the blast effects on occupants. For example, day care centers should be located in inconspicuous places, rather in plain sight, and away from streets and front entrances.

4. Protect the utility services such as manhole covers, electrical vaults, fiber optic, telephony rooms, and T1 lines. Information about security in these areas can be found in Chapter 15. Whenever possible, provide redundant electrical, telephony, and computer cabling like T1 and fiber optic services.

5. Studies done in Israel indicate that there needs to be blast-resistant areas of refuge in buildings that can accommodate the occupants. The studies were conducted during the 1991 Gulf War on a missile that landed near apartment buildings. It was found that, even if a missile landed near the building and caused heavy damage, the building did not collapse. What occurred after the war was to construct buildings with an inner tower of protective space to shield the occupants from effects of a blast. One bedroom of the apartment is made of reinforced concrete with a light blast-resistant window and door. There is a steel shutter that will cover the blast window. The tests were done for the effects of car bombs as well missiles on the tower of protective space concept. The tests seem promising and there is a paper by the Israeli Engineering firm that conducted the tests at http://www.dtic.mil/ndia/technology/amit.pdf. The paper goes into detail about the design specifications for the protective space and the tests.

6. According to the US Army Technical Manual TM 5-1300, controlled venting is an option to help minimize the effects of an accidental explosion caused by chemicals or high explosives. The same concept is used to relieve the pressure of a dust explosion by using blow out panels. The panels, walls are designed to blow out with a pressure build up like that which occurs during an explosion. The wall or blowout panel is an exterior wall and it is the weak side so it gives during an explosion and the all of the pressure is vented out through the wall preventing the pressure to vent upward and to all the other sides causing significant damage.

There are also fire suppression systems that are designed to suppress an explosion which will be discussed in Chapter 17. The systems use fine water spray open head sprinklers and a fast reacting detection system.

7. Windows can use laminate to minimize the possibility of large shards being produced during an explosion. The American Society of Civil Engineers in a 1995 Task Group Report on the Structural Design for Physical Security in Chapter 5 provides information on the design of windows using laminate for blast protection.

8. For information on retrofitting existing buildings look at The American Society of Civil Engineers in a 1995 Task Group Report on the Structural Design for Physical Security Chapter 8 *"Retrofitting Existing Buildings"*. Retrofitting existing buildings is important since there are a large number of buildings that have been built before the information on explosion protection was available and may need to be protected because they are considered high risk buildings. On the other hand some building cannot be retrofitted due the original construction of the building like the older wall load-bearing buildings.

9. A method to help to control access to a building is the use of barricades. The barricades are usually concrete K rail or Jersey barriers. They are placed strategically around the building to prevent a vehicle form getting too close to the building. Ramming the barricades will not easily breach them. The placement of the barricades is in a pattern so that you cannot drive straight through the barricades. All of the barricades are offset from each other. If one barricade is breached a vehicle cannot get up enough speed to penetrate the next barricade since there is not a straight line between the barricades. The vehicle will not be able to accelerate to a speed to cause damage to the next barricade due to the angle and the close proximity of the barricades. Protective barriers are discussed in more detail in Chapter 4.

10. The US Air Force has doing testing on composite polymers to retrofit existing concrete exterior walls to strengthen them against blasts. These tests have shown promise that the polymers can provide blast protection to exterior concrete walls. The type of polymers used in the tests can be found in the bed lining of some pick up trucks and the lining for municipal water tanks.

11. Using blast resistant doors to protect the opening from the effects of a blast. Chapter 11 has more detail on blast resistant doors. Figure 16-1 is a sample design specifications document from Sandia National Laboratory for a blast resistant rolled steel door and frames.

12. Eliminate underground parking that is underneath of the building for new or planned structures. Sometimes this is at odds with local ordinances addressing parking but permitting parking under buildings presents a higher

(text continues on page 310)

SPECIAL SPECIFICATION

SECTION 08394S

BLAST RESISTANT DOORS

PART 1 - GENERAL

1.01 SECTION INCLUDES

    A.   Section includes Blast Resistant rolled steel doors and frames.

1.02 REFERENCES

    A.   ASTM A 123 - Zinc (Hot-Dip Galvanized) Coatings on Iron and Steel Products.

    B.   ASTM A 653 - Steel Sheet, Zinc-Coated (Galvanized) or Zinc-Iron Alloy-Coated (Galvannealed) by the Hot-Dip Process.

    C.   ASTM C 236 - Test Method for Steady-State Thermal Performance of Building Assemblies by Means of a Guarded Hot-Box.

    D.   ASTM E 152 - Methods of Fire Tests of Door Assemblies.

    E.   DHI - Door Hardware Institute: The Installation of Commercial Steel Doors and Steel Frames, Insulated Steel Doors in Wood Frames and Builder's Hardware.

    F.   NFPA 252, Fire Tests of Door Assemblies.

    G.   SDI-100 - Standard Steel Doors and Frames.

    H.   SDI-105 - Recommended Erection Instructions for Steel Frames.

    I.   SDI-107 - Hardware for Steel Doors (Reinforcement - Application).

    J.   UL 10B - Fire Tests of Door Assemblies.

1.03 QUALITY ASSURANCE

    A.   Conform to requirements of SDI-100.

Blast Resistant Doors

Issue Date: December 9, 2002   08394S - 1

FIGURE 16-1 Sample design specifications document for a blast resistant rolled steel door and frames
(continued on next page)

B.   Installed frame and door assembly to conform to UL 10B for fire rated class indicated or scheduled.

C.   Manufacturer Qualifications: Company specializing in manufacturing the Products specified in this section with minimum three years documented experience.

1.04   REGULATORY REQUIREMENTS

A.   Conform to applicable local building codes for fire rated requirements of metal door/metal frame.

B.   Fire Rated Door Construction: Conform to ASTM E 152, NFPA 252, UL 10B.

C.   Fire Rated Door Construction: Rate of rise of 250 degrees F across door thickness.

1.05   SUBMITTALS

A.   Shop Drawings: indicate frame configuration, anchor types and spacings, location of cutouts for hardware, reinforcement, and finish.
     Indicate door elevations, internal reinforcement, closure method.

B.   Manufacturer's Installation Instructions: Indicate special installation instructions.

C.   Manufacturer's Certificate: Certify that Products meet or exceed specified requirements.

1.06   DELIVERY, STORAGE AND PROTECTION

A.   Protect doors and frames with resilient packaging.

B.   Accept doors on site in manufacturer's packaging. Inspect for damage.

C.   Break seal on-site to permit ventilation.

1.07   FIELD MEASUREMENTS

A.   Verify that field measurements are as indicated on shop drawings

1.08   COORDINATION

A.   Coordinate the work with door opening construction, door frame and door hardware installation.

Blast Resistant Doors

Issue Date: December 9, 2002   08394S - 2

FIGURE 16-1   Sample design specifications document for a blast resistant rolled steel door and frames
(continued)

PART 2 - PRODUCTS

2.01 MANUFACTURERS

A. Blast Resistant Doors and Welded Unit Frames:

1. Overly Door Company, Greensburg, PA 15601-0070 or approved equal.

2.02 BLAST RESISTANT DOORS

A. Design Basis and Type: Blast resistant pre-engineered door system designs shall be based on the VLRB series as manufactured by the Overly Door Company, Greensburg, PA 15601-0070 or approved equivalent

B. Design Criteria: The door, frame and restraining hardware shall be designed to withstand pressures up to 250 psf seating the door into the frame and 250 psf unseating the door from the frame (rebound). The door system shall be fully operable after application of the specified loads.

C. Product Description: Doors and frames shall be constructed of 14 gauge low carbon steel. Doors shall be a nominal 1 3/4" thick, full flush, constructed and reinforced to resist the blast forces specified. Design door hardware and reinforcements to transfer all applicable loadings to frame. Design frame anchors to transfer all loadings to walls or structural sub-frame embeds. Frames shall be hollow metal formed steel with formed stops, three sided, single or double rabbet, factory reinforced and tapped for hardware. Frame anchorage shall be concrete expansion anchors.

D. Fire rating: Those openings scheduled as fire rated shall have been tested by and bear the labels of Underwriters Laboratories marked for 3 hour, A label for flush doors.

E. Lockset: Refer to section 08710 – Finish Hardware, for Lockset.

F. Door Closer: Refer to section 08710 – Finish Hardware, for Door Closer.

G. Exit Device: Refer to section 08710 – Finish Hardware

H. Weather stripping: Provide solid elastomer seals.

I. Hinges: Hinge shall be heavy duty ball bearing butts of sufficient size and quantity to withstand blast loadings and door weight. Hinges shall conform to ANSI Standard A156.1. Refer to section 08710 – Finish Hardware, for Hinges.

Blast Resistant Doors

FIGURE 16-1 Sample design specifications document for a blast resistant rolled steel door and frames *(continued)*

2.03   FABRICATION

    A.   General: Assemble work using all welded construction conforming to the applicable requirements of AWS D1.1 and D1.3.

    B.   Materials: Construct from formed sheet conforming to ASTM A366 or ASTM A569. Steel plate and shapes for reinforcing and/or framing members shall conform to ASTM A36 and bars shall conform to ASTM A108 Grade 1018. Hardware shall be corrosion resistant steel of the appropriate design for the function intended.

    C.   Painting and Cleaning: After fabrication, remove all tool marks and surface imperfections, and dress all welded joints smooth and coat with a rust-inhibitive primer.

2.04   FINISH

    A.   Steel Sheet: Galvanized to ASTM A 653, G60

    B.   Exterior Units: over 2.0 ounces per square foot galvanizing, in accordance with ASTM A 123.

PART 3 - EXECUTION

3.01   EXAMINATION

    A.   Verify that opening sizes and tolerances are acceptable.

    B.   Verify surfaces and conditions are ready to receive work of this section. Notify Architect of any existing conditions which will adversely affect execution. Beginning of execution will constitute acceptance of existing conditions.

    C.   Installation: Install work in strict accordance with approved shop drawings and recommended installation instructions of the manufacturer. Any required field welding must be performed by certified welders in accordance with AWS D1.1 and D1.3.

3.02   INSTALLATION

    A.   Install frames in accordance with SDI-105.

    B.   Install doors in accordance with DHI.

Blast Resistant Doors

FIGURE 16-1   Sample design specifications document for a blast resistant rolled steel door and frames *(continued)*

C. Install roll formed steel reinforcement channels between two abutting frames. Anchor to structure and floor.

D. Set frames plumb, level, and true alignment, securely fastened to the floor and adjoining walls.

E. Install doors accurately in frames, maintaining specified clearances.

3.03 <u>TOLERANCES</u>

A. Maximum Diagonal Distortion: 1/8-inch measured with straight edge, corner to corner.

3.04 <u>ADJUSTING AND CLEANING</u>

A. Adjust hardware and door movement for smooth, quiet and balanced door movement.

END OF SECTION

Blast Resistant Doors

Issue Date: December 9, 2002 08394S - 5

FIGURE 16-1 Sample design specifications document for a blast resistant rolled steel door and frames *(continued)*

risk especially if the shipping and receiving dock is also part of the underground parking structure. Loading docks for shipping and receiving that are underground are high risk because the clearances for vehicle heights will be much higher to allow trucks to enter to go to and from the loading dock.

The issue can be addressed administratively by searching every truck that enters the garage and verifying the delivery with shipping and receiving. The searching would include exterior and inside the truck, the cargo. The searching needs to be done by trained security personnel who know what to look for. The driver and any other passengers in the truck need to be questioned. This may not be practical for a multi-tenant building using a common loading dock but a security plan should be put in place to minimize the risk especially for high value targets. Any security plans to address the threat that are put in place should remain as anonymous as possible and not become public, otherwise there is no security plan.

Hardened and Protected Structures

There is a difference between a hardened and protected structure. A hardened structure is designed to able to perform its intended function even after a wartime attack. The structure is hardened against chemical/ biological/radiological (CBR) attacks. The majority of the cost of construction is focused on hardening the structure to withstand CBR attacks. The structure is not only protected so are its occupants from the effects of the attacks. These include air blast, ground shock, penetration, fragmentation and damage to the structure from the effects of an explosion that is external to the building. The building does not need to be the target to sustain heavy damage or total destruction and recent events of the last several years has shown this to be true. For example, in the Oklahoma City bombing, the surrounding buildings sustained extensive damage from the blast even though they were not the intended target. The buildings in close proximity to the Murrah Federal Building in downtown Oklahoma City, a congested urban area, sustained substantial damage to total collapse. Three hundred and twenty-four (324) were either destroyed or damaged in the bombing.

Protected structures on the other hand are designed to minimize the effects of a blast to assets mainly people. The structure is hardened or protected to minimize the damage from the effects of an explosion. The building or structure may be destroyed but the injury and death to people is minimized as is the damage to other assets. Since the likelihood of a terrorist attack is minimal the cost of protecting or hardening a structure is not something that was historically a widely accepted practice but that is changing due to the events of recent years.

Site planning should address the following elements if possible:

1. Separation of the structures on the site. Buildings or structures should not close enough to permit one device take out more than one building especially critical structures. This is not practical solution in congested urban areas.

2. The orientation of hardened buildings should be such that the most vulnerable sides face away from other critical structures or buildings, assets, etc.

The building layout for a hardened structure should include redundancy of utilities, telecommunications, and the like so if one system is disrupted or severely damaged the building or structure can still operate.

The footprint for a hardened structure should be a square, rectangle or some other regular geometric shape that attenuates the effects of a blast. By attenuating the force of the blast it will lessen the force and the damage will minimized as well.

All exterior openings like ventilation, doors, windows, air intakes, and exhaust stacks should be protected. When designing the structures, consideration should be given to blast pressure, heat, fragments, dusts, and toxic gases entering the protected or hardened structure through the openings.

Other design considerations include:

1. Minimize flying debris hazards

2. Progressive collapse avoidance

3. Direct design approach

4. Indirect design approach

Minimizing flying hazards is important first to keep the injuries to people to a minimum, and secondly, keep damage to other assets to a minimum. The high velocity wind that is produced by the blast drag loading will create missiles out of the flying debris. Since the winds are high velocity the materials being tossed about will have greater force than normally and will be more destructive.

Progressive collapse is a chain reaction of failures that results from damage to a relatively small part of the building. The progressive collapse causes severe damage to the structure that is not in proportion to the initial damage. A consequence of a progressive collapse is the unnecessary loss of life and the trapping of survivors under the rubble of the collapsed structure. Progressive collapse is also an issue during natural disasters such as an earthquake or hurricane.

Direct deign approach considers the alternative path method so when a structural member is damaged or removed the load will find an alternate path to absorb the loads created by the missing or damaged structural member. The loss of one structural member will not cause a progressive collapse since the load is distributed across other structural members.

The indirect design approach uses a redundant structural member system with continuity across joints so each member can develop the full structural capacity of the connected structural members. If a large displacement of structural members occurs it can be accommodated by those left intact. In other words the load is distributed across the remaining structural members without the complete loss of strength resulting in a collapse.

CHAPTER 17

Fire Protection

ire protection is a part of the overall security of the facility. Fire protection is
something that is required by local codes and ordinances and is part of he
perimeter and interior protection systems of the facility. There are fire codes
that dictate what must be done to make the building safe from fire for new structures or modifications to existing structures. The code review process is part of getting a building permit. Building codes also describe requirements for building safety.

Fire protection consists not just detecting and suppressing a fire but also the life
safety aspect of notification and the safe evacuation of a building during a fire
emergency. The safe evacuation by the building occupants also involves the use
of a back up emergency power system or exit sign lights that will illuminate when
there is a loss of power. Emergency lights that light up the exit path during a
power loss. These are usually battery operated lights that are found in stairwells.
The unit has two lights both pointing to exit pathway.

Entire books have been written about fire protection and life safety and so one
chapter devoted to fire protection will not be all inclusive instead it is offered as
a summary to fire protection.

FIRE CODES

No discussion of fire protection and fire systems would be complete without a
brief look at the fire codes. There are several main fire codes used in the United
States today. Fire standards are not fire codes, for a fire standard to become a code
the local jurisdiction must adopt the code in part or in its entirety as an ordinance.
Depending on the jurisdiction it usually takes three readings of the ordinance to
become law. During the reading of the ordinance the council, board of supervisors or whatever the local governing body is will vote to accept the ordinance.
The ordinance will be read and voted on at two more consecutive meetings before it is adopted.

Now that the fire code is law it will be used in the permit review process and all new construction seeking permits will be reviewed for compliance with the code. Until 1994 there main fire codes used on the United States were:

1. Uniform Fire Code

2. Standard Fire code

3. National Building Code

The following are the fire codes used in the United States since 1994:

1. International Fire Code (IFC)

2. National Fire Code (NFPA 5000)

The fire codes are now consolidated into two main code making and distribution bodies, The International Code Council (ICC), and the National Fire Protection Association (NFPA).

The fire codes cover such topics as:

1. Fire detection systems

2. Fire alarms

3. Fire sprinklers

4. Fire extinguishers

5. The Life Safety Code (r) NFPA code
   a. Number of exits required by occupancy
   b. Exit pathways
   c. Signage (backup power)

6. CO_2 systems

7. Water spray systems

8. Hazardous materials storage and handling

9. Chemical systems

10. Foam systems

11. Storage of flammable and combustible liquids

12. Smoke detection systems

The topics that are outlined above are a sampling of the items that are addressed by the fire codes. There are other items addressed in the fire codes and it is recommended that a copy of the local fire codes be obtained and reviewed.

The fire codes are the regulations that determine what is necessary to be in a building based on the occupancy. Occupancies are broken based on what goes on in the building. For example if the building is a movie theatre, it is Assembly Occupancy, and if it is a school, it is in an Educational Occupancy. There are others but the fire codes identify them so look at the code to see what occupancy the building that is being planned will fall under.

The building codes have information related to the materials of construction and some relate directly to the fire rating of walls, doors, floor coverings and paint. The architects designing the project will have access to the building and fire codes and the design will meet the requirements set forth in the codes. All drawings will be presented to the local jurisdiction for approval as part of the permit process.

FIRE SUPPRESSION SYSTEMS

There are a variety of fire suppression systems, water sprinklers, CO2, Dry Chemical, and FM 200 (Halon replacement). The most common system is the wet pipe fire sprinklers.

Automatic fire sprinklers were originally designed to control a fire until the arrival of the fire department for final extinguishment and where first used in the United States in 1874. Now there are sprinkler systems designed to actually extinguish the fire.

There are two main types of fire sprinkler systems:

1. Wet pipe

2. Dry pipe

Before we continue our discussion there are some myths about automatic fire sprinklers that need to be dispelled.

1. The first myth is that all the sprinkler heads will flow water at the same time.

    When a wet pipe automatic fire sprinkler system activates, all the heads flow water one time. This is not true that only the heads over the fire area will be activated and most cases only one head will flow water during a fire. It has been shown in studies of numerous fires that in 93% of the fires one sprinkler head will handle the fire, two sprinklers in 4% of the fires, and 3 sprinklers in the remaining 3% of the fires. Heads that are not directly over the fire will not be activated since the liquid in the glass bulb or the fusible link will not be heated so that water is released from the head. The system is designed with designated design area which is usually 10-12 sprinkler heads.

2. Sprinklers will go off accidentally causing water damage.

   Sprinklers do not go off accidentally since the heads can only flow water when the glass bulb breaks or fusible link melts which can only happen by heat of a real fire.

Wet Pipe Sprinkler Systems

A wet pipe sprinkler system is where water fills the entire system piping and is up to the sprinkler heads. This means the valve for the wet pipe fire sprinkler system has water on both sides of it. When a sprinkler is activated and starts flowing water the main sprinkler valve will open and water will flow into the pipe from the fire water source. The source can be the municipal water system or a private fire water system of tanks and ponds, etc. The sprinkler heads have a fusible link which is made from two metal pieces and solder to hold them in place in the opening of the head to hold back the water. Most of the newer sprinkler heads today have a glass bulb instead of the fusible link made of lead. The fusible link is set at predetermined temperature to melt causing the two metal rods holding the cap over the orifice to hold the water back to fall out. The newer sprinklers have glass bulbs which are filled with a glycerin-based liquid that expands when heated, at a predetermined temperature causing the liquid to expand bursting the bulb allowing water to flow out of the head.

Wet pipe sprinkler systems are used to protect the following types of buildings:

- Offices
- Hospitals
- Schools
- Stores
- Hotels
- Residences

There is another type of wet pipe sprinkler system which a foam system. Foam sprinkler systems are used to protect flammable and combustible liquid storage areas. The foam sprinkler system consists of sprinkler piping with closed or open sprinkler heads and at the main valve there is a foam injection system and a foam tank.

How automatic fire sprinklers work is simple. When the temperature of the ceiling over the fire reaches the temperature of the fusible link or the liquid in the glass bulb then the head is activated and water will flow out of the pipe on to the deflector of the sprinkler head. The deflector breaks the water into a spray to extinguish the fire.

Sprinkler heads are upright, pendent, or side wall mount. Upright heads are used to protect the underside of the floor or roof decking and the name suggests the deflector is facing upright. Pendent heads are the ones you see hanging from the ceiling in most buildings with the deflector facing down toward the floor.

The sprinkler heads have different size orifices with most heads in office buildings having a 1/2-inch orifice. Some systems have larger orifices to flow more water, for example the Early Suppression, Fast Response (ESFR) heads have a 3/4-inch orifice. The ESFR fire sprinkler system is used in warehouses to eliminate the need for in-rack sprinklers. The ESFR heads are placed at the ceiling using pendent or upright heads. The ESFR system is a wet pipe system.

The fire sprinkler systems are designed in two ways, either pipe schedule or hydraulic design. Pipe schedule systems are based on the piping size and each hazard classification listed below has a different pipe schedule for the design of the system:

- Light hazard

- Ordinary hazard

- Extra hazard

Most fire sprinkler systems are designed using hydraulic calculations. A hydraulically designed system saves money because the piping sizes are based on flow and friction loss. The calculations used to be done using by hand, now they are designed using computer programs. The programs calculate the required flow and friction loss of the system. By calculating the flow and friction loss of the system the piping sizes are determined that will deliver the flow accounting for the friction loss.

Dry Pipe Sprinkler Systems

The dry pipe system does not have any water in the piping to the sprinkler heads. The piping system is filled with air. The sprinkler heads are closed and have fusible links or glass bulbs with liquid. Dry pipe systems are used in places where freezing temperatures are a problem. The purpose of the air in the system is to hold the sprinkler valve known as the clapper valve down to hold back the water from the source.

There are two types of dry pipe systems:

1. Closed head

2. Open head or water spray systems

The closed head system is described above where there is air in the pipe and the sprinkler heads have a glass bulb with liquid at set temperature or a fusible link a set temperature. When the heat from a fire reaches the set temperature to melt the fusible link, or expand the liquid in the glass bulb bursting it, the air is released out of the open head opening the valve allowing water to flow into the pipe and out of the open sprinkler head. The closed head dry pipe system is used in areas where freezing temperatures are an issue. If the water freezes in the sprinkler pipe, ruptures of the pipe occur causing leaking.

The system that has the open sprinkler heads (nozzles) or water spray system has all the heads open and there is a pilot head (small diameter pipe filled with air with closed sprinkler heads) or detection system that when one head is heated by the fire to the pre-determined temperature, the air in the pipe of the pilot head system is released opening the valve to allow water to flow through the heads. The other detection system is either a rate of rise detector or protector wire also set at a pre-determined temperature. The valve is then opened electrically flowing water through the pipe.

The purpose of the design of the dry pipe system is to have all the heads flow at one time since they are all open. Dry pipe systems are used to protect such things as:

• Large electric transformers

• Protection on tanks such as anhydrous ammonia

• Pumps

The dry pipe system with open heads is sometimes called a deluge system since all the heads are open. The purpose is to get a large amount of water on the fire quickly or to protect an exposure from a fire. The exposure could be an adjacent transformer. If one transformer catches fire the adjacent transformer will be protected from the heat of the fire by the automatic dry pipe water spray system.

Another system that uses the dry pipe concept is the pre-action system. In a pre-action system the piping is dry to the heads and there is a detection system that open the valve to flow water to the pipes and sprinkler heads. The detection system used is usually smoke or heat detectors. For water to flow out of the sprinkler head the fusible link or glass bulb must be heated to the pre-determined temperature for the sprinkler head. Pre-action sprinkler systems are used to protect computer equipment and rooms.

Gaseous Fire Suppression Systems

Gaseous fire suppression systems are special systems for applications such as protecting switchgear rooms, unoccupied computer equipment rooms, flammable liquid storage areas, etc.

Gaseous systems are as follows:

• Carbon Dioxide

• FM 200 and other halon replacement systems

• Dry Chemical

Carbon Dioxide Systems are designed to displace the oxygen in the room to extinguish the fire. The smothering of the fire is one of the ways in which fires are extinguished. The use of CO_2 systems in occupies rooms is not advisable because the displacement of oxygen is dangerous to human life.

CO_2 systems are designed to be total flooding systems or local application systems. This means that the room or other enclosure is flooded with CO_2 to extinguish the fire. The total flooding systems consists of fixed supply bottles of CO_2, piping, nozzles for delivery of the agent into the enclosure. When a total flooding system is to be used in an enclosure or room the room must be airtight so that the design concentration of the system must be achieved within seven minutes. A local application system consists of a fixed supply of bottles which contain the CO_2, piping and nozzles directed at the hazard independent of any enclosure that may exist.

The CO_2 system is activated by a detection system that uses two different types of detectors like smoke and heat rate of rise detectors. The first detector the smoke detector will initiate an alarm so the area can be evacuated. The second detector the heat detector will trigger the flow of the CO_2 into the protected enclosure or room. These types of detection systems are called crossed zoned systems and one detector from each zone needs to be activated before the CO_2 system will flow out of pipe to suppress the fire.

CO_2 systems are used for flammable and combustible liquid storage areas electric turbine generators oil seal areas, and electrical switch gear rooms and vaults.

Since Halon is no longer permitted to be used for fire suppression systems there have been replacements developed. The replacements include the following gasses:

1. Inergen®

2. FM 200®

Inergen is a halon replacement agent that works the same way halon does in extinguishing the fire by breaking up the chemical chain reaction of the fire. Inergen systems are similar to the CO_2 systems consisting of a fixed supply of bottles of the agent, piping and nozzles to deliver the agent to the fire. The system is activated using the same type of detection as the CO_2 systems do; cross-zoned using smoke and heat detectors. Inergen systems are used to protect computer rooms, equipment rooms, etc.

FM 200 is another Halon replacement gas and it extinguishes the fire in the same way as Halon and Inergen does by breaking up the chemical chain reaction. FM 200 is used to protect computer rooms and equipment.

Dry chemical fire suppression systems consist of fixed supply bottles, piping and nozzles with nozzles to deliver the agent to the fire. The detection system used to activate the dry chemical agent is the same as those used for the CO2, FM 200, and Inergen.

A final note on fire suppression systems is the fire sprinkler systems designed to suppress an explosion. The system is water that is broken to very fine spray. The detection system is a system using fast acting ultraviolet detectors to sense an explosion in its beginning stage. All explosions are the sudden release of rapid burning so as the explosion starts it starts with a flame so the ultraviolet detector is designed to detect the flame signature. The detector then will release the water sprinkler system as fine spray to suppress the explosion. The explosion suppression system is expensive but effective in suppressing an explosion in critical equipment or filling room for flammable or combustible aerosol cans.

SMOKE AND FIRE DETECTION SYSTEMS

Detection systems do not suppress any fires that may work in conjunction with fire suppression systems but the detection system alone does not suppress fires. Smoke detectors are a fire detection system that provides an early warning to occupants that there is a fire in the building.

Smoke detectors come in two main types.

1. Photoelectric

2. Ionization

Photoelectric smoke detectors sense a charge in the intensity of light received by a photo receptor built into the detector. Photoelectric smoke detectors are fast response:

• To smoke

• To smoldering fires

• To overheated PVC wire insulation

Photoelectric smoke detectors have a slow response to:

• To a fast flaming type fire

• To particles of combustion that have diameters that are smaller than the wavelength of the light source in the detector

• To particles of combustion that absorb light rather than scattering it

Ionization principle detectors sense a change in the electrical properties of a chamber that employs a very small radioactive source. The ionization detector has a fast response:

• To fastflaming fires
• No flame present; only small aerosols (products of combustion) are present
• Does not depend on the color of the smoke to respond

Ionization detectors have a slow response to:

• To a heavy smoldering fire

Since smoke detectors are an early warning system to alert occupants to a fire in the building, they are often connected to the audible and visual alarm system of the building. As previously mentioned, smoke detectors are also used in conjunction with heat detectors in a cross-zoned detection system to alert the occupants and then to actuate a fixed fire suppression system. The smoke detectors are used to sound the alarm and the heat detector is used to actuate the suppression system.

Heat detectors are designed to detect the heat produced by a fire. Heat detection is accomplished using different heat detection principles. The heat detection principles used are for different types of heat detectors as follows:

• Fixed temperature
• Continuous line detectors
• Rate-of-rise heat compensated

The fixed temperature detector is set to alarm when the temperature reaches a specific point. Fixed temperature heat detectors start at 135 degrees F and go up from there. There are several types of fixed temperature detectors.

• The eutectic which is the fusible metal made of either bismuth or lead and will melt at a predetermined temperature. These are detectors are one-time use only and need to be replaced after the metal has melted.

• The glass bulb type uses a glass bulb to maintain a switch in the open position. The bulb has a vapor pressure liquid and air and when heated the liquid expands which compresses the air bubble until it ruptures the glass. The rupturing of the glass closes the switch. These type of detectors are rarely used.

• The bimetal type detector has two different metals and when the metals are heated, the coefficients of the thermal expansion cause bending or flexing toward the metal of the lower expansion rate. This closes the normally open circuit sending an alarm.

The fixed temperature detectors described above are known as spot detectors because they are designed to detect heat in one location.

Another type of fixed temperature detector is the line type detector that uses semiconductor material and a stainless steel capillary tube. The tube has a center coaxial center conductor separated from its wall by a temperature sensitive fiber optic. Under normal conditions there is small current that flows to the circuit. When the temperature increases the resistance current supplied by the fiber optic cable decreases, the circuit current will increase and the increase in current at a set point in the circuit will send an alarm. So this type of detection measures changes in resistance.

There is a line detection system that is at a fixed temperature and has two wires separated by insulation. When the temperature is reached the two wires inside the detector come into contact with one another closing the circuit sending an alarm. This is called Linear Thermester cable.

The rate-of-rise detector will detect the change at the ceiling a predetermined increase in temperature usually 15 degrees F per minute rise above the ambient temperature. Most rate-of-rise detectors are deigned to compensate for normal rise in temperatures.

Flame Detection

Flame detectors are also available to detect the heat waves or radiation that is produced by a fire. Infrared and ultraviolet detectors are two types of these kinds of detectors that detect flame. Flame detectors are the fastest with respect to detection times and have the highest false alarm rate from non fire-related sources than of any other detector. Flame detectors detect flame at its ignition.

Flame detectors are used in high hazard areas such flammable liquid loading platforms and other areas where very rapid fires known as explosions can occur.

Infrared detectors are deigned to block out unwanted wavelengths and focus on the incoming energy on a photovoltaic or photo resistive cell sensitive to the infrared. Sometimes infrared detectors are in combination with flame flicker in the frequency range of 5 to 30 hertz. Flame flicker is added to minimize the false alarm rate caused by the solar interference. Solar interference is a problem with the infrared detectors that receive total IR radiation without flame flicker.

Ultraviolet detectors are used when the distance from the detector to the hazard is a short distance. The flame selectivity is accurately set to respond to the specific ultraviolet wavelength produced by the flame.

EMERGENCY BACKUP POWER

Emergency backup power is critical to the operation of the fire protection equipment and the security systems. The fire protection systems can operate on UPS (Uninterruptible Power Supply) but some of the security systems do not operate well on a UPS system. To augment the UPS a generator is usually installed. The generator is a diesel generator that is sized to generate the power needed for the emergency equipment including the computers during an outage. The diesel motor runs the power generator and can run for up to 72 hours depending on the storage capacity of the diesel fuel and how quickly more fuel can be delivered to the site. The diesel driven generator will have a battery backup to start the generator during a power outage. The backup generator power system is designed to come online after the normal power has been disrupted for 30 seconds or more. The UPS system will keep things running until the generator power comes online.

The backup power system is designed to meet the demand for providing the electrical power to operate the essential equipment at the site or in the building. The backup power systems are designed like the power systems by electrical engineers who are registered professional engineers in electrical engineering. There are calculations that the engineer does to determine the power needs and to calculate what will be needed to provide those power needs.

The backup fire pumps, if the site has them, will also run on electricity and should be included in the equipment list for backup power requirements. The other fire pump is usually a diesel driven fire pump which will run on the diesel fuel and the diesel fire pump will run independent of the backup generator power. The diesel fire pump will have storage batteries to start the pump when it is needed during a power outage. The fire pumps must be deigned to meet the National Fire Protection Association Standard 20 to be accepted as being a fire pump by the local authorities and to be given credit by the property casualty insurance companies.

DEIGNING FIRE DETECTION AND SUPPRESSION SYSTEMS

Fire detection and suppression systems need to be deigned by a registered fire protection engineer. The architect doing the design work will contract with a fire protection engineer to design the fire detection and suppression systems for the project.

Sound Control **18**

S ound control may not be an issue for every company or location. Companies that have lost confidential information and trade secrets are usually more receptive to developing a sound control program as part of the perimeter security program. These losses of confidential information and trade secrets can cost a company millions of dollars and market share in the competitive markets of today. It is less costly and reason enough for some to steal the trade secrets (intellectual property) and confidential information of other companies then it is to develop their own.

Depending on the industry it could be years and cost millions of dollars of research and testing to develop trade secrets also known as intellectual property. This makes the information an attractive target for thieves to steal since the payment for such property is substantial and there are willing buyers. To protect a company's assets, especially intellectual property, there are things a company can do and one of them is to roll sound control into the perimeter security design or re-design depending on the circumstances.

Who is listening? That is the question that needs to be answered and the answer maybe, "It depends". What is important to the company? Does the company do defense or other work that may have national security implications or homeland security implications?

By answering the questions above as a part of the vulnerability assessment you can start to develop a plan for providing sound control. Not every location will need sound control but for those that do, there are methods to help mitigate the issues of losing confidential and intellectual property through the use of listening devices.

EAVESDROPPING DEVICES - THE EXTENT OF THE THREAT

The threat from illegal eavesdropping devices is widespread, each year there is 800 million dollars worth of eavesdropping devices sold and installed in corporations annually in the US. The majority of the illegal eavesdropping equipment is imported from outside the US. Each day over 6 million dollars worth of surveillance equipment is sold to the public in the US. The equipment is sold over the counter through mail order and from the Internet. There are numerous companies in New York City that will not only sell the equipment but they will also gladly break into and install the equipment at the customer's target location.

So the question is, what can companies do to protect their assets from falling into the wrong hands? There are things that can be done and it is not a good idea to just ignore the problem or pretend it doesn't exist.

Industrial espionage is illegal. It is still being done because the benefits, the rewards for doing are great. It helps a company gain a competitive edge by knowing pricing, strategy, and research and intellectual property, so those that engage in industrial espionage feel the rewards out weigh the risks and the chances of getting caught are not high.

There are things companies can do to help protect themselves from the onslaught and availability of eavesdropping devices:

1. Learn what devices are being used

2. Know what countermeasures are available

3. Sound control methods and devices

The Devices

The first eavesdropping device is called a Parabolic Microphone which looks like a TV satellite dish. The dish around the microphone is called a parabolic reflector which is used to focus and collect sound waves onto a microphone. The range of the parabolic microphone is around 300 feet. The parabolic microphone can be handheld or mounted on a tripod.

Second is the shotgun microphone. The shotgun microphone is a narrow tube and is a line-of-sight device. The shotgun microphone can only pick up sounds or conversations in the direction the microphone is pointing to. The microphone is handheld and can pick up conversations up to 50 feet away for most commercial brands. There are shotgun microphones that are mounted on booms and used in movies and television production. There are probably others that have a longer range but the device is line-of-sight and being too far away may cause interference with the intended target.

For listening "through windows" the third device is the laser bounce listening device. When conversations take place in rooms with windows the conversation sound waves will cause the window to vibrate slightly. The waves of the conversation causing the window to vibrate can be captured so everything that is said is then heard and recorded. There are other bugging devices that are designed to be planted in a room to pick up any conversation. Contrary to popular belief, as seen in movies, turning up the stereo and whispering will not prevent the conversation from being captured since there are ways to filter out the background noise. These bugging devices are small and if properly deployed will not be seen with the naked eye. They can be hidden almost anywhere even in plain sight but not be noticed. These devices can be delivered in a gift such a clock radio to the office; it could be in the fresh cut flowers that were placed in the board room or meeting room, or the new telephone jack in the wall of the meeting room.

Here are the eavesdropping principles:

1. A device to pickup the sound known as the pickup device. This is usually a microphone of some sort that picks up the sound and converts it to electrical impulses. Images can be picked up by a video camera. If the device can be planted with an available power source it will eliminate the need for whoever is doing the eavesdropping to go into the room to change the batteries in a battery-operated device. Some listening devices can store the information digitally to be transmitted to the listening station at predetermined time. There are tiny microphones that can be used with a tiny amplifier to block out background noise and provided better quality conversations.

2. A way to transmit the signal picked up by the listening device to a location known as the listening post for analysis. This is done by wire or radio frequency transmission. The unused telephone wires which are readily available can be used to transmit what is picked up be the listening device. Unused electrical wires or the underground electrical conduit can all be used to covertly transmit the signal to the listening post. Transmitters need power and may be connected to an existing available power source or to a battery operated source. The transmitter may be designed to operate continuously or operated from a remote location usually the listening post.

3. The location where the signals are transmitted to from the listening device is called the listening post. At the listening post the signals can be recorded, monitored, or transmitted to another location for further analysis. The physical location of the listening post can be in the next room or several blocks away. Voice actuated recorders are used to record only when there is activity in the target room. The will minimize how the tapes need to be changed since the tape can hold about 12 hours of recordings. With the advent of digital recording it may be even longer time between disk changes and the amount of information that can be stored on a disk is greater than on tape.

The devices used for eavesdropping are numerous in size, shape, and capabilities but all follow the basic principles listed above. More and more devices are becoming available to the general public albeit these devices are illegal to own as well as use. The penalties for using an unauthorized device that is a court order for wire tapping and carries a fine of $10,000 and 10 years in prison if convicted. The stakes are high and the gains are high in the world of industrial espionage so there are those willing to take the chance to do eavesdropping. Most never get caught because the sophistication of the devices makes it hard to find them.

One way to find the devices is to have a technical security assessment performed by a company that is qualified to perform the sweeps of area using special equipment to find the bugging devices. Another defense against eavesdropping is to conduct meetings in rooms that have been cleared of any devices and to soundproof the room.

SOUNDPROOFING A ROOM

With the laser bounce device the conversations in a room can be picked up outside of the building and the device does not need to be in the room. There is a difference between soundproofing and acoustical conditioning. Acoustical conditioning is used to control reverberation in a room. Soundproofing on the other hand, is designed to keep sound out or in a room. Keeping sound in is important to controlling the sensitive information that will discussed in the room.

For sound to travel there must be air movement and a vacuum cannot transmit sound. Air transmits sound effectively over large bandwidths of frequencies because of its low mass. This "catch-air" is not as effective at moving sound at high frequencies.

There are two issues when considering soundproofing:

1. At high frequencies is not a problem but is a problem at low frequencies.
2. There must a medium to transmit sound from one area to another unless there is continuous transmission from one area to another.

In rooms the transmission of sound from one room to another is usually done by the construction materials of the walls. For example, wood and drywall are good conductors of sound and will transmit any conversations and other sounds through the walls. Try this little experiment to see for yourself how sound can travel through the walls. Place your ear up against the wall in an apartment or hotel room and listen. You will probably hear the TV, radio, and some conversations. Sometimes if the people next door in a hotel room are loud, you can hear the entire conversation as clearly as if you where sitting in the room with them. So it is no surprise that the wall construction materials, wood and drywall, transmit the sound waves extremely well.

Floors are also an issue when it comes to transmitting sound. The floor carries a great deal of sound waves or energy. There is no to keep it out once the sound waves enter the room or building.

Now let's turn to the task at hand, the requirements for soundproofing a room. First it is important to note that 100% room soundproofing cannot be achieved.

To soundproof the walls it is best to have two walls with an intervening space that is filled with a fibrous material which will help deaden the sound and not permit the sound to travel between the rooms. Care must be taken to make sure that there are no holes, no matter how small, in the either wall structure into the intervening space because the sound waves will travel through the opening defeating the purpose of the specially constructed walls. The ceiling and floors will need to be built with the same goal in mind. That is to have an intervening space filled with fibrous material to deaden the sound. The fibrous material in the floor, walls, and ceiling spaces will help minimize the amount of vibration that rigid structures have because the sound will cause these stiff structures to vibrate and the dampening material will help minimize this problem. The more layers that are used will require different dampening materials since each one has its own vibration frequency known as resonant frequency.

Lead is another substance used to prevent vibration. Lead is so dense that it does not vibrate however lead is very expensive and, with environmental regulations around lead, it is probably not a feasible alternative to the fibrous material as a dampening material. For the fibrous material to be effective it needs to fill the space between the two walls.

Concrete can also be used to fill the space between the walls. Concrete does transmit sound from one wall structure to the other because of its density. Make sure that there are not any leaks for sound to pass from one wall through the concrete to the other wall or the concrete fill will be useless. Before you decide to use concrete as a fill material for soundproofing material make sure that the floor and walls can carry the extra load. For example, if the room is on a higher floor than the first or if the first floor sits on the slab and there is not a basement under the first floor. A civil engineer can do the calculations required to ensure that the floor can take the extra loading safely and will not fail under the load.

We have discussed soundproofing the walls, floors and ceilings of a room. Below is a summary of the information:

1. Wall, ceiling and some times floor plates (floors made from concrete will not transmit sound); structural materials will vibrate sound from one location (room) to another. Drywall and wood vibrate readily and transmit sounds easily.

2. To eliminate the issues of two walls, ceiling, and floor plates, from coming in contact with one other from different rooms, a space can be placed between the walls, ceilings and floor plates. The space needs to be filled with a fibrous

material to dampen the sound otherwise the sound will be transmitted through the space between the walls. The same can be constructed for ceilings using two plates with an intervening filled space between them.

3. Materials for filling the space between the walls also include concrete and not just fibrous materials. The important note is that there must not be any leakage in the intervening material in the wall or ceiling space or the fill will be rendered useless as sound will be transmitted through the space and the two wall or ceiling structures.

The room shouldn't have any windows but if there are then a shutter or a plug can be installed to block the sound from exiting through the window. A plug is made of Plexiglas® cut to fit over the window like a shutter on the outside. The sounds from the room will be dampened. A plug can is made of stiff material that is cut to fit in the window frame and is installed inside the window. For larger windows a backing is placed on the mat to hold it in place. Caulking around the edges will keep the plug in place.

Another solution is installing double pane windows which also reduce sound leakage but do not completely eliminate it. Double pane windows reduce the sound leakage about 20%. Laminating windows will reduce the sound leakage since the laminate which is plastic sits between the two pieces of glass that make up the window this helps to reduce sound leakage through the window.

There are soundproof windows that are made to be used with existing windows. The soundproof windows are designed to be installed on the interior side of the existing windows. The existing windows become the exterior windows. For better results use double pane windows. The soundproof windows are installed leaving an air space between the windows. The air space between the windows cannot be filled in as is the case in the walls with fibrous materials or any other material since that will block the light through the window and the window will be blocked. The air space will cut down on the vibration of the windows and therefore minimize the amount of leakage. Another method to soundproof windows is to use thicker glass.

To soundproof windows there are only the following options since filling the gap between the windows panes will also block out the window since it will not be transparent any longer:

1. Use thicker glass

2. Use an a large intervening air space between the window panes

3. Use laminate glass

4. Use more panes of glass

Soundproofing doors can be accomplished by one of the following methods:

1. Install a solid core door

2. Install a drop sill at the bottom of the door

3. Install a thicker heavier door

4. Install gaskets at the top and sides

The door to a soundproof room needs to be soundproof as well or there will be sound leakage from the room. A solid core door will provide some sound dampening since the door has come density. A hollow core door is hollow in the center and the sound will leak through the door.

Placing a drop sill at the bottom of the door will close any gaps at the bottom so that sound will not be lost through the door bottom. The drop sill will make a tighter seal at the bottom of the door.

Thicker doors provide more sound dampening than thinner doors. This follows what happens with the walls or windows, the more soundproofing can be realized with the thicker heavier walls. Concrete is good at sound dampening because it is so dense.

Installing gaskets at the top and sides of the door will seal any gaps that will permit leakage of sound from the room. The gaskets are like weather stripping for the door except instead of trying to keep the heat or air conditioning in the room the gaskets are keeping the sound from leaking out of the room. The gaskets are made of neoprene and when the door is closed the neoprene compresses to form an airtight seal. The airtight seal prevents sound leakage through the gasket and any space that would otherwise be at the top and sides of the door.

A cam hinge is also used on doors that are designed to soundproof. The cam hinge is deigned to drop the door down when it is closed making a tight seal to prevent sound leaking out of the bottom of the door.

By adding the gaskets around the top and sides of the door and the cam hinge, the door becomes more soundproof because sound can leak through the smallest hole defeating the soundproofing of the door which in turn causes the room to not be soundproof. Care must be taken to avoid adding any bumpers to the door frame to soften the closing of the door since it is designed to close completely, the door will have a tendency to slam, making noise. The bumpers will cause air gaps around the door rendering the door useless for soundproofing. A solution is to adjust the door closer so that it positively latches the door (closes tightly) without out slamming it closed which is an annoyance. If no one will be entering the room during meetings, then it may ok to have the door slam closed to ensure a proper seal.

Remember any leakage of sound from a room either through the walls, ceiling, floors, windows, or doors, will nullify any soundproofing that has been done.

It does not make any difference how small the hole is, sound will leak through the hole.

Another measure that can be taken to help soundproof a room is called active noise cancellation. What active nose cancellation does is it adds more noise known as white noise to cancel out any noise that may come from the room. This works because when two sound waves arrive together at 180 degrees out of phase they cancel each other out. This same concept is used in noise cancellation headphones. Apparently they do a good job of blocking out background noise from getting into the earphones and interfering with what is coming into the headphones such a playing a CD.

Remember to sweep the soundproof room frequently to make sure there are not any covert listening devices installed. Next check for leakage of sound regularly, semi-annually or more frequently if necessary, to make sure that there are not any holes for the sound waves to escape the room through.

CHAPTER 1

Shipping and Receiving

The shipping and receiving areas; loading dock storage and processing need to be secured like any other part of the facility. Doing a vulnerability assessment is the best way to find out what the security needs are for an existing or new shipping and receiving area. There is no one physical security program that will be right for all shipping and receiving locations either existing or new. However by using good physical security tenents which consist of the basics of perimeter security, access control, instruction detection, and CCTV that can be applied to the shipping and receiving area some level of protection can be achieved. The approach of defense–in–depth is one that can be used to help make the shipping and receiving and warehouse operations more secure by hardening the target. Procedures are important as well but we will only be reviewing and applying some of the physical security measures that have been discussed throughout the book.

Warehouse operations security is handled differently because of the volume of packages being received and shipped rather than the shipping and receiving for a building or facility which receives and ships less packages than a warehouse operation does. The warehouse security is on a larger scale but still employs the same principles that are needed for the shipping and receiving areas. Either one, the warehouse or the shipping and receiving for a building or facility is an area that is vulnerable to being exploited for sending a package bomb. Theft in shipping and receiving of packages and materials is also an issue that has to be monitored and methods on how to better protect the packages needs to be explored. Thefts have a greater probability of occurrence than does a bomb event. However by protecting the area from thefts some of the same physical security measures can be used to help minimize the risk of a bomb slipping through in one of the packages. Screening the packages is something that should be considered when designing security for shipping and receiving. The shipping and receiving area has been in the past an overlooked area for applying physical and procedural security standards. Some agencies and companies have written security policies and procedures for the shipping and receiving departments to follow and although there were some physical security features added, like CCTV, there had not been a concerted effort to increase the physical security. There has been greater focus on physical security measures for shipping and receiving because of the events of the last several years that have brought more attention to the shipping and receiving areas as being vulnerable. Shipping and receiving areas have always been vulnerable and if not properly protected they could become the soft spot in an otherwise hardened target.

The shipping and receiving area should be designed with physical security in mind. For example, access to the interior of the shipping and receiving area can be controlled by using the building or site access control system. Only those that need to have access will; all others will not be permitted access. The access control can also be used to control access to high value shipments either incoming or outgoing. This can be similar to the high value storage area for warehouses which is a caged area with limited access.

PHYSICAL SECURITY FOR SHIPPING AND RECEIVING

The physical security of the shipping and receiving (S&R) area should be included in the design of the facility or building physical security since it is a continuation of the building or a part of the facility. The physical security for the S&R would include the following.

1. Access control

2. Intrusion detection

3. CCTV

4. Lighting

ACCESS CONTROL

The access control system that is used for the building and/or site will also be used to control access to the S&R area. From inside the building or site there would be a card reader installed to enter into the S&R where the packages are stored and shipped out and access would limited to those who need access only. Not everyone will be permitted to enter the S&R area where the packages are staged. Company personnel needing access to ship something will go to a window to drop off the package or to pick up a package. The window would be large enough for a package but not for someone to jump over to gain access. The window will have a way to lock it when the S&R area is closed.

The doors leading to the package area will have access control using a card reader with a PIN. The card and the PIN must match or no entry will be granted. The doors from the loading dock to the inside of the building will have card and PIN access.

The high value area for incoming and outgoing packages can be controlled using the access card and a PIN. The high value area will have a barcode on the package for tracking that will be used to log packages in or out.

Access to the loading dock for a building's shipping and receiving area can be limited to those who are making scheduled deliveries. All others will not be permitted to enter. Drivers of delivery trucks or vehicles will not be permitted to enter the shipping and receiving area. The shipping and receiving personnel will check the paperwork from the delivery driver at the window for deliveries then the shipment will be unloaded.

The access control for shipping and receiving will use proximity cards and readers just like the rest of the facility or building. The system can be connected to the building or facility's enterprise security system for monitoring. Access is to be granted only to those who work in the shipping and receiving department. All the doors that have access control readers will have a REX for exiting each door but the REX will not unlock the door, it will only be used to shunt the alarm.

To enter the garage, if shipping and receiving is in the basement of the building, there will an access control point for all delivery trucks. All the trucks will be stopped and inspected manually by a security officer. The carriage of the truck will be inspected using a mirror on a telescoping pole that has a light on it. The delivery trucks will be held back by a protective barrier that will retract when entry is permitted but will remain in the up-and-ready position. A truck attempting to ram the barrier will be kept from entering by the barrier. A protective barrier will be used on the outgoing traffic side to prevent a vehicle from entering the wrong way. As the vehicle approaches the wrong side of the entry, sensors in the ground will cause the protective barrier to be placed in the defensive position automatically.

Facilities that do not have an underground garage where shipping and receiving is located can use the protective barrier system as well. When deliveries are to be made, they go to a gate that is for deliveries to enter the facility. A protective barrier will be used at the gate and before entering the delivery will be verified and the truck or vehicle will be inspected. The barrier will be lowered to allow the truck to enter. When the truck has completed the delivery it will drive up to the protective barrier on the exit side of the gate. The protective barrier will be lowered and the truck will leave. The protective barriers are in the set position on both sides at all times.

INTRUSION DETECTION

Intrusion detection system can be installed to help secure the shipping and receiving area. The intrusion detection system can be installed in the shipping and receiving area to monitor during off hours as well as during business hours. IDS sensors installed on overhead dock doors will alert security of an attempted intrusion. The sensors will be balanced magnetic switches and will alarm when contact is broken or if an outside magnet is used to attempt entry. All emergency exit doors will have alarms that will sound if the door is opened from the inside and contact switches to alert if the door is forced from the exterior. The switches used are balanced magnetic switches. All of the emergency exit doors will have a blank face on the exterior if not needed for re-entry. This will help make the door harder to force from the exterior. All access-controlled doors will be alarmed and have contact switches as well. As previously stated the REX on each access-controlled door will shunt the alarm for proper exiting so a forced door alarm is not received.

Dual technology motion sensors will be used in the interior of the shipping and receiving area. The motion sensors used would be infrared and ultrasonic. The sensors used as a dual technology solution along with the door contact switches will provide layers of security. The purpose of layering the detection is to make it a little harder for an intruder by having more obstacles to overcome to gain entry.

Intrusion detection would also be on the interior facing doors of the shipping and receiving area. These interior doors are the doors that lead into the shipping and receiving area from inside the building and would have door contact switches using balanced magnetic switches. The doors that are access-controlled doors would have door contacts and a REX on each access-controlled door for exiting to shunt the alarm and not the exit as a forced door alarm.

In addition to the door alarms and motion dual technology glass break sensors would augment the other systems and add another layer. Fence Motion sensors would be used in the high value storage area. The sensors would sense anyone entering the caged area without using a valid access card and PIN. The swiping of a valid access card and punching in a valid the PIN that matches the access card disables the motion sensors. So the motion sensors are armed all the time except for valid entries to retrieve and place packages in the storage area.

Another layer of protection is the use of bar codes. All packages have a bar code on them and to remove a package it must be read by a valid bar code reader to be removed or an alarm will sound. To be a valid bar code reader it will be connected via a wireless network to the server where the information about the package resides. Once the information is swiped from the bar code and a few questions are answered such as:

1. Access code (password) to gain access

2. Name of person removing the package and date/time

3. Order number or Invoice number

When packages are checked in and stored in the high value area the following is done:

1. Access code (password) to gain access

2. A bar code is added

3. Name of person removing the package and date/time

4. The package information is entered into the data base

After the bar code is added and the information about the package is entered into the data base the package is then stored in the high value storage area. This will help track high value packages that are received and shipped by the company.

As a part of checking in packages for shipping and receiving for a building or facility all packages will go through an explosives detector. The packages will be checked for explosives residue and the packages will be placed on a conveyor that goes through the explosives detection machine. The explosives detection will be used for packages being received only. For warehouse operations the explosive screening of all packages being received may not be practical.

Intrusion detection can be used to help monitor the perimeter of the building or facility near the shipping and receiving. Motion detectors can be used after hours to detect any movement near the area of shipping and receiving. The motion will alert the security officers at the console and the CCTV cameras in the area near where the motion sensors will come up on the screen. The security officers will be able to zoom and pan the cameras manually to see what is going on.

CCTV FOR SHIPPING AND RECEIVING

CCTV is used a surveillance tool and can be used to help with surveillance of the shipping and receiving area. CCTV cameras can be used in conjunction with access control system to verify who is entering and to make sure the picture of the person entering matches the picture on the access card. As the person presents the access card to the reader the access control system will pull up the picture of the card holder in the access control data base and the CCTV camera will send the picture of the person presenting the card to match the two. If there is a match the person then enters their PIN number. If there is not a match then the person is not permitted to enter their PIN number and access is denied. The security officers will receive an alarm at the security console if there is not a match between the pictures. The screening of card holders using the match of the picture from the access control data base is a good way to keep people from using another person's access control card to enter a restricted area. Access control systems are sophisticated tools that can be used to control access to areas of the facility and alert security personnel that someone is attempting access that may not have it.

CCTV can also be used to monitor the shipping and receiving during off hours if there are any. The CCTV cameras can be set to record on motion. All of the indoor cameras can color and the outdoor cameras can be day/night to compensate for low light. Outdoor cameras can also be set to record on motion for after hours and alarm at the security console. During business hours, the cameras can be remotely operated and record at the request of the security officer. The perimeter intrusion detection on or near the perimeter fence will activate the cameras near the perimeter fence to the building or facility and then to record what is taking place. Also CCTV can be integrated into working with the exterior motion sensors in the area outside the shipping and receiving area. When the motion sensors are tripped it will bring up the cameras on the security console screen with an audible alarm.

The CCTV recordings can be made on digital recorders rather than VHS tape. It makes it easier to find an incident on the disk than the old tape. On a digital recording all you have to do is to scan the disk and then go the spot on the disk that says alarm and then view the recording. All recordings should be done in real time which them easy to view and analyze.

CCTV cameras can be placed inside the shipping and receiving area to record what is going on. The cameras in the shipping and receiving area can be set to record when there is activity in the area. For example, if the dock doors are open and deliveries are being made the cameras on the loading dock will record the events and archive the recordings for future reference if necessary.

CCTV can also be used to help monitor the activities in the high value storage area. The cameras can be placed in the caged area and can record personnel entering and leaving. The cameras can be deigned to record when the access control system to enter the cage is used or if the intrusion detection system is triggered.

LIGHTING

Security lighting is an important part of the physical design. Without good lighting the CCTV system will not be as efficient. The types of lighting that can be used to help monitor the area are as follows:

- Continuous lighting

- Glare lighting

Continuous lighting is on poles throughout the facility or outside of the building. If the lighting is for an underground parking garage that leads to the shipping and receiving area the lights will be continuous and the garage can have painted surfaces to that reflect the most light making it bright and easy to see anyone in the garage. The type of luminaries to use in the lights in the garage is quartz lamps which produce a bright white light.

Continuous lighting in the garage will be illuminated at all times. In other locations outside the garage the lighting will come on using a timer or photo cell sensor that will turn on the lights at dusk and turn off the lights at sunrise.

The other type of lighting that can be used is glare protection especially around the loading dock doors for shipping and receiving areas. The lights will come on using a motion sensor that is set to only work after it gets dark. When an intruder approaches the overhead loading dock doors, the motion sensor will pick up the movement and the lights will come on. The lights can be pointed directly at the approaching person. Quartz bulbs can be used as the luminary since they produce a bright white light and come on quickly and do not need a warm time. The objective of the lights is to project glare out toward the perimeter so the intruder is blinded by the glare but the security officers approaching the area will have the light to their backs so the officers will not be affected by the light.

If glare protection cannot be used because the light will also blind the security officers then use lights that will light up the area but not project glare. The lights can still come on using a motion sensor which can also be part of the intrusion detection system to alert the security officers that there is an intruder in the area.

SECURING SHIPPING AND RECEIVING

As we have seen the physical security measures that are used to help secure the facility or building can be used to secure the shipping and receiving area although there is no way that one system of physical security can work for all shipping and receiving locations. The same can be said for the physical security of any facility, building, etc. that one way is the best way for all. This is why designing in the physical security at the time the facility or building is being designed makes good sense. The same techniques of using perimeter motion sensors in conjunction with CCTV that are used elsewhere can be used to monitor the shipping and receiving area as well. Motion sensors will work to monitor any movement in the area after hours and alert security personnel to the possibility of intruders gaining access to the area. After notification security would respond to the area to do a check of the area.

Exit and entry door contact switches can send an alert to the security console that a break in may be in progress since the door contacts may have been separated sending an alarm. CCTV will help in the monitoring of the area and can be used by security officers to assess an alarm. The overhead dock door alarm contact switches will alert the security officers if an attempted breakin is occurring at the dock doors after hours.

Access control will keep those who do not have need to be in the shipping and receiving area out and most buildings and facilities are already using access control systems. Using dual technology access adds another layer of security. Dual access control technology would be the use of a card access and a PIN number, or card access and biometric. Another part of access control is to limit one card, one entry by using revolving doors or "mantraps" for entry. This will help keep the number of people with access to a minimum and help reduce the exposure of the area to pilfering and other thefts. By minimizing the number of personnel that have access, it will be easier to track anyone who has entered the area after hours using a valid access card and PIN.

Security lighting will help by making it harder for an intruder to enter without being seen because of the lights. It is important to remember that there must not be shadows for the intruder to hide or the purpose of the security lighting is lost.

High value storage areas enhance the security of those packages by making it harder to remove them from the shipping and receiving area. High value storage works well in a warehouse setting and can work in a building or facility storage area as well. High value storage would consist of:

1. Computers, both desktop and laptop

2. Computer parts

3. Blank check stock

4. Any other item that is considered valuable.

High value cargo or packages have a high probability of being stolen because of the high value. Keeping the high value cargo and packages separate from the other packages and cargo will help make it more secure since there will be more scrutiny and accountability of the high value storage area through the use of physical security controls and monitoring. Pilfering will kept to a minimum by securing the high value storage area and limiting access to only those who need access and monitoring the movement of the packages and personnel in the high value storage area.

Checklists and Forms

This chapter will have all the checklists and forms that are discussed in all the chapters of the book. They categorized by type for easy reference. Checklists and forms make doing security surveys easy and they are a good way to capture the information.

SECURITY SURVEY FORMS

SECURITY SURVEY

PART 1

BUILDING and/or SITE PHYSICAL FEATURES

1. Location of facility: _____

2. Job: _____

3. Street Address and Zip: _____

4. Telephone: _____

5. Number of structures on the Site:
   (a) 1 story _____ (b) 2 story _____ (c) 3 story _____ (d) 4 story _____ (e) 5 story or higher _____

6. Number of structures interconnected:
   (a) At grade level or higher _____ (b) Below grade _____

7. Total working population on:
   (a) First (day) shift _____ (b) Second shift _____ (c) Third shift _____

8. Estimated number of daily visitors: _____

9. Number of automobiles parked daily: _____

PART 2

SOCIAL and POLITICAL ENVIRONMENT

10. Is the facility in a: (a) City _____ (b) Town _____ (c) Incorporated village _____ (d) Agricultural _____
    (e) Unincorporated hamlet _____ (e) Rural area _____

11. Estimated percentage of neighboring area:
    (a) Residential _____ (b) Commercial _____ (c) Industrial _____ (d) Agricultural _____ (e) Undeveloped _____

12. Estimated percentage of residential area:
    (a) One family homes _____ (b) Two family homes _____ (c) Multiple dwellings _____
    High rise multiple dwellings _____

13. Police department having jurisdiction: _____

14. Total sworn officers in the department: _____

15. Average response times for emergency calls: _____

16. Is the jurisdiction separately reported in the Standard Metropolitan Statistical Area section of the Uniform Crime Reports?
    _____

17. If 16, is yes, what are the most recent indexes for:
    (a) Total crime _____   (b) Violent crime _____
    (c) Property crime _____   (d) Murder and Manslaughter _____
    (e) Rape _____   (f) Robbery _____
    (g) Aggravated assault _____ (h) Burglary _____
    (i) Larceny over $50 _____   (j) Car theft _____

Explanation of Element Scoring

(X0) - Score No = Zero; Yes = Points Indicated
(%) - Score up to the points indicated based on the percent compliance
(Part Whole) - Award points indicated for each part up to the whole number indicated.
(PJ) - Score up to the points indicated based on your professional judgment.

	PART 3 Physical Security Survey Perimeter		
1. GROUNDS (66)			
		Yes	No
1.1	Is there a perimeter fence? (X0-5)		
1.2	Does the fence meet the minimum specifications for security fencing? (.5/3)		
	(1) Chain-link?		
	(2) No. 11 gauge or heavier wire?		
	(3) Mesh opening not larger than 2 inches square?		
	(4) Selvage twisted and barbed at top and bottom:?		
	(5) Fence bottom is within 2 inches of solid ground?		
	(6) Is the fence top guard strung with barbed wire & angled outward & upward at a 45-degree angle?		
1.3	Are boxes or other items placed a safe distance from the fence? (X0-5)		
1.4	Is there a cleared area on both sides of the fence? (X)-5		
1.5	There are not any unsecured overpasses or subterranean passageways near the fence?		
1.6	Are fence gates solid and in good condition? (X0-5)		
1.7	Are fence gates' hinges secure and non-removable? (X0-5)		
1.8	Have unnecessary gates been eliminated? (X0-5)		
1.9	Are locks and chains used to secure gates? (X0-5)		
1.10	Do you regularly check those gates that you have locked? (X0-5)		
1.11	There are not weeds or trash adjoining the building that should be removed? (X0-5)		
1.12	Is shrubbery near windows, doors, gates, and near entrances kept to a minimum? (X0-5)		
1.13	Stock, crates, pallets, etc. are not allowed to be piled near the building? (X0-5)		
2. EXTERIOR DOORS (55)			
2.1	Are doors constructed of sturdy material? X0-5)		
2.2	Are all hinge pins located on the inside? If No, are they pinned or welded? (X0-5)		
2.3	Are all door hinges installed so that it would be impossible to remove the closed doors without seriously damaging the door or Jam? (X0-5)		

		Yes	No
2.4	Are all door frames well constructed and in good condition? (X0-5)		
2.5	Are the exterior locks double cylinder, dead bolts, or jimmy-proof type locks? (X0-5)		
2.6	The breaking of glass or a door panel then will not allow the person to open the door? (X0-5)		
2.7	Are all locks working properly ? (X0-5)		
2.8	Are all doors properly secured or reinforced? (X0-5)		
2.9	Are all unused doors secured? (X0-5)		
2.10	Are all padlocks, chains, and hasps case hardened? (X0-5)		
3. EXTERIOR WINDOWS (20)			
3.1	Are all windows securely fastened from the inside? (X0-5)		
3.2	Are windows within 14 feet from the ground equipped with protective coverings? (X0-5)		
3.3	Do those windows with locks have locks that are designed and located so they cannot be reached and/or opened by breaking the glass? (X0-5)		
3.4	Windows cannot be removed without breaking them? (X0-5)		
4. OTHER OPENINGS (25)			
4.1	Are all ventilators or other possible means of entrance to the buildings) covered with steel bars or wire mesh? (X0-5)		
4.2	Are exposed roof hatches properly secured? (X0-5)		
4.3	Are the accessible skylights protected with bars or an intrusion alarm? (X0-5)		
4.4	Do fire exit doors have a portable alarm mounted, to alert if door is opened? (X0-5)		
4.5	Entrance cannot be gained from an adjoining building? (X0-5)		
5. EXTERIOR LIGHTING (45)			
5.1	Is the lighting adequate to illuminate critical areas? (X0-5)		
5.2	Is there sufficient lighting over entrances? (X0-5)		
5.3	The protective lighting and the working lighting system are not on the same circuit? (X0-5)		
5.4	Is there an auxiliary power source for protective lighting? (X0-5)		
5.5	Has the system been tested? (X0-5)		
5.6	Is the auxiliary system designed to go into operation automatically when needed?: (X0-5)		
5.7	How are the protective lights controlled? (5/10) 1. Automatic timer 2. Photo cells		
5.8	Are the switch boxes and/or automatic timer secured? (X0-5)		

PART 4 INTERIOR		
I. INTERIOR LIGHTING (20)	Yes	No
1.1 Is there a back-up system for emergency lights?: (X0-5)		
1.2 Is the lighting provided adequate for security purposes? (X0-5)		
1.3 Is the lighting at night adequate for security purposes? (X0-5)		
1.4 Is the night lighting sufficient for surveillance by the police department? (X0-5)		
2. INTERIOR DOORS (30)		
2.1 Are doors constructed of a sturdy and solid material? (X0-5)		
2.2 Are doors limited to the essential minimum? (X0-5)		
2.3 Are outside door hinge pins spot welded or bradded to prevent removal? (X0-5)		
2.4 Are hinges installed on the inward side of the door? (X0-5)		
2.5 Is there at least one lock on each outer door? (X0-5)		
2.6 Is each door equipped with a locking device? (X0-5)		
3. OFFICES (20)		
3.1 Are offices locked when unattended for a long period of time? (X0-5)		
3.2 Are maintenance people, contractors, vendors, other visitors, required to show identification? (X0-5)		
3.3 Are desks and files locked when left unattended? (X0-5)		
3.4 Items of value are not left on desks in an unsecured manner? (X0-5)		
4. KEYS (33)		
4.1 Are methods taken to control the issuance and management of keys? (X0-20)		

4.2 Do these controls include: (1/13)
  1. Total keys issued?
  2. Total master keys?
  3. Is there an adequate log maintained of all keys that are issued?
  4. Key holders are not permitted to duplicate keys?
  5. Are keys marked "DO NOT DUPLICATE"?
  6. If master keys are used, are they devoid of markings identifying them as such?
  7. Are losses or thefts of keys promptly reported to security?
  8. Is there a person responsible for issuing and replacing keys?
  9. Are visual audits made of the keys?
  10. Are locks changed immediately upon loss or theft of keys?
  11. Are the duplicate keys stored in a safe and secure place?
  12. Are keys returned when an employee resigns, is discharged, or suspended?
  13. Are records maintained indicating buildings and entrances for which keys are issued?		

		Yes	No
5. LOCKS (35)			
5.1	Are entrances equipped with secure locking devices? (X0-5)		
5.2	Is the lock designed or the frame built so that the door cannot be forced by spreading the frame? (X0-5)		
5.3	Are all locks in working order? (X0-5)		
5.4	Are the screws holding the lock firmly in place? (X0-5)		
5.5	Is the bolt protected or constructed so it cannot be cut? (X0-5)		
5.6	Are locks' combinations changed or rotated immediately upon resignation, discharge, suspension of an employee having possession of master keys?		
5.7	Are locks changed after a major security violation resulting in large loss?		
6. ACCESS CONTROL (20)			
6.1	Are methods taken to control entry and movement of people and vehicles?		

6.2	Do these controls include: (1/10):
	  1. Employees?
	  2. Service people?
	  3. Truck, rail, and other delivery/pickup vehicle operators?
	  4. Outside contractors?
	  5. Visitors?
	  6. Sales personnel?
	  7. Employees' vehicles?
	  8. Other vehicles?
	  9. Intruders?
	  10. Other:		

7. ALARM SYSTEMS (25)			
7.1	Does the alarm system have an intrusion alarm system? (X0-5)		

7.2	Does the alarm system have the following features: (2/20)
	  1. Is it connected to a central station?
	  2. Is it a proprietary system?
	  3. Is the system tested before activating it for non-operational periods?
	  4. Is the alarm system inspected and tested annually?
	  5. Is the system tamper resistant?
	  6. Is the system weather resistant?
	  7. Is there an automatic emergency power supply?
	  8. Is the alarm system properly maintained by trained technical specialists?
	  9. Are frequent tests conducted to determine the adequacy and promptness of response to alarm signals?
	  10. Other:		

PART 5			Yes	No
1. WAREHOUSE ACTIVITIES (30)				
1.1	Are methods taken to control entry and the movement of people and finished products and raw materials? (X0-16)			
1.2	Do these controls include: (2/14) 1. Is there separate lounge facilities for truck drivers? 2. Trash collectors are not permitted in the warehouse? 3. Employees/vehicles? 4. Contractor's vehicles? 5. Are shipping and receiving platforms free of trash? 6. Are pin locks used for loaded trailers parked on company property? 7. Other? N/A			
PART 6				
1. EMPLOYEE TRAINING (50)				
1.1	What percentage of employees receive an orientation to security program standards? (%-10)			
1.2	Are written materials included in the orientation? (X0-5)			
1.3	Are signs and notices posted in appropriate places to reinforce knowledge of security standards? (X0-5)			
1.4	Are training manuals used to aid and reinforce security training?			
1.5	Are records kept to verify security training and identify employees who need training?			
PART 7 **SECURITY LOSS REPORTS (24)**				
1.1	Are security losses investigated with the findings and actions reported on a standard incident report form? (X0-10)			
1.2	Does the security program require a complete investigation of incidents involving the following: (2/14) 1. Cash funds? 2. Irregularities in financial accounts? 3. Equipment and materials shortages? 4. Production losses from disturbances? 5. Expendable supplies and inventories shrinkage? 6. Computer theft? 7. Other security losses:			
PART 8 **SECURITY POLICY (50)**				
1.1	Is there a written policy signed by the site manager emphasizing the importance of protecting people, property, and intellectual property against loss by taking or intentional destruction? (X0-15)			

		Yes	No
	3. Equipment and materials shortages? 4. Production losses from disturbances? 5. Expendable supplies and inventories shrinkage? 6. Computer theft? 7. Other security losses:		
PART 8 SECURITY POLICY (50)			
1.1	Is there a written policy signed by the site manager emphasizing the importance of protecting people, property, and intellectual property against loss by taking or intentional destruction? (X0-15)		
1.2	Does the security policy include: (1/10) 1. Theft of property? 2. Burglary? 3. Theft of process or trade secrets? 4. Assault on employees and visitors? 5. Bomb threats? 6. Arson? 7. Civil disturbances? 8. Other security losses?		
1.3	Is the security policy: (2/10) 1. Communicated in writing to all employees? 2. Referred to during new employee orientation? 3. Referred to in group meetings? 4. Contained in some manual? 5. Referred to in management program?		
1.4	Does senior management support the security policy: 1. By periodic written communications? (X0-5) 2. By regular security tours? (X0-5) 3. By participating in security program audits? (X0-5)		
2. SECURITY STANDARDS AND PROCEDURES			
2.1	Are there written standards for management performance in the security program? (X0-5)		
2.2	Are security program standards communicated to all levels of management? (X0-10)		
2.3	Are security instructions and procedures defined in a program manual? (X0-5)		
Total Points Scored for Security Total Possible Points: Percentage Score for Security: (Total points scored divided by total points possible multiplied by 100. Figure to nearest 1/10 of 1%)			

Figure 20-1 is a sample physical security form used by FORSCOM (The US Forces Command).

FORSCOM PHYSICAL SECURITY SURVEY
(FORSCOM Reg 190-13)
(See FORSCOM Reg 190-13 for instructions on completing this survey.)

PART I - ADMINISTRATIVE DATA

1. INSTALLATION	2. DATE OF SURVEY	3. DATE OF PREVIOUS SURVEY

4. OVERALL EVALUATION OF PHYSICAL SECURITY OF THE INSTALLATION. *(Attached as Enclosure 1 is a list of current installation security vulnerabilities, with a discussion of each. The discussion will contain recommendations to counter each vulnerability.)*

☐ EXCELLENT ☐ SATISFACTORY ☐ MARGINAL ☐ POOR

5. NAME(S) OF PERSONNEL CONDUCTING SURVEY

NAME	RANK	TITLE	ORGANIZATION

PART II - INSTALLATION DESCRIPTION

6. INSTALLATION MISSION STATEMENT *(Attach as enclosure if necessary)*

7. INSTALLATION COMMANDER	8. INSTALLATION PROVOST MARSHAL OR DIRECTOR OF SECURITY

9. INSTALLATION ACREAGE

10. POPULATION

MILITARY	FAMILY MEMBERS	CIVILIAN EMPLOYEES	TOTAL

11. NUMBER OF DESIGNATED MISSION ESSENTIAL OR VULNERABLE AREAS (MEVAs). *(Attach MEVA list as Enclosure 2, indicate date of last risk analysis for each MEVA.)*

12. NUMBER OF BUILDINGS	13. NUMBER OF TENANT ACTIVITIES *(Enclose list of tenants)*

14. TYPE INSTALLATION ACCESS

OPEN POST	CLOSED POST	NUMBER OF GATES MANNED		NUMBER OF GATES UNMANNED
		Full Time	Part Time	

15. ARE RESOURCES AVAILABLE TO PROVIDE CONTROLLED OR RESTRICTED ACCESS TO INSTALLATION AND MEVAS IAW APPROPRIATE THREATCON MEASURES? *(Barriers)*

PART III - INSTALLATION LAW ENFORCEMENT AND SECURITY FORCES

16. LIST SECURITY FORCES AVAILABLE TO SUPPORT INSTALLATION SECURITY REQUIREMENTS

TYPE	AUTHORIZED	ASSIGNED
MILITARY POLICE		
OTHER MILITARY GUARD FORCES (BMM)		
CONTRACT GUARDS		
DOD POLICE		
DOD CIVILIAN GUARDS		
OTHER		
TOTAL		

FORSCOM FORM **190-R**, 1 AUG 99

8-1/2x11

FIGURE 20-1 Sample physical security form

(continued on next page)

PART III - INSTALLATION LAW ENFORCEMENT AND SECURITY FORCES (CONTINUED)	YES	NO
17. ARE SECURITY FORCES AVAILABLE TO PROVIDE REQUIRED SECURITY/LAW ENFORCEMENT SUPPORT?		
18. ARE SECURITY FORCES TRAINED AND EQUIPPED?		
19. ARE GUARD ORDERS PUBLISHED, CURRENT AND ADEQUATE? *(For questions 16-19, if deficiences exist, provide discussion as enclosure.)*		

PART IV - PHYSICAL SECURITY PERSONNEL

20. LIST NUMBER AND GRADES AUTHORIZED/ASSIGNED

a. MILITARY SUPERVISOR *(Name, Rank)*	b. CIVILIAN SUPERVISOR *(Name, Grade, Title)*

c. MILITARY INSPECTOR/PHYSICAL SECURITY INSPECTOR *(Name, Rank, MOS)*

d. CIVILIAN PHYSICAL/SECURITY SPECIALIST(S) *(Attach list as enclosure if necessary)*

NAME	GRADE	TITLE

21. IS STAFFING LEVEL SUFFICIENT TO SUPPORT INSPECTION REQUIREMENTS? *(If staffing not sufficient, attach discussion as enclosure.)*

PART V - INSTALLATION PHYSICAL SECURITY PLAN

22. DATE OF CURRENT PLAN

23. DOES PLAN COVER PEACETIME, DEPLOYMENT/ MOBILIZATION CONTINGENCIES?

24. DOES PLAN CONTAIN REQUIRED ANNEXES IAW AR 190-13?

25. DOES ANTI-TERRORISM ANNEX CONTAIN PROVISIONS FOR IMPLEMENTING THE THREATCON SYSTEM?

26. ARE RESOURCES FOR IMPLEMENTING THREATCON MEASURES IDENTIFIED AND AVAILABLE?

27. DATE ANTI-TERRORISM ANNEX TO PLAN LAST EXERCISED

28. ASSESSMENT OF ADEQUACY OF PHYSICAL SECURITY PLAN AND ANNEXES *(Attach discussion as enclosure.)*

☐ ADEQUATE   ☐ INADEQUATE   ☐ MARGINAL

PART VI - THREAT STATEMENT

29. DATE OF INSTALLATION THREAT STATEMENT *(Attach current Threat Statement as enclosure.)*

30. DOES THREAT STATEMENT PROVIDE ADEQUATE ASSESSMENT OF LOCAL THREAT?

31. HAS THREAT STATEMENT RESULTED FROM COORDINATED EFFORT OF CID, MILITARY INTELLIGENCE, PROVOST MARSHAL, AND APPROPRIATE LOCAL LAW ENFORCEMENT AGENCIES?

PART VII - ENGINEERING/IDS

32. DOES ENGINEER/PUBLIC WORKS EMPLOY A SYSTEM THAT IDENTIFIES SECURITY RELATED WORK ORDERS?

FORSCOM Form 190-R, 1 Aug 99   2

FIGURE 20-1   Sample physical security form *(continued)*

(continued on next page)

PART VII - ENGINEERING/IDS (CONTINUED)			
33. NUMBER OF PENDING SECURITY RELATED WORK ORDERS			
34. ARE IDS INSTALLED IN ALL LOCATIONS AS REQUIRED BY REGULATION?			
35. TYPES OF IDS ARE INSTALLED *(Check all appropriate boxes)* ☐ J-SIIDS ☐ J-SIIDS WITH AMG ☐ ICIDS ☐ OTHER			
PART VIII - CRIME DATA			
36. NUMBER OF CRIME RELATED SIRs			
CURRENT CY	PREVIOUS CY		PREVIOUS 2D YEAR CY
37. INSTALLATION CRIME RATES OVER 3 YEAR PERIOD. *(Data will be graphic depiction which covers both crimes against property and against persons.)*			
38. ENCLOSURES			
INSTALLATION VULNERABILITIES AND RECOMMENDED COMPENSATORY MEASURES *(Required)*			
MEVA LISTING *(Required)*			
LIST OF RESTRICTED AREAS *(Required)*			
LIST OF TENANT ACTIVITIES *(Required)*			
DISCUSSION OF SECURITY FORCE DEFICIENCIES *(Required if significant deficiencies are found)*			
DISCUSSION OF PHYSICAL SECURITY PERSONNEL *(Required if significant deficiencies are found)*			
DISCUSSION OF SECURITY PLAN *(Required if plan is assessed as less than adequate)*			
DISCUSSION OF THREAT STATEMENT *(Required if significant deficiencies are found)*			
LIST OF WAIVERS AND EXCEPTIONS *(Required if any waiver or exception exists)*			
FACILITIES REQUIRED BY REGULATION TO HAVE IDS WITH NO IDS INSTALLED *(Include explanation for each, i.e., resources, new construction, etc.)*			
CRIME RATE CHARTS *(Required)*			
OTHER			
REMARKS			

FIGURE 20-1 Sample physical security form *(continued)*

There are other forms used for capturing the information when completing a security survey or you can make up your own based on the information in this book.

Risk Assessment Forms and Checklists

The risk assessment steps table in Table 20-1 will help guide the process of doing a risk assessment.

Table 20-2 below is a risk assessment matrix used for classifying the potential risk and the probability of occurrence.

TABLE 20-1 Risk Assessment Steps

STEP	DESCRIPTION
Identification of the assets	People, equipment, buildings, etc.
Identification of the threats	CAP Stats, etc.
Analyze the threats (risk assessment)	Probability of occurrence
Choose Countermeasure	Alarms, access control, etc.
Cost analysis of countermeasure	
Cost benefit, ROI	

TABLE 20-2 RISK MATRIX

	PROBABILITY OF OCCURRENCE		
SEVERITY	HIGH	MEDIUM	LOW
High	1	2	3
Medium	4	5	6
Low	7	8	9

Index